Women Singer-Songwriters in Rock

A Populist Rebellion in the 1990s

Ronald D. Lankford Jr.

THE SCARECROW PRESS, INC.

Lanham • Toronto • Plymouth, UK

2010

Published by Scarecrow Press, Inc.
A wholly owned subsidary of The Rowman & Littlefield Publishing Group, Inc.
4501 Forbes Boulevard, Suite 200, Lanham, Maryland 20706
http://www.scarecrowpress.com

Estover Road, Plymouth PL6 7PY, United Kingdom

British Library Cataloguing in Publication Information Available

Library of Congress Cataloging-in-Publication Data
Lankford, Ronald D., 1962–
  Women singer-songwriters in rock : a populist rebellion in the 1990s / Ronald D. Lankford Jr.
    p. cm.
  Includes bibliographical references and index.
  ISBN 978-0-8108-7268-4 (pbk. : alk. paper) — ISBN 978-0-8108-7269-1 (ebook)
  1. Rock music—1991–2000—History and criticism. 2. Women rock musicians. I. Title.
  ML82.L35 2010
  782.42166082'0973—dc22
                          2009028649

∞ ™ The paper used in this publication meets the minimum requirements of American National Standard for Information Sciences—Permanence of Paper for Printed Library Materials, ANSI/NISO Z39.48-1992.

Printed in the United States of America

To Elizabeth C. S. Lankford

Contents

Acknowledgments

I would like to thank Elizabeth C. S. Lankford for reading the various drafts of the manuscript and offering feedback, as well as putting up with endless discussions on third wave feminism and the music of women singer-songwriters in the 1990s. I would also like to thank my editor Renée Camus for her support for my initial proposal and encouragement to broaden the scope of the project.

There were various other people and institutions that offered generous support. I received grants from Sophia Smith College and Duke University, which allowed me to visit both schools. The special collections staff at both colleges helped locate and sort through a wide variety of zines and other materials. I would also thank the library staffs of Sweet Briar College and Lynchburg College for the liberal use of materials. Two public libraries, the Rustburg branch of the Campbell County Public Library (Virginia) and Lynchburg Public Library (Virginia), helped track down a number of hard-to-find books and articles. Special thanks to Beth E. Eby (at Rustburg) and Candy Thompson (at Lynchburg) for help with interlibrary loans.

I would like to thank several other people who either read the manuscript or helped locate materials. Theodore Gracyk, Ann M. Savage, and Ray Pratt offered valuable feedback on early chapters. Both Alyssa Isenstein Krueger and Gail O'Hara were kind enough to forward hard-to-find materials from zines they had been involved with during the 1990s (*Second Skin* and *Chickfactor*, respectively). Finally, I would like to thank both Karen Zarker and Zeth Lundy for feedback and encouragement during the earliest stages of this project.

Introduction

The fact is that gender will remain an issue as long as the music industry is dominated by men, and female musicians remain an exception to the rule.

—Amy Raphael[1]

Rock music provides women with a chance to break out of their social order, to wallow in a passionately sexual chaos of their own making, to blow up the law and roam through spaces where femininity has been throttled.

—Liz Evans[2]

If you had asked a fan or music critic about women in rock around 1992 or 1993, it's doubtful that anyone would have noticed a trend, much less a movement. They might have noted a number of performers who had emerged in the mid- to late 1980s—Tracy Chapman, Suzanne Vega, and Melissa Etheridge—who continued to record. But "the year of the woman," as the singer-songwriters' movement was tagged in 1988, seemed to have lost its momentum by 1989–1990. Fans and critics might have also noted riot grrrl bands like Bikini Kill and Bratmobile, members of a women-based punk movement that had emerged in Washington DC and Washington State in the summer of 1991. While media shy, riot grrrl would flourish for two to three years as a musical style and a broader philosophy, spreading its feminist assault through independently recorded albums and homemade zines. But while the movement would infiltrate towns and cities across the American continent, it remained a small, underground phenomenon. Others might have called attention to promising college bands like the Throwing Muses or alternative performers like Lydia Lunch. But even if a listener put these various strands together in 1992–1993, there was little evidence of a movement of women in rock.

In 1994–1995, however, it became evident that a movement of women singer-songwriters was in motion. It also became evident in retrospect that the movement had emerged as early as 1992. Released in 1993, Sarah McLachlan's *Fumbling towards Ecstasy* and Sheryl Crow's *Tuesday Night Music Club* were slow growers that continued to generate singles in 1994–1995 (McLachlan's "Possession" would reenter the charts in 1997). The success of both performers in the mid-1990s also helped fans and critics look back to 1992–1993—seemingly lean years for women in rock—and note the release of Tori Amos' *Little Earthquakes* and PJ Harvey's *Dry* in 1992, along with the issue of Harvey's *Rid of Me* and Liz Phair's *Exile in Guyville* in 1993. Other releases, Amos' *Under the Pink* and Hole's *Live through This* in 1994, reinforced the idea of a trend. There were many other releases, but the album that pulled all of these strands together and underlined the reality of the movement was Alanis Morissette's *Jagged Little Pill*, released in the summer of 1995. For anyone who had not been paying attention to recent developments in music in 1995, Morissette's album served as a wake-up call.

There were many other women working within pop and rock during the early to mid-1990s, from rappers like Lil' Kim to mainstream pop stars like Mariah Carey. What separated Morissette, Crow, Phair, Harvey, Amos, Courtney Love, and McLachlan from the others, however, was the fact that they wrote and sang their own material, building on thirty-plus years of the singer-songwriter tradition. This element gave these performers cohesion despite the seeming gulf between Hole's pop-punk assault on *Live through This* and McLachlan's ethereal New Age pop on *Fumbling towards Ecstasy*.

In the broadest sense, the singer-songwriter was anyone who wrote and performed his or her own songs, which meant that John Lennon and Paul McCartney were singer-songwriters, even within the Beatles. Labeling someone a singer-songwriter, however, implied that the performer carefully crafted material that was richer lyrically and philosophically than the average pop song. This meant that Lennon and McCartney would be more properly seen as singer-songwriters on singles like "Yesterday" (1965) than "Love Me Do" (1962). While there had always been the implication that these self-penned songs related to the singer-songwriter's personal life, the tradition at its most expansive made room for other approaches. A number of rock performers like Lennon, Bruce Springsteen, and Heart, for instance, offered more generalized lyrics. Lennon's "In My Life" (1965) and Springsteen's "Born to Run" (1975) may have given general insight into each singer's philosophy of life, but the lyrics were not particularly revelatory about either writer's personal life. Still, even in this broad singer-songwriter category, good lyrics and performances by singer-songwriters represented their own kind of truth, a felt authenticity that related to lived experience.

In the narrower sense, the singer-songwriter penned confessional lyrics that seemed to express the writer's innermost thoughts. In a sense, they were the musical equivalent of confessional poets like Sylvia Plath and Anne Sexton, crafting poems drawn from the experience of their own lives. Carole King's *Tapestry* (1971) was a popular example in the early 1970s, with songs like "So Far Away" and "You've Got a Friend" exploring love, romantic conflicts, and friendship. On the album's cover, King sat with her cat in a homey interior, inviting the listener into her private space. The quintessential example of a woman singer-songwriter as an artist, however, was Joni Mitchell, and if *Blue* (1971) covered many of the same themes as *Tapestry*, it did so in a way that was more personal and, seemingly, more revealing. From the opener, "All I Want," to the closer, "The Last Time I Saw Richard," Mitchell took the listener on a journey of the heart, from the warm embrace of love to bitter disillusionment. This confessional quality gave the impression that there was no distance between the singer and the song.

It was this narrower version of the singer-songwriter that, musically and lyrically, became a perfect fit within popular music as the politically charged 1960s faded into what Tom Wolfe would refer to as the Me Decade. During the 1970s, Mitchell and King were joined by James Taylor, Cat Stevens, Carly Simon, and many others in the first half of the decade. Janet Maslin wrote in *The Rolling Stone Illustrated History of Rock & Roll*, "Indeed, the form's clearest hallmark became self-absorption complete enough to counterbalance the preceding era's utopian jive."[3] The genre, to its critics, also quickly became a cliché in the early 1970s. Singer-songwriters were "navel gazers," revealing and reveling in failed love affairs and pretentious observations about life against a soft rock background. Rock critic Lester Bangs noted of an early James Taylor album, "He doesn't care about anything in particular except himself, the love he's found, his dog, and the lanes and pastures in his neighborhood which he finds great contentment ambling through."[4]

Focusing on the personal instead of the political, the singer-songwriter genre became culturally conservative by default, seemingly disconnected from the broader social sphere. It also lacked the rebellious nature of its rock pedigree. While the style seemed to promise more than the typical three-minute love song, it was difficult to describe the moody "Fire and Rain" by Taylor as rebellious. Because the singer-songwriter style was ultimately harmless regarding its social impact, it also proved a safe and acceptable place for women who wished to enter the music business. A woman who expressed personal feelings about love and life while accompanying herself on piano or acoustic guitar had little room to flaunt her sexuality or protest an unequal gender system.[5] Many other strands of women in rock—women within punk during the late 1970s, women within classic rock during the 1970s and 1980s—ultimately became dead ends. But the singer-songwriter proved perennial. Even when MTV seemed to open up an arena for a number of women like Madonna, Cyndi Lauper, and Annie Lennox during the 1980s, the safer singer-songwriter (Suzanne Vega and Tracy Chapman) would reemerge as a popular and critically lauded movement in 1987–1988.

Drawing from both traditional rockers and navel gazers, women singer-songwriters during the 1990s would turn these clichés upside down, combining alternative, classic, and punk rock with lyrics that retained their political bite. With a louder and/or more complex musical backdrop, the new sound provided an attractive and forceful way to deliver a message that was charged with personal politics. If the "feminine" singer-songwriter genre, with its focus on gentle voices, messages, and sounds, had been an easy entry port for women within the music business, women in the 1990s reimagined the genre for a new generation. Author John Covach wrote in *What's That Sound? An Introduction to Rock and Its History*,

> Perhaps the most significant development for the [singer-songwriter] style in the 1990s was the emergence of a new generation of female singer-songwriters—artists whose lyrics dealt with issues that are important to women generally, and with specifically feminist issues as well. Influenced by well-known singer-songwriters like Carole King, Joni Mitchell, and Carly Simon, as well as lesser known but critically celebrated artists such as Kate Bush, Tracy Chapman, and others, the music of this new generation of younger women ranged from quiet and contemplative to angry and aggressive.[6]

While adapting many of the traditional trappings of the singer-songwriter style, these women also pushed hard against old boundaries, demanding the right to be angry and sexual, the right to play electric guitar and scream, and, finally, the right to combine the political and the personal in myriad ways.

The movement of women singer-songwriters in rock also seemed to arrive at the same time as, and share many qualities with, third wave feminism. Many believed that second wave feminism had dissipated with the failure of the Equal Rights Amendment in 1982. This was set against the backdrop of what would come to be defined as a conservative backlash against women during the 1980s, seemingly supported by the Reagan and George H. W.

Bush administrations (1980–1992) in the United States. The new feminist movement would emerge in the twilight of the Reagan-Bush years, and some commentators would pinpoint third wave's birth to the Clarence Thomas Supreme Court nomination hearings in 1991. Third wave represented a significant shift within feminism, partly because the movement represented a new generation of women. Born between the late 1960s and mid-1970s, these young women were—both symbolically and literally—the daughters of second wave feminists. It has often been said that because of this, third wave would take many of second wave's advances for granted. They also rebelled against what they perceived as second wave's shortcomings.

Even attempting to define third wave feminism risks simplifying a complex movement that, depending on the source, was too diffuse to qualify as a movement or is still unfolding today. Historian Rory Dicker wrote, "The designation 'third wave' is a broad one . . . and though it may seem to include an ever-growing group of people, the same could have been said of the first wave."[7] Generally speaking, third wave feminism breaks into two broad philosophies.

On one side, third wave embraces politics and political action, and can be seen as both a continuation and expansion of second wave's commitment to political issues during the 1970s. An example of this could be seen in Third Wave Direct Action Corporation, an organization that helped register voters during the early 1990s; after transforming into the Third Wave Foundation in the mid-1990s, the group funded projects including reproductive health and justice initiatives. While sharing many commitments with second wave, however, politically based third wave breaks with the earlier movement by also focusing on issues of race, ethnicity, colonization, and class. Leslie Heywood and Jennifer Drake noted in *Third Wave Agenda: Being Feminist, Doing Feminism*, "The definitional moment of third wave feminism has been theorized as proceeding from critiques of the white women's movement that were initiated by women of color, as well as from the many instances of coalition work undertaken by U.S. third world feminists."[8] The complaint against second wave feminism and feminists, then, centered on the perception that the earlier movement concentrated on the concerns of white, middle class women, mostly living in the United States. Third wave would continue the legacy of second wave's political commitment, but it would expand that work to an international, multiracial, and classless movement.

The other side of third wave feminism was more entrenched in popular culture than politics, experiencing its feminism through television, magazines, movies, music, and fashion. It was perhaps more intertwined with the consumption of popular culture than an overtly expressed form of feminism.

The cultural-based third wave embraced television shows like *Buffy the Vampire Slayer*, *Xena: Warrior Princess*, and *Gilmore Girls*; magazines like *Sassy*, *Bust*, and *Jane*; movies like *Thelma & Louise*, *Fried Green Tomatoes*, and *G.I. Jane*; politicized figures like Anita Hill, Monica Lewinsky, and Lorena Bobbitt; and women musicians and festivals like Sarah McLachlan and Lilith Fair.[9] These third wave women were sometimes referred to as girlie or lipstick feminists because they embraced many aspects of femininity within the consumer culture that second wave feminists had seemingly rejected, including fashion and make-up; they also rejected the often negative portrayal of heterosexual relationships and heterosexual sex by feminists like Catharine MacKinnon and Andrea Dworkin. Jennifer Baumgardner and Amy Richards noted in *Manifesta: Young Women, Feminism, and the Future*, "Girlie says we're not broken, and our desires aren't simply booby traps set by the patriarchy. Girlie encompasses the tabooed symbols of women's feminine enculturation—Barbie dolls, make-up, fashion magazines, high heels—and says using them isn't shorthand for 'we've been duped.'"[10]

Both sides of third wave had significant Achilles' heels. On the political front, third wave seemed a marginal and fragmented movement at best, with no real public presence. The most persistent argument for a politically based third wave came from within the movement itself, as though repeating a mantra could revitalize feminism in the 1990s. Culturally based third wave had the opposite problem. Almost any woman who combined traditional femininity with slogans like "girl power" could be called a lipstick or girlie feminist. Even shopping, it seemed, empowered women, leaving no line between consumerism and feminism. Many within third wave feminism nonetheless embraced and celebrated these contradictions, and there would even be a great deal of crossover between politically and culturally based feminists during the 1990s.

To muddle matters even more, feminism in the 1990s was sometimes defined and identified in the public arena by women who were often referred to as postfeminists but could more accurately be described as antifeminists. These spokeswomen included Katie Rolphie, Christina Hoff Sommers, Camille Paglia, and, later in the decade, Naomi Wolf. Historian Rory Dicker noted, "In the early 1990s, when third wave feminism was first discussed in the media, self-proclaimed feminist authors promoted their own writing by rehashing the idea that feminism was outmoded and that feminists were whiny victims."[11] Like third wave in general, these women criticized what they perceived as the faults of second wave feminists, but they also offered reactionary positions on issues like affirmative action and date rape. For the antifeminist, second wave feminism had leveled the playing field for all women; now it was up to women to make their way in the world. For anyone not immersed in the finer points of feminism during the 1990s, these multiple positions were contradictory and confusing.

In general, the culturally based third wave was more likely to embrace popular women singer-songwriters during the 1990s, and the basic reasons for this boiled down to ideology and commercialism. Culturally based feminists formed an intricate and intimate relationship with the music of women who wrote and performed their own songs, utilizing these songs to explore issues revolving around relationships, identity, gender, and female sexuality. They were not concerned that Morissette, McLachlan, and Amos recorded for major labels or that these women seldom offered overt feminist views. It was also significant that these performers—in age, class, gender, and race—shared many of the same experiences as their listeners; by presenting these private experiences in the public realm (on record, in concert), then, this music served a similar function to consciousness-raising during the second wave. By making these social connections, music by women singer-songwriters became the soundtrack to the lives of many culturally based third wave feminists during the 1990s.

For many politically based feminists along with riot grrrl purists, however, popular women singer-songwriters were opportunists and culturally conservative. In *Cinderella's Big Score: Women of the Punk and Indie Underground*, Maria Raha expressed what many within punk and riot grrrl believed:

> And out trotted a string of attractive young women armed with guitars and a softer, cleaner feminist bent that tidied up riot grrrl's grit. Enter: Jewel, Alanis Morissette, Fiona Apple, Tracy Bonham, Sheryl Crow, Joan Osborne, et al. The "women in rock" years were now under way—and the public devoured it.[12]

Popular women singer-songwriters refused—politically based feminists and riot grrrls believed—to connect with more substantive women's issues: they wrote about relationships, but only heterosexual relationships; they explored masculinity and femininity, but were unwilling to completely discard the traditional categories; and, finally, they sang about the world from a mostly white, middle class perspective, but refused to analyze their own privilege. According to their critics, popular women singer-songwriters had watered down the feminist punk of riot grrrl for mass consumption. Put simply, they were sell-outs.

While these criticisms may have identified certain truths about the movement, especially as record labels attempted to jump on the bandwagon in the mid-1990s by offering Morissette clones, these opinions were overstated and unbalanced. Popular women singer-songwriters in rock presented a clear trajectory during the 1990s and this trajectory included addressing women's issues in a substantive manner. And in regard to the riot grrrls, many of these singer-songwriters were contemporaries who simply chose to express their art in a less confrontational manner. Ann M. Savage noted in *They're Playing Our Songs: Women Talk about Feminist Rock Music*, "Female music artists made a convincing impact on the music scene in the 1990s. More noteworthy was that many of these artists gained mainstream acceptance despite their political and/or feminist sensibility."[13] Once again, part of this acceptance seemed to relate to the ability of these artists to connect with a broad, mostly female audience who were grappling with the same issues. While different singer-songwriters approached these issues with different degrees of commitment, each artist at least offered an entry point into the everyday workings of relationships, sexuality, and gender from a woman's point of view. Even if the mainstream singer-songwriter had toned down the riot grrrl message, a message nonetheless remained. Writing about Lilith Fair and Meredith Brooks' "Bitch" (1997), Kalene Westmoreland noted, "A moderate feminist message is an effective strategy for a top ten hit and a music festival; the celebration of femininity which 'Bitch' and Lilith Fair have stimulated challenges traditional ideas of women in rock."[14] The mainstream may have often equaled mediocrity and a softer spin on women's issues, but it also proved capable during the 1990s of absorbing, introducing, and spreading feminist ideas. This in itself was radical.

Writing about Women in Rock

The idea of writing about women singer-songwriters in rock during the 1990s only occurred to me over time. I had listened to Tori Amos, Hole, Sheryl Crow, Liz Phair, and Sarah McLachlan for years, but it only later occurred to me that what they were saying (about women's issues and feminism in the 1990s) and how they were saying it (with a rich pop-rock tapestry) deserved a more detailed exploration. Part of what intrigued me was a basic attempt to better understand the issues that singer-songwriters like PJ Harvey, Tori Amos, and Courtney Love were exploring and, in doing so, to gage how much feminist thought could be inserted into popular culture at any given time. I was also curious about the music itself. I understood that singer-songwriters like Crow could be accused of drawing too heavily from rock's past, but I still found it fascinating that Crow, Harvey, and Amos deviated from the singer-songwriter cliché—a quiet girl singing self-absorbed lyrics with piano/acoustic guitar backing—by drawing from indie rock and punk. Simply put, these women seemed to have something to say and a new way of saying it.

Other people had written articles, essays, and books about women singer-songwriters, and I'd learned a lot from books like Simon Reynolds and Joy Press' *The Sex Revolts: Gender, Rebellion, and Rock 'n' Roll*. But I also believed that certain things were either not being covered or had been too easily dismissed. For one, it always surprised me that a great deal of writing about music skipped over the music—the sound—itself. It's one thing to say that Phair's *Exile in Guyville* was voted album of the year by the *Village Voice* in 1993, but you're no closer to comprehending how it sounds. And while describing sound with words may be an imperfect task, it seemed that the author owed it to the reader to at least try. It also seemed problematic to me that many critics were willing to dismiss the more popular singer-songwriters like Alanis Morissette as lightweight rip-offs of earlier riot grrrl bands. It is easy to gain the impression from books like Maria Raha's *Cinderella's Big Score: Women of the Punk and Indie Underground* that mainstream music by women during the 1990s was both aesthetically and politically bland. This seemed unfair.

By drawing from my own appreciation of women singer-songwriters and looking at these issues, *Women Singer-Songwriters in Rock* finally became a book about two things. First, it focuses on a popular movement of women in rock music that mirrored the rise of third wave feminism between 1992 and 1999 (chapters 1, 5, and epilogue). Historically, the women singer-songwriters' movement in the United States opened up in the wake of a changing political and social climate during the early 1990s, grew and came into its own during the mid-1990s, and crashed and burned in the late 1990s as the political and social climate changed once again. The women in rock movement, then, could be loosely described as a popular countermovement against the cultural conservatism as described by Susan Faludi in *Backlash: The Undeclared War against American Women* in 1991.

Second, *Women Singer-Songwriters in Rock* focuses on the work of six women singer-songwriters—Harvey, Phair, Love (Hole), Amos, McLachlan, and Crow—within the movement. Here, I wanted to get a better idea of what each songwriter had to say about women's issues and how she chose to say it through her music, lyrics, and cover art. I also wanted to understand whether feminism within popular music became more diluted in relation to an artist's popularity. How does Harvey's less popular early work (like *Dry*), where male/female relationships often turn violent, compare to Crow's more mainstream work (as on *Tuesday Night Music Club*)? Or how does Phair's early work (*Exile in Guyville*), constructed from bare-bones rock and raw language, compare to McLachlan's ethereal soundscapes and "pretty" vocals (*Fumbling towards Ecstasy*)? How much feminism could filter into the mainstream?

There are a number of reasons to study women singer-songwriters in rock during the 1990s as a separate movement, to isolate the women rockers from the men. The main reason is that women singer-songwriters during the 1990s were drawing from a similar pool of experiences and ideas, exploring the personal and social complications of sexuality, gender, and relationships. The movement, then, included songs written by women that focused on the personal issues that women lived with every day, as well as songs that openly questioned the repercussions of these issues within the broader social sphere. This gave a thematic unity to singer-songwriters like Harvey, Phair, Love, Amos, McLachlan, and Crow, and created an intricate bond with the mostly female fans of these performers. If *Women Singer-Songwriters* had focused on aesthetics alone, then it would have made sense to talk about Harvey and Nirvana, or Phair and the Smashing Pumpkins. Philosophically, however, the grunge and the women singer-songwriters movements seem mostly disconnected. Another much simpler reason for covering women separately is purely personal. I had listened to most of these singer-songwriters for years before I planned to write *Women Singer-Songwriters in Rock*, and I seldom listened to grunge or rap or other kinds of music from the 1990s. It was music that I knew and music that I liked, and music that I believed I had something to say about.

Women Singer-Songwriters in Rock argues that the movement by women in rock made a significant social and aesthetic contribution during the 1990s, a contribution that in essence pushed feminism into mainstream American culture. The pop, rock, and punk that these performers utilized added a fresh sonic imprint to a genre that had often seemed exhausted, while the mix of the personal and political updated consciousness-raising for a new generation of mostly women listeners. It was a combination that was commercially viable while simultaneously offering a persuasive countermovement to the ongoing backlash against women. Simply put, women singer-songwriters in rock during the 1990s found the perfect combinations of lyrics and music, delivering an attractive message in an attractive package to create something we might think of as populist feminism. These women would rely on rock's long legacy of rebellion to generate a vision that questioned the traditions, social conventions, and hierarchies that had relegated them—on the basis of gender—to second class citizenship. Between 1992 and 1999, it was also a vision that would be embraced by millions of listeners.

Notes

1. Amy Raphael, *Grrrls: Viva Rock Divas* (New York: St. Martin's Griffin, 1995), xxx.

2. Liz Evans, *Women, Sex and Rock 'n' Roll* (San Francisco, CA: Pandora, 1994), viii.

3. Janet Maslin, "Singer-Songwriters," in *The Rolling Stone Illustrated History of Rock & Roll*, ed. Jim Miller (New York: Random House, 1976), 312.

4. Lester Bangs, *Psychotic Reactions and Carburetor Dung* (New York: Alfred A. Knopf, 1987), 115.

5. Steve Chapel and Reebee Garfolo, *Rock 'n' Roll Is Here to Pay* (Chicago, IL: Neslon-Hall, 1977), 276–77.

6. John Covach, *What's That Sound? An Introduction to Rock and Its History* (New York: W. W. Norton, 2006), 534.

7. Rory Dicker, *A History of U.S. Feminisms* (Berkeley, CA: Seal Press, 2008), 125.

8. Leslie Heywood and Jennifer Drake, *Third Wave Agenda: Being Feminist, Doing Feminism* (Minneapolis: University of Minnesota Press, 1997), 8.

9. Jennifer Baumgardner and Amy Richards, *Manifesta: Young Women, Feminism, and the Future* (New York: Farrar, Straus and Giroux, 2000), 136–37.

10. Baumgardner and Richards, *Manifesta*, 136.

11. Dicker, *A History of U.S. Feminisms*, 130.

12. Maria Raha, *Cinderella's Big Score: Women of the Punk and Indie Underground* (Emeryville, CA: Seal Press, 2005), 223.

13. Ann M. Savage, *They're Playing Our Songs: Women Talk about Feminist Rock Music* (Westport, CT: Praeger, 2003), 14.

14. Kalene Westmoreland, "'Bitch' and Lilith Fair: Resisting Anger, Celebrating Contradictions," *Popular Music and Society* 25, no. 1 (Spring/Summer 2001), 205–20.

CHAPTER ONE

1995: "You Oughta Know"

Like a woman with a gun, a woman with a very loud guitar is an immediate thwarting of the social status quo.

—Karen Schoemer[1]

We're definitely in a time of gender war.

—Naomi Wolf[2]

In the summer of 1995, an angry song by a twenty-year-old woman from Canada surprised radio listeners and MTV watchers. The lyrics of "You Oughta Know" hurled angry words like weapons against an ex-lover, and while the most offending word was partially censored on radio and MTV, everyone knew that the singer said "fuck." It was an angry fuck, too, the kind of outburst listeners might have expected from Guns N' Roses in 1987–1988 or Nirvana in 1991–1992. But the song's narrator was mad, sounded mad, and seemed unconcerned that someone might find shouting "fuck" objectionable or unladylike. Writing in the *Guardian*, Amy Raphael called "You Oughta Know" "one of the most confrontational songs ever written."[3]

It was also the kind of direct, angry song one might have expected from a Seattle riot grrrl band, the kind of confessional lyric that felt good to get off one's chest, but that would nonetheless never receive radio play. Instead, "You Oughta Know" ascended on three *Billboard* charts: number 3 on Mainstream Rock Tracks, number 7 on the Mainstream Top 40, and number 1 on Modern Rock Tracks. And while many objected to the singer's crude references to sex and her angry vocal, the song and the story it told resonated with a young and primarily female audience.

Alanis Morissette relaunched her music career in the fall of 1994, cutting the tracks for *Jagged Little Pill* in the studio with producer Glen Ballard. She had recorded two albums previously, *Alanis* in 1991 and *Now Is the Time* in 1992, and was compared to Tiffany and Debbie Gibson. Now, she seemed determined to move beyond her teen image. Morissette would eventually be signed to Maverick, an American label operated by Madonna, and the decision would be made to release "You Oughta Know" as the first single from the album. "You Oughta Know," then, would be the single that reintroduced Morissette to the broader public.

The snapshot left behind from "You Oughta Know" is sharp but narrowly focused, a snapshot that concentrates on specific elements while leaving others obscured. Below the residue of anger, Morissette describes a relationship gone awry, one in which a young woman is left behind without warning for an older woman. We are offered no physical description of the older woman, or why she was chosen over the narrator; only that she appears, through the narrator's eyes, as more sophisticated (the narrator has the impression that she speaks eloquently) and is perhaps better prepared for motherhood. These details, along with other lyrics, draw a sketch of domestic tranquility in the male's residence—he seems more peaceful now; the narrator calls and interrupts him during dinner—suggesting he left Morissette's persona for a more mature woman with whom he could settle down and begin a family.

Because the lyric describes the narrator's sexuality so overtly, it is also easy to gain the impression that he considered her a sexual plaything, someone to pass time with until he found a mature woman. And because his departure from the relationship seems so sudden, a listener may also wonder whether he was already involved with the second woman, but had continued to use the narrator.

The story of a love affair gone awry was hardly a new one, but Morissette's presentation was shocking and had a great deal to say about women's experience in the 1990s. It was shocking, first and foremost, because she was a woman expressing anger very publicly. Her righteous anger, however, was not just directed toward the person who had left her: it was directed toward a traditional masculine attitude that allowed men to exploit women (perhaps for sex) and then leave them behind for other women without concern over the emotional consequences. Also, by leaving a sexually adventurous, outspoken young female for an older woman with a more traditional view of femininity (a potential for motherhood, domesticity, and conservative sexual mores), the male who embodies these attitudes passes judgment on femininity and feminine behavior. Certain behaviors are approved or disapproved of according to how well they meet the needs of the man.

In 1995, Morissette was joined on the airwaves by many other women singer-songwriters who were exploring the same issues and likewise finding a sympathetic audience. On the heels of *Fumbling towards Ecstasy* in 1993, Sarah McLachlan had released *The Freedom Sessions*, which rose to number 78 on the Billboard 200. "Hold On," from *Fumbling towards Ecstasy*, rose to number 29 on Modern Rock Tracks in 1995, and "I Will Remember You," from the soundtrack *The Brothers McMullen*, rose on four charts, including the Billboard Hot 100 (number 14). The title track to Liz Phair's *Whip-Smart*, issued by Matador in 1994, rose to number 24 on the Modern Rock chart, while PJ Harvey's *To Bring You My Love* reached number 40 on the Billboard 200 and produced one hit ("Down by the Water," number 2 on Modern Rock Tracks). Hole's 1995 EP, *Ask for It*, reached 172 on the Billboard 200, and the band continued to chart singles ("Asking for It," "Softer, Softest," and "Violet") on Modern Rock Tracks from 1994's *Live through This*. Morissette herself followed "You Oughta Know," which rose on three different Billboard charts, with hits of "All I Really Want" and "Hand in My Pocket."

These women were joined on the charts in 1995 by a healthy cast of women singer-songwriters as soloists and within bands: No Doubt's *Tragic Kingdom* and "Just a Girl"; Poe's single from *Hello*, "Trigger Happy Jack (Drive by a Go-Go)"; Heather Nova's *Oyster* and "Walk This World"; Joan Osborne's *Relish* and "One of Us"; Jewel's *Pieces of You*; and Garbage's self-titled release along with the singles "Queer" and "Vow." Women may not have been on the verge of leveling the historic inequality in the music business, nor were women the only significant trend in popular music during the 1990s; but women singer-songwriters were creating a large and vibrant body of work that explored a multitude of issues that resonated deeply with Gen X women.

"You Oughta Know" shocked listeners in 1995, but not because it revealed anything new: other women singer-songwriters had been exploring similar issues since at least 1992. It was shocking because of the way Morissette's narrator delivered her complaint, because it was aired so publicly, and because she was a woman. If she had been a more traditional singer-songwriter, she might have introduced the song's content more organically or indirectly, with the narrator discussing the problem with a friend or perhaps writing a letter. Instead, Morissette's persona openly challenges her oppressor, openly offers her own moral indictment against his behavior, and openly expresses these thoughts through the least feminine of emotions, anger. And while one might point to other songs with similar content and presentation (PJ Harvey's "Rid of Me"), none had registered so broadly on the popular culture scene. On CD, as a single, as an edited cut on the radio, as performed live, and as an edited video on MTV, "You Oughta Know" reached millions of listeners and viewers, making its challenge to traditional feminine and masculine roles a public one that was difficult to avoid. Because of this direct, very public challenge, "You Oughta Know" served as a battle cry for a new generation of women, giving notice that the rules of engagement between the sexes were in flux.

The New Women Singer-Songwriter: From Joni to Patti

"You Oughta Know" was born into a thirty-year-old singer-songwriter tradition that dated back to the mid-1960s. While blues and folk singers had always penned songs and drawn material from personal experience, designating someone a singer-songwriter implied a predilection toward personal reflection and a serious attitude toward song craft. The genre had deep roots in the folk music and left wing politics of the 1940s. In this sense, Woody Guthrie, writing about life on the road and penning odes to Depression-era America, was something of a singer-songwriter prototype. In the early to mid-1960s, many songwriters, including Bob Dylan, Phil Ochs, and Buffy Sainte-Marie, wrote folk songs protesting the Vietnam War, nuclear weapons, and the treatment of Native and African Americans. By 1964–1965, however, a gradual shift occurred, with songwriters turning away from politics to more personal concerns.

While the singer-songwriter would continue to evolve over the next thirty years leading up to Morissette's "You Oughta Know," the genre's signature elements—simple folk accompaniment and autobiographical lyrics—have helped define and sometimes stigmatize the genre for many listeners. But the genre, even from its very inception, had always been more expansive than the cliché of a woman performing in a coffeehouse with an acoustic guitar and a sad story of love gone wrong. When the women singer-songwriters' movement exploded in the 1990s, it drew from a broad tradition that included both quiet folk singers and noisy punk rockers.

The Myth of the Folk Madonna

In certain circles, the singer-songwriter had always been suspect, a sensitive type who was so consumed with love and self-reflection that she had lost contact with the world. Born in the midst of political turmoil in the mid-1960s, she turned her back on the Vietnam War, the civil rights movement, and the proliferation of nuclear weapons to pen melancholy paeans that compared the various stages of love to the seasons. From this critical point of view the sensitive singer-songwriter, whether female or male, expressed the feminine opposite of masculine hard rock in the late 1960s. With a lyrical concentration on personal relationships and emotion, backed by acoustic guitars and pianos, the singer-songwriter was the spiritual child of confessional poets like Sylvia Plath and Anne Sexton, and a prototype to Tom Wolfe's self-absorbed Me Generation of the 1970s. In an article about James Taylor from *Newsday*, rock critic Robert Christgau noted,

> Essentially . . . Taylor is leading a retreat, and the reason us rock and rollers are so mad at him is simply that the retreat has been so successful. We assume that there is something anarchic in all of us, something dangerous and wonderful that demands response, not retreat.[4]

For many, these prejudices remain even today, and it is easy to trace this model of the singer-songwriter from Joni Mitchell in the 1960s to Carole King in the 1970s to Suzanne Vega in the 1980s to Jewel in the 1990s. In its mainstream incarnation, the style has had a strong presence in multiple *Billboard* charts, which include Mainstream Rock Tracks, Modern Rock Tracks, Adult Contemporary Tracks, the Billboard Hot 100, Mainstream Top 40, and Adult Top 40; in its less commercial incarnation, the genre has a strong presence on Triple A and college radio. But the idea of the singer-songwriter as placid, nonpolitical or politically naïve, and traditionally feminine is quite limited when a listener considers singer-songwriters like Laura Nyro and Patti Smith. Furthermore, even a typical singer-songwriter like Joni Mitchell continued to expand her themes and complicate her musical arrangements throughout the 1970s. In reality, the genre has proved one of the most versatile in rock, even when traveling back to the mid- to late 1960s when the term *singer-songwriter* first came into common usage.

In 1968 when Mitchell issued her debut, *Song to a Seagull*, Nyro released her second album, *Eli and the 13th Confession*. While Nyro, like Mitchell, avoided direct political statements, she nonetheless treated broader social subjects in songs like "Poverty Train," and, as a contemporary to the budding second wave feminist movement, offered a bold exploration of female sexuality in "The Confession." Unlike the musical simplicity of *Song for a Seagull*, these songs were delivered with innovative, full-band and orchestrated arrangements that supported everything from gentle ballads like "Emmie" to abandoned pop-rock in "Women's Blues." And finally, unlike Mitchell's full-vocal range and pristine delivery, Nyro added a touch of soul and, caught up in the emotion of the lyric, sometimes sang beyond her range. By 1968, then, the new genre was broad enough to encompass the early, quiet work of Mitchell and the more expansive pop-oriented work of Nyro.

Despite the potential range of aesthetic choices, popular women singer-songwriters mostly devolved during the late 1970s and throughout the 1980s, relying on the genre's more conservative elements. In the late 1970s, it was easy to place albums like the Roches' self-titled release in 1979 within the folk-based singer-songwriter tradition and perceive Rickie Lee Jones's self-titled release in 1979 as an updated version of Mitchell's *Court and Spark*. Likewise, Tracy Chapman, Suzanne Vega, and many others offered a 1980s version of the plaintive folk Madonna with and without a social conscience. And while each of these performers was well received by critics, and while each of these artist's works touched upon issues that resonated with women listeners, musically and lyrically, something was missing.

These singer-songwriters seldom suggested the expansive musical vision of Nyro's early work, or of Mitchell's mid-1970s work including *Court and Spark* and *The Hissing of Summer Lawns*. Instead, many of these singer-songwriters reinforced the cliché of the sensitive poet on the coffeehouse circuit. A small number of women within rock and punk during the 1970s, however, would offer a broader idea of the singer-songwriter. Punk rocker–poet Patti Smith, for instance, serves as a fine example of just how this minority of women threw the sensitive singer-songwriter into relief.

It is difficult to step back in time in order to understand the impact of Smith's *Horses* on listeners in 1975. Janis Joplin had been dead for five years, and even Mitchell's full-band work never rocked. Women within rock music were still somewhat rare in 1975. And while blues-rocker Bonnie Raitt recorded a series of albums in the 1970s, the more commercial pop-country-rock sound of Linda Ronstadt was much better known. Smith stepped into this vacuum, literally exploding singer-songwriter clichés and opening myriad possibilities for both men and women within the genre.

For those who lived outside of New York City and had never seen Smith live, putting the needle down on *Horses*' first track—"Gloria"—must have been startling. Built around the skeleton-riff and chorus of Van Morrison's "Gloria," Smith and her band married surreal stream-of-consciousness poetry to muscular, stripped-down rock, creating a tour de force of punk energy. The opening lyrics—noting that Jesus might have died for somebody's sins, but not hers—seem tailored to either grab the listener's attention or simply offend her (thus, also gaining her attention). Smith's performance was self-assured and her delivery unwavering, while Lenny Kaye's bluesy electric guitar added sway and swagger. Here was a woman singing about her obses-sion with another woman, the same androgynous woman who had directly returned the viewer's gaze on the album's black-and-white cover. Arty and visceral, Smith's *Horses* offered a provocative blueprint for any singer-songwriter brave enough to make use of it.

Smith would record three more albums—*Radio Ethiopia* (1976), *Easter* (1978), and *Wave* (1979)—before taking a hiatus from the music business. Critics praised her work, and she stood as an equal among American punks. She also found moderate success when *Easter* rose to number 20 on the Billboard Pop Album chart and "Because of the Night" reached number 13 on the Pop Singles chart. But punk was a short-lived and nonpopular movement in America, and few female artists followed in Smith's musical footsteps. Exceptions like Heart, a group that included the songs of Ann and Nancy Wilson, would find a niche within classic rock during the mid- to late 1970s. It would be easy to assert, though difficult to prove, that record labels and radio stations were simply unwilling to, respectively, take chances or provide air time for multiple women performers.

Why were the aesthetic choices for women singer-songwriters so limited? In *Rock 'n' Roll Is Here to Pay*, Steve Chapple and Reebee Garofalo offered a reason for the initial success of singer-songwriter Joan Baez:

> It was no coincidence that the first woman to reach the status of culture heroine was a folksinger performing in a notoriously asexual genre. In a society founded on double standard . . . it is much harder for a woman than a man to project her sexuality in a way that contributes positively to her image.[5]

Margot Mifflin, referring to singer-songwriters like Suzanne Vega and Tracy Chapman, would emphasize a similar point in *Keyboard* in 1990:

> Close your eyes and listen to the "new" women in rock; you'll find that for all their alternative accolades, they sound frighteningly homogenous: humble, sentimental, and harmonically uninventive. They're living proof that our current dilemma has less to do with being asked to show a little leg than with being *forbidden* to show our fangs.[6]

Overall, the idea of a woman singer-songwriter who could balance both rock and poetry would have to wait for another generation.

The Myth of the Confessional Songwriter

There are things that I have gone through that I chose not to write about because they were too personal and while it may seem that I don't have any boundaries, I do.

—Alanis Morissette[7]

Joni Mitchell served as the prototype for the confessional songwriter in the late 1960s and early 1970s, the spiritual child of Plath and Sexton, penning diary entries or transcribing confessions disguised as songs. For baring her soul—exposing her doubts, hopes, dreams, and love affairs—in public, Mitchell gained authenticity, "a kind of strength-through-vulnerability," noted Joy Press and Simon Reynolds in *The Sex Revolts: Gender, Rebellion, and Rock 'n' Roll*.[8] *Clouds* (1969) and *Blue* (1971) impressed listeners as the musings of a poet brave enough to plumb her own depths for psychological and spiritual truths, and then, without concern for her own privacy, share them publicly with her fans. As fans listened to each new album, they believed that they knew the real Mitchell, that she, by baring her soul, had shared her life and loves with each listener personally. "The Last Time I Saw Richard" was rumored to be about Chuck Mitchell, her ex-husband, while "Little Green" may have referenced the child that she gave up for adoption. The myth of the confessional singer-songwriter would endure: that there was no line, and that there should be no line, between a songwriter's personal life and music, and the more painful the confession, the more real the results.

Singer-songwriters have frequently supported the myth. Mitchell, speaking of perhaps her most autobiographical album *Blue*, told writer Bill Flanagan,

> I'll just tell you what you have to go through to get an album like that. That album is probably the purest emotional record that I will ever make in my life. . . . All I knew was that everything became kind of transparent. I could see through myself so clearly. And I saw others so clearly that I couldn't be *around* people. I heard every bit of artifice in a voice. Maybe it was brought on by nervous exhaustion. Whatever brought it, it was a different, un-drug-induced consciousness. . . . I was so thin-skinned. Just all nerve endings. As a result, there was no capability to fake.[9]

When asked by Cameron Crowe whether she had ever been bothered by the fact that she had revealed so much of her life in song, Mitchell only regretted the times that she allowed artifice and infection to enter her work and dilute her style.

Some twenty-four years later, the pattern for the singer-songwriter had not changed. As soon as "You Oughta Know" received airplay, people became interested in the identity of the man in the song. Several names were mentioned and debated in public, and reporters even spoke to men with whom Morissette had been involved. Morissette made no secret that the song was about a specific person, but also stated that she had no intention of revealing his name. Furthermore, she even stated that she had reason to believe that the person she had based the lyric on was unaware that the song was about him. And while the identity of Morissette's ex has never been revealed, the debate did reassure fans of a central singer-songwriter truth: this was a song about a real relationship between Morissette and someone else, and that the events within it were more or less true.

Because of the personal nature of many singer-songwriters' work, and because of the statements singer-songwriters have made concerning their work, it has been easy for fans and critics to read lyrics like "You Oughta Know" as autobiographical. Similarly, this connection is reinforced because singer-songwriters frequently record and perform their own songs. But a literary critic might argue that song lyrics, no matter how truthfully they relate to a personal event, no matter how emotionally true they may seem to be, are not necessarily autobiographical. A reader might assume, for instance, that a confessional poet included autobiographical material within a poem, but not assume that all information within the poem was meant to be taken literally; likewise, even when we find autobiographical content in confessional poems, like Plath's "Daddy," we cannot assume that Plath is the narrator of the poem. Plath is the author who has created a persona to narrate her poem; how much of Plath resides in her personas is impossible to discern. While a lyricist like a poet may draw from her personal experience, then, the listener should accept the result as a filtered experience that works in tandem with a number of creative or fictional elements.

The critic's argument is strengthened in relation to "You Oughta Know." Morissette wrote the song as an imagined response to a man she had been in a relationship with: in reality, according to Morissette, she never made the phone call. So while the man behind the song may have been real, the dialogue between him and Morissette was fabricated. A narrator, then, not Morissette, delivers the lyric; a fantasy persona derived from Morissette, not Morissette herself. Even if "You Oughta Know" had related to an actual phone conversation between Morissette and her ex-boyfriend, the listener should still accept the narrator as a persona. First, there seldom seems a way to validate the information in a song, and a song lyric, like poetry, is not a diary entry.

For many, however, the idea of referring to the entity who delivers Morissette's lyric as a narrator is distancing and may seem unrepresentative of how the song is delivered—in Morissette's voice, by Morissette. Perhaps the easiest way to cut through the autobiography/fictional split would be to think of the entity who delivers a singer-songwriter's lyric as a persona or character, a mask or voice that represents, more or less depending on the performer, the singer-songwriter. Sometimes the voice may even represent the singer-songwriter's reading of a person or her observations about the lives of others. Whether Morissette's persona has detailed an autobiographical or fictional event is immaterial. As far as the listener is concerned, the success of a song like "You Oughta Know" is measured by its emotional resonance and honesty, by its ability to connect with the listener—not by its literal truthfulness.

The signature trait of the women singer-songwriters during the 1990s, then, may have been founded on autobiography, but it was experience that relied on literary conventions including the limitations of expression within a verse-chorus-bridge structure. The broader success of the movement, however, rested upon the emotional truths that resonated with millions of listeners, allowing individual women to see a social dimension to personal issues. Ann M. Savage underlines the importance of the connection between women singer-songwriters and women listeners during the 1990s in *They're Playing Our Songs: Women Talk about Feminist Rock Music*:

> Arguably, an artist's life experience influences her songwriting and performance style. In turn, a female artist's music is bound to ring true for, and be relevant to, other women's lives. Female audience members are drawn to female artists' music because of similar lived experiences. The music, lyrics and the artist become relevant to the listener's life.[10]

By spilling her own guts in a fantasy phone call based on a failed relationship, Morissette's "You Oughta Know" tapped into a generation of women who were ready to make their own angry phone calls. The song, like many others by women singer-songwriters that had preceded it, was much more than the musings of one pissed-off woman who needed to get something off of her chest. It was an emotional cry that resonated with millions of mostly female listeners, reminding women, whether they wore the feminist label or not, that the personal was still very political. In an article in the *Irish Times*, Morissette was asked whether she believed that her music was speaking to "those who have yet to find their own voices": "Definitely. And people do say 'thank you' for specific songs and I know that's because of what I've tapped into, in their lives. On stage, too, it's less about me being up there than what they see in me that reminds them of themselves."[11]

Art and Artifice

Morissette's personal politics may have found a match in a generation of angry women, but it was the sound of "You Oughta Know" that guaranteed the song would receive a sympathetic hearing. As "You Oughta Know" begins, Morissette's voice quivers against an easy drum shuffle, seventeen seconds of relative stillness before the storm breaks loose. While she delivers the first half of each verse in quiet restraint, leaving the emotion to simmer beneath the surface, she allows the bitterness of her feelings to ripen in the second half of each verse. But it is only with the choruses that she comes clean, pushing the intensity and force of her anger to a wail of anguish. Her vocal carries the lyric in all of its splendid fury. It is less singing than an acid-laced growl, less pretty than the cry of an unrelenting emotion. As Morissette totally immerses herself into the passion of the moment, the venom of the rage practically drips from the recorded track, creating a presence that seems to live beyond the song.

The crescendos of electric guitars, played by David Navarro of the Red Hot Chili Peppers, creates a complementary voice, while Flea's (also from the Red Hot Chili Peppers) bass-line balances Morissette's higher vocal range by providing a punchy bottom end. With the addition of drummer Matt Laug (organ has also been added to the track), Morissette, producer Glen Ballard, and the band have created a nicely balanced track with a full range of sounds. The sonic imprint may be hefty and loud, but it matches the intensity of Morissette's vocal and the drama of the lyric. All of these elements work in tandem, energizing "You Oughta Know" with an aural vigor.

The powerhouse performance supported and extended the song's social content, presenting the song's message in an attractive package that easily communicated to larger audiences. It is rhythmic and catchy, but also loud and in your face; it is private and emotive, but also communal and cathartic; and it is direct and hard-hitting, but also conversational and politically understated. "You Oughta Know" is a powerful rock song that communicates its social politics through lived experience, stylish and uncompromising. This combination of sheer sound and lived experience gave the singer-songwriter genre a new edge and power that made the music more attractive both aesthetically and commercially. But it was a combination that was not always understood, and it was even easy for someone as successful at it as Morissette to fall back on a number of clichés of the singer-songwriter genre.

At the beginning of 1996, Morissette radically rearranged "You Oughta Know" for a live performance at the Grammy Award ceremony. She would use a similar arrangement when she performed the song for MTV Unplugged in 1999. Unlike the original, the newer version was an acoustic ballad with strings, one that made its emotional argument very quietly. The only emotional fireworks occur on the choruses, which are similar—save for the quieter acoustic instruments—to the choruses on the original version. Morissette has stated that she wished to communicate the confusion she had experienced more clearly with the rearranged version of "You Oughta Know," expressing the vulnerability she had felt in the aftermath of the relationship. This would prove as a corrective, since many listeners only seemed to connect with the anger of the original version:

> That song is more vulnerable than upset and angry. Anger is an extension of hurt to me. It's a cowardly way of dealing with pain. When I sing the song now, I think back to the original emotion. The acoustic version with strings at the Grammys was my way of carrying it back to its first emotion, feeling hurt and confused. So, when I see the Angry Young Women label, it's completely missing the point of what the song is about.[12]

The mellower version, however, evoked Mitchell and Vega more than the new singer-songwriter of the 1990s, and the raw references to sex and profanity seemed out of place for this rock ballad. In this instance, Morissette seemed to have misunderstood both her own lyric and the change that she and other women singer-songwriters had ushered in during the 1990s. Even more problematic, she gave the appearance of joining those who had criticized or disliked the song because of its depiction of female anger. By offering a new performance that was more in line with the traditional idea of a singer-songwriter, Morissette had attempted to declaw "You Oughta Know" and to offer a more conservative, reasonable image of herself: she was more than an angry young woman. Seemingly for most listeners, however, the original version of "You Oughta Know" remained the better-known track, and it would continue to define Morissette and offer perhaps the best-known example of the women singer-songwriters' new visceral sound during the 1990s.

Singer-Songwriter Building Blocks

The change initiated by women signer-songwriters in rock during the 1990s had required a lengthy gestation period. While a small handful of women singer-songwriters followed in the footsteps of Patti Smith between the mid-1970s and very early 1990s, few found the right combination of lyrics and music needed to deliver a powerful sound and sharp social message to a popular audience. Instead, women singer-songwriters either conformed to the more conservative idea of the folk Madonna, offering an acceptable feminist message wrapped in a familiar musical package, or they ignored all the rules, offering a radical feminist message wrapped in a noisy, noncommercial musical package.

    In the mid- to late 1980s, the woman singer-songwriter made her strongest comeback since the popular heyday of the genre in the early 1970s. Vega and Tracy Chapman led a group of women singer-songwriters who seemed to follow in the spiritual footsteps of Mitchell and Joan Baez. With soft feminism and a nostalgic roots sound, they inhabited an acceptable niche for women during a conservative era both within and without the music industry. The progressive politics and roots music approach of Chapman, Shocked, and others, however, was polite, safe, and seldom rocked. The idea of a folk Madonna quietly mining the nostalgic qualities of protest folk and singer-songwriter self-absorption was both acceptable to the music industry and, for a short time, marketable. It was, however, overly familiar, an old aesthetic that had little to add to the history of the woman singer-songwriter or to music in general.

This is not to argue that these performers were apolitical. Chapman's self-titled debut was broadly seen as a slap against the complicity of the conservative Reagan era, and the set's most passionate song, "Behind the Wall," addressed issues of violence against women. The lyrics on *Tracy Chapman*, however, were seldom as daring as "Behind the Wall," and all of the words were wrapped in a gentle folk-rock; Chapman's musical approach might have been better described by the press as quietly intense than angry. In many ways, singer-songwriters like Chapman and Michelle Shocked were throwbacks to the 1960s, adding a layer of nostalgia to even their most acute political songs. For people who missed or idealized the 1960s, and for those who disliked the mainstream music of the 1980s, these women singer-songwriters offered an intelligent if predictable alterative. Commenting on the music industry during the 1980s in *Keyboard*, Margot Mifflin wrote, "Despite occasional magazine articles celebrating the changing roles of women in rock and pop, the progress of feminism in this industry was negligible in the eighties."[13]

Three or four years after the media grew tired of this trend in women's music, a new movement erupted in Washington DC and Washington State called riot grrrl. Borrowing from 1970s punk DIY (do-it-yourself) aesthetic, riot grrrl rejected everything the earlier quiet girl movement had stood for: it was abrasive, radically feminist, and purposefully noncommercial. Instead of poetic lyrics and acoustic-electric arrangements, riot grrrls explored a full range of women's issues against a backdrop of industrial punk noise. They refused to sign to mainstream record labels, and after the press became interested in the movement, expressed ambivalence toward media coverage. Riot grrrl seemed to pick up the baton dropped by women punks after the mid- to late 1970s and build a strong underground market through music and zines during the early 1990s.

While the movement possessed an integrity lacking in the women's singer-songwriter movement of the mid- to late 1980s, its uncompromising punk sound and profane, direct lyrics seemed tailor-made for the small audience it reached. More problematic, however, was that while the movement clearly energized an underground community mostly consisting of girls and young women, the music that surrounded these political messages often seemed an afterthought. Simon Reynolds and Joy Press wrote, "These women are not necessarily *interested* in making a contribution to rock history or the evolution to the form. Riot Grrrl is foremost about the *process*, not product."[14] As a result, the music of bands like Bikini Kill and Bratmobile was rudimentary and lacked originality. "From a rock critical perspective, most Riot Grrrl bands seemed to be engaged in a reinvention of the wheel: they sound like very traditional hardcore or late '70s punk bands."[15] Riot grrrl, then, bravely advanced the idea of feminist politics within loud rock and punk, but seemed to have little interest in presenting this vision in a manner that might reach a popular audience.

The woman singer-songwriter in rock during the 1990s would negotiate the difference between these two extremes, with each songwriter finding her niche along the continuum, somewhere between abrasive and melodic, poetic and visceral. Historically, she would borrow her punk-fueled anger from Smith and X, but borrow her sharply observed lyricism from Mitchell and Vega; her smart sense of song craft from the Go-Go's and the Pretenders, but her jagged rock edge from the Throwing Muses and Mary Margaret O'Hara; and her sense of the theatrical from Kate Bush, but her political righteousness from Sinead O'Connor. The earlier version of "You Oughta Know" from *Jagged Little Pill* successfully navigated the new aesthetic, finding an equilibrium between the harsh assault of Bikini Kill and the fragile lyricism of Vega. While the forging of a new aesthetic would take many twists and turns during the 1990s, the central elements—the combination of loud rock or sophisticated pop, self-penned lyrics, and social commentary—gave the women singer-songwriters' movement cohesion despite many individual styles.

During the 1990s, this new aesthetic would allow the woman singer-songwriter a broader range of emotional and musical colors on her palette. This ensured that her angry song sounded angry, but not so angry as to register as no more than an aural assault; this ensured that her lyrics truthfully expressed her personal politics, but not so directly as to register as no more than a slogan set to music. No longer simply a songbird or an underground insurgent, the woman singer-songwriter unleashed an original musical rebellion in the 1990s that would redefine women within the contemporary music scene.

Riding the Third Wave

Despite the fact that Morissette connected with millions of women and touched on issues of sexuality, gender, and relationships, many questioned her and other singer-songwriters' feminist credentials. It was easy to ignore the criticism of conservative commentators who had never embraced feminism as a legitimate philosophy. Hearing songs from *Jagged Little Pill* on the radio in the presence of her twelve-year-old twins, singer Debbie Boone complained about lyrical content.[16] This, however, was to be expected. It was more complicated to respond to criticism from progressive women who might have been seen as Morissette's potential allies.

Part of the problem was generational. As Carrie Borzillo noted in *Billboard*, songwriters like Morissette wrote lyrics "so strikingly personal that they seem more suited for a therapist's ear than for millions of strangers."[17] And although feminist critics were sympathetic to Morissette's outrage, they argued that her protagonist's inability to let go of an unhealthy relationship clung to the conservative ideas of traditional femininity. Kristen Schilt noted in *Popular Music and Society*,

> [Morissette] offers no examples of a woman receiving sexual pleasure, which casts women back into the traditional sexually passive role. Also, if Morissette is truly a feminist rock heroine as the papers claim, is being unable to let go of a relationship a positive message for young girls?[18]

For many second wave feminists, "You Oughta Know" failed to present a positive image of an independent woman.

For politically minded third wave feminists and punk rock purists, Morissette and her peers presented other problems. Morissette, Liz Phair, Sheryl Crow, Courtney Love, PJ Harvey, Tori Amos, and Sarah McLachlan were white, mostly middle class, and heterosexual, thus representing only a narrow point of view on women's issues. Because of their privileged positions within the culture, they were incapable of offering a radical critique of patriarchal culture or of comprehending how racism, colonialism, classism, and homophobia supported patriarchal authority. There was also a backlash against Morissette's popularity within the punk/alternative rock community: she, critics charged, reaped the benefits of the foundation that had been laid down by earlier bands like Bikini Kill and Bratmobile. These critics argued that Morissette's anger was little more than a watered-down version of riot grrrl. Maria Raha wrote in *Cinderella's Big Score: Women of the Punk and Indie Underground*,

> When word got out that riot grrrls' affection could not be bought or co-opted easily . . . , mainstream music seemed to trip over its own version of the "angry girl." And out trotted a string of attractive young women armed with guitars and a softer, cleaner feminist bent that tidied up riot grrrl's grit.[19]

For these critics, Morissette's music represented a step back for women.

Many women, however, were focused on popular culture, not politics, and for these third wave feminists, these criticisms against Morissette were either old-fashioned or beside the point. "You Oughta Know" was simply a gut-level reaction aimed at a man who had betrayed a woman, not a treatise on how to properly end a relationship or be a good feminist. Morissette's outraged vocal and the crunchy electric guitar sounded as angry as the lyric, and many women related to that anger. If Morissette's persona reminded one of an irrational Glenn Close in Fatal Attraction, so be it. But unlike Close's Alex, who was interpreted from a male director's point of view, Morissette offered her story from a woman's point of view. Author Elizabeth Wurtzel noted of the song in Bitch: In Praise of Difficult Women, "And the funny thing is, by the end of the song, I do get the feeling that Alanis Morissette has achieved a great deal more dignity by being true to herself, her impulses, however idiotic, than any of us are by staying in control."[20]

By purging her bad energy, by expressing her personal turmoil, and by sharing her turmoil with other women who had experienced the same thing, Morissette's "You Oughta Know" provided a portrait of an empowered woman for a new generation.

But "You Oughta Know" also provided a deeper underpinning for third wave philosophy in general. By painting a portrait of a sexually active young adult woman, and by sketching an unresponsive, insensitive adult male, Morissette explored a number of cultural expectations regarding women's sexuality along with masculine and feminine stereotypes. In "You Oughta Know," the young woman defies traditional feminine social rules by being openly and unapologetically sexual and angry. Her intense affection for the male antagonist is measured against the more traditional femininity of her imagined replacement: the new woman is older, articulates her speech more clearly, and is seen as potentially being a good mother. Because she has been replaced, Morissette's character believes her ex-boyfriend is judging her as immature and insufficient, and that he has perhaps viewed her as a sexual plaything. The ex-boyfriend, then, can accept women as sexual aggressors temporarily, but not as permanent mates. The heaviest criticism, however, falls on a type of masculinity that allows a male to make promises, leave someone behind without explanation, quickly find a new love interest, and have no qualms about the emotional wreckage in the rearview mirror.

Many feminists might object that Morissette's criticism fails to radically alter the traditional male/female dynamic: while her persona complains bitterly in "You Oughta Know," she remains more or less a victim of the male's behavior and choices. Within third wave feminism, however, the victory rests in her refusal to remain silent. While Morissette's character may be a victim, she, by speaking out, shows that she will not remain one. On the cover of the single for "You Oughta Know," a blurry, closely framed shot reveals a partial female face and, in the foreground, a small frog pressed between her index finger and thumb. Psychologically, the woman on the cover appears in control, a control that extends to inflicting harm if and when she chooses. Far from remaining static, the traditional male/female dynamic has been reversed: within her power, the frog has little chance of becoming a prince.

The anger of "You Oughta Know," then, represents much more than one woman and her relationship problems: it is an outburst by any woman who has been wronged; it is a rebellion by any woman who has been taught by her societal upbringing to keep her feelings to herself; it is a cry of anguish against a limited style of masculinity that refuses to accept responsibility for its actions; and it is an outburst by any woman who is no longer willing to remain a victim or no longer willing to sacrifice herself for masculine requirements.

This connection between singer-songwriter and audience extended to many other women's issues during the 1990s, and even Morissette's vision expanded beyond sexuality and gender expectations. Over the course of *Jagged Little Pill*, Morissette examined a number of women's issues that lay at the heart of third wave feminism, including sexism ("Right through You"), social expectations/emotional violation ("Perfect," "Forgiven," "All I Really Want"), and relationships ("Head Over Feet," "Not the Doctor"). These songs, then, would become part of the fabric of women's lives during the 1990s, working as touchstones for exploring personal issues in both the private and public realms. In Ann M. Savage's *They're Playing Our Songs*, one young woman that she interviewed underlined this point when speaking of Morissette's "Hand in My Pocket": "I love that song. . . . I can identify with [the lyrics]. She's talking about contradictions within herself. . . . Why do you have to be one thing? Why can't you be a million things rolled into one?"[21] These connections and the public airing of these issues worked like a populist version of consciousness-raising, encoding a popular cultural movement with feminist politics.

Other women singer-songwriters in rock would echo and expand these issues during the 1990s, exploring the clichés of masculinity and femininity (Liz Phair, PJ Harvey), the potential trauma of growing up female (Tori Amos), and the acts of betrayal and emotional assault within relationships (Sarah McLachlan, PJ Harvey). As women singer-songwriters in rock sang out their lives, these issues reverberated and validated both the singer's and the listener's communal experiences.

Rebellion

Upon its release, "You Oughta Know" caused a knee-jerk reaction from many listeners, offering support for the idea that Morissette's song had hit a sensitive spot in the culture. Rock critic Greil Marcus wrote, "Late last summer, when Alanis Morissette's 'You Oughta Know' was hitting the radio left, right, and center, five people sat around a table trying to figure out what this horrible piece of bleating na-na-na was doing in our lives."[22]

In *Playboy*, Charles M. Young seemed to be attempting to live up to feminist opinion of the magazine by describing "You Oughta Know" as "a harrowing howl of rage about being dumped for a more fabulous babe."[23] Young also wondered about Morissette's future relationships: "[She would] have to find lovers with real low SAT scores or go to bed with guys who are so intimidated at the prospect of getting ripped in her next song that they will just lie there staring at the ceiling."[24]

Others commented on Morissette's shrill vocals, noted the importance of producer Glen Ballard to the success of *Jagged Little Pill*, and called attention to her earlier work, when she had been seen as the Debbie Gibson of Canada.

There also seemed to be a gender divide between those who liked and who disliked "You Oughta Know." "Women, by and large, love the song," wrote Ian Shoales in the *Milwaukee Journal Sentinel*. "Men, by and large, seem terrified by it."[25] Anger and sexual aggressiveness, after all, were supposed to be male attributes, and, from a cultural point of view, healthy ones within limits. Presented by Morissette and representing a woman (any woman) who had been wronged by a man (any man), though, the lyric and presentation of "You Oughta Know" proved threatening and destabilizing to accepted male/female gender roles. By questioning these roles publicly, Morissette and her singer-songwriter peers had broken a silent pact between the sexes.

In one sense, the rebellion of women singer-songwriters in the 1990s was nothing new: youth cultures had frequently rebelled against the previous generation. But the fact that these singer-songwriters were women who were rejecting a gender system that had never benefited them threw a monkey wrench into what might have been seen as normal rebellion.

To a generation that came of age listening to a different kind of rock during the 1950s and 1960s, the typical rebellion was a rite of passage for the middle class male. The idea that rock might really mean something, however, that rock might actually threaten a social system, was somewhat passé by the 1970s, though many social conservatives continued to worry about the effect of the music's sexual content and profane language on the

American family. By the 1970s, it was easy to see that middle class rebellion amounted to little more than a phase that a young man passed before attending college, joining the work force, and then joining his parents, with his own family, in the suburbs. Temporarily rejecting the values of one's parents, then, had become part of growing up in America, a middle class privilege that parents could afford to indulge. Few Americans, however, seemed to want their teenage daughters to be as sexually free, foul mouthed, and as angry as Morissette, and few wanted their children to call basic assumptions of gender into question.

Questioning these assumptions gave the movement the potential, however, to be a new kind of rebellion, one that permanently altered the way women thought about identity, gender, and relationships. By exploring these issues and dismantling traditional thought, the women singer-songwriters in rock movement promised no less than a rebellion in how women lived their lives and related to the world around them. This gave the movement both a personal and social dimension: as women singer-songwriters enriched the lives of a new generation of women, they also provided a powerful countermovement to the ongoing backlash against women. The social tremor that accompanied Morissette's "You Oughta Know" represented a deep shift in feminist politics and gender relations within popular culture during the 1990s. "You Oughta Know," then, served as a battle cry for the new movement as it gained ascendency in the summer of 1995, empowering sympathetic listeners and informing everyone else that the rules had changed.

Notes

1. Karen Schoemer, "Kitten, Bikini Kill and Boss Hog Maxwells," *New York Times*, February 6, 1992, C20.

2. Farai Chideya (with Melissa Rossi and Dogen Hannah),"Revolution, Girl Style," *Newsweek*, November 23, 1992, 85.

3. Amy Raphael, "Women: Look at Me I'm Famous," *Guardian*, October 10, 1995, 7.

4. Robert Christgau, "James Taylor," *Newsday*, November 1972; reprinted at Robert Christgau's website, www.robertchristgau.com/xg/bk-aow/taylor.php.

5. Steve Chapel and Reebee Garfolo, *Rock 'n' Roll Is Here to Pay* (Chicago, IL: Nelson-Hall, 1977), 276.

6. Margot Mifflin, "The Fallacy of Feminism in Rock," *Keyboard*, April 1990; reprinted in *Rock She Wrote: Women Write about Rock, Pop, and Rap*, ed. Evelyn McDonnell and Ann Powers (New York: Delta, 1995), 78.

7. T. L. Khoo, "Up Close with Alanis Morissette," *New Straits Times*, November 27, 1996.

8. Simon Reynolds and Joy Press, *The Sex Revolts: Gender, Rebellion, and Rock 'n' Roll* (Cambridge, MA: Harvard University Press, 1995), 249.

9. Bill Flanagan, *Written in My Soul: Rock's Great Songwriters Talk about Creating Their Music* (Chicago, IL: Contemporary Books, 1986), 242, 243.

10. Ann M. Savage, *They're Playing Our Songs: Women Talk about Feminist Rock Music* (Westport, CT: Praeger, 2003), 25.

11. Joe Jackson, "Jagged Little Lady," *Irish Times*, April 12, 1996.

12. "Vulnerable, Not Angry," *Winnipeg Free Press*, August 4, 1996, B4.

13. Mifflin, "The Fallacy of Feminism in Rock"; reprinted in McDonnell and Powers, *Rock She Wrote*, 77.

14. Reynolds and Press, *The Sex Revolts*, 327.

15. Reynolds and Press, *The Sex Revolts*, 327.

16. Paul Cantin, *Alanis Morissette: You Oughta Know* (Toronto: Stoddart, 1997), 162.

17. Carrie Borzillo, "Maverick Finds Smooth Going for Morissette's 'Pill,'" *Billboard*, July 15, 1995, 1 (2).

18. Kristen Schilt, "'A Little Too Ironic': The Appropriation and Packaging of the Riot Grrrl Politics by Mainstream Female Musicians," *Popular Music and Society* 26, no. 1 (February 2003): 5–16.

19. Maria Raha, *Cinderella's Big Score: Women of the Punk and Indie Underground* (Emeryville, CA: Seal Press, 2005), 223.

20. Elizabeth Wurtzel, *Bitch: In Praise of Difficult Women* (New York: Anchor Books, 1998), 32–33.

21. Savage, *They're Playing Our Songs*, 75.

22. Greil Marcus, "Days between Stations," *Interview*, April 1, 1996, 80.

23. Charles M. Young, "Alanis Morissette Is a Big Deal," *Playboy*, May 1, 1996, 141.

24. Young, "Alanis Morissette Is a Big Deal," 141.

25. Ian Shoales, "'You Oughta Know,'" *Milwaukee Journal Sentinel*, March 3, 1996, 8.

CHAPTER TWO

Rid of Me: PJ Harvey

The reason I started to do music instead of what I was doing before, which was sculpture, was because I feel that music is a better, more physical way to reach people. Pieces of artwork can make you think, but they don't grab you by your stomach, shake you around for three minutes, and then leave you feeling exhausted and drained.

—PJ Harvey[1]

I'm always looking for extremes in things. That's what I try to do in my music, push something as far as you can take it. Until it becomes almost unacceptable.

—PJ Harvey[2]

Elvis Costello once commented that it seemed like a lot of PJ Harvey's songs were about blood and fucking.[3] And while his comment may have seemed overly critical and simplistic, it did distill the minimalism of the subject matter: in Harvey's early songs, her characters are often trapped by elemental desires that keep them locked in combat with themselves and with the opposite sex.

In "Snake," PJ Harvey reinterprets the Fall, with Eve narrating her sexual betrayal by the snake, a dramatic story with dramatic presentation. Harvey's lyric crudely describes the snake crawling between Eve's legs, and her anguished vocal embodies the pain of the betrayal, with Eve listing the promises made by the snake—that she would no longer need God or "him" (Adam)—promises that will never be kept. The propulsive guitar and shouted vocal pound the listeners' senses, more an assault than musical in any traditional sense. In a second version of "Snake" from *4-Track Demos* (1993), Harvey's Eve literally stops mid-song to release an extended moan-cry, completely breaking down and bringing the song to a temporary halt.

In "Snake," and many other songs from *Dry* (1992) and *Rid of Me* (1993), Harvey draws a bleak sketch of a world where women and men are born to desire one another emotionally and physically. But pure desire honestly expressed has a short shelf life; soon desire is thwarted or betrayed by complications and entanglement, leading to desperation, revulsion, and violence. A man or woman may indulge in escape fantasies that shed sheer physicality, but the impossibility of escaping desire burdens even fantasies. It is a world that might feel overly determined and fatalistic were it not for the fact that Harvey's female characters frequently rebel against what may seem like the natural order of male-female relationships.

While "Snake" clearly sounds like a rock song (albeit a particularly emotionally strained one), it is easy to see traces of the blues (Howlin' Wolf, John Lee Hooker) that influenced Harvey in her youth in both the lyric and performance.[4] Likewise, it is easy to see the direct influence of the blues in many 1960s and 1970s rock performers, from Eric Clapton and Cream to Led Zeppelin. And as for blues performers in general, sex and betrayal was a frequent subject matter. But noting that Harvey's early work focused on relationship turmoil and sexual desire is not the same thing as saying that many early Led Zeppelin (from *Led Zeppelin I* and *II*, 1969) songs were about relationship turmoil and sexual desire.

When listening to Led Zeppelin's "The Lemon Song" from *Led Zeppelin II*, for instance, the listener never feels entangled in a claustrophobic life that consists of physical pain and emotional sorrow. Instead, the listener notes the style of Robert Plant's frenzied vocal and his persona's request, despite his relationship with a woman he considers deceitful, for sexual gratification. Sexual release, like rock music itself, is an act of liberation, and "The Lemon Song" above all else embodies the liberation of rock.

Unlike Plant's persona in "The Lemon Song," Harvey's Eve remains earthbound in "Snake," a slave to her desires with no chance of emancipation. After she has been betrayed by the Snake, Eve can only improve her situation by making peace with another oppressor, Adam. Even if the listener concentrates on how a man suffers when saddled with an ungrateful woman in "The Lemon Song," Plant's persona is still able to identify himself, no matter how bad things appear, as a man. For Harvey, an Eve made of flesh can never boast of being a woman, but is damned to imprisonment within her own flesh.

There is also a sense in which the listener would never take the blues of Led Zeppelin seriously, unless he was either very young or committed to a traditional masculine code. "The Lemon Song" is less a blues song, then, than a facsimile of a blues song performed by four young men who were perhaps familiar with the genre but far removed from its origins in time and space. The blues form Led Zeppelin inherited or borrowed from was already sexist; the band, however, reduced the form to its most sexist elements and then left out the traditional cultural markers of the genre. Because of the exaggeration of the blues form, it may even seem comical that the man in the song falls out of bed when the woman squeezes his lemon. Likewise, it might be less easy to sympathize with the supposed hardship the narrator experiences, that he has to work a day job and that his woman is deceitful, because these elements seem more fantastic than real. In the end, approximating or appropriating the blues in "The Lemon Song" seems like a good excuse to present a male fantasy within the rock idiom, not a chance to relate to a black sharecropper's life in the Mississippi Delta in the 1930s.

It would also be easy to note that Harvey's "Snake" is far removed from the Mississippi Delta, but this misses a central point: Harvey's blues, wherever the listener locates them in place and time, feel like a true lament, not an imitation. She may borrow from myth, but she dresses the myth in a woman's flesh and blood. Far from comical or titillating, Harvey has distilled Eve's grief into a chilling, universal cry. A woman, unlike Led Zeppelin's man, is cursed to be betrayed, not to betray; betrayed by her own body to desire men and betrayed by the men she desires. And while "Snake" may have had little in common musically or lyrically with the great Delta blues masters, it nonetheless offered a new kind of blues with a distinctive feminine point of view, fully worthy of the Delta. It was late twentieth-century blues for a new kind of woman.

In this sense, if Liz Phair's *Exile in Guyville* was a deconstruction of the Rolling Stones' *Exile on Main Street*, then Harvey's early work might be seen as a deconstruction of the classic rock and heavy metal albums in the mold of *Led Zeppelin II*. Imaginatively borrowing from the classic rock blueprint, Harvey's characters inhabit a constricted world when compared to the typical Led Zeppelin male. Her characters may be as unapologetically sexual as those in Led Zeppelin's work, but because of traditional culture and biology, they are left to bear the brunt of sexual responsibility. Between 1991 and 1993, Harvey offered a corrective, exploring masculinity and femininity both lyrically and sonically from a woman's point of view.

Early Releases

In the beginning, "PJ Harvey" worked as both the name of a band and the name of its primary songwriter, guitarist, and singer. The band formed in 1991, and first consisted of Harvey, bassist Ian Oliver, and drummer Robert Ellis, before solidifying when Stephen Vaughan replaced Oliver. In a short time, the band would record its first set of songs on a five thousand pound budget, which would be released as *Dry* on the Too Pure label in 1992.

Singles

Harvey issued her first single, "Dress," on Too Pure in 1991. In the song, Harvey relates a somewhat elliptical tale of a woman, a man, and a dress. Like a blues lyric, many of Harvey's lyrics only provide a bare sketch of a song's drama. While the emphases and inflections of her recordings help clarify certain intent, her songs still frequently remain open to multiple readings. Lyrically, the listener might observe that the inferences in "Dress" are somewhat obvious, though there is also a powerful subtext that is difficult to read. Also, no matter how obvious the content may appear, the song's theme—the conflict between a woman's desire to be attractive to men by wearing a dress and the fact that a dress constricts a woman's movement—was an unusual subject matter for a single in 1991 and, perhaps, any other time.

At the beginning of "Dress," Harvey's character is putting on a red, sparkling dress to go out dancing, wondering how she can dress to please her man. This is juxtaposed by the fact that her dress is difficult to walk in, that she describes herself as toppling over like a tree heavy with fruit. Feminist Susan Brownmiller wrote,

> Feminine clothing has never been designed to be functional, for that would be a contradiction in terms. Functional clothing is a masculine privilege and practicality is a masculine virtue. To be truly feminine is to accept the handicap of restraint and restriction, and to come to adore it.[5]

At the beginning of the second stanza of "Dress," however, her initial optimism seems daunted by loneliness. Still, she believes the music, which is good for romance, will make everything okay. But quickly, the lyric becomes unclear, the meaning murky. The man arrives, tells her that she looks good, but also reminds her that he is the one who bought the dress. In the last stanza, she notes that the tight dress is now dirty, that she wishes to leave, and that she is a fallen woman. It is easy to read a sexual exchange between the two characters into the song though one is never stated; that because she received a dress from him, she was now indebted. But Harvey never clarifies the exchange, leaving it submerged within the lyric.

Sonically, "Dress" is on the edge of explosion, with bass guitar and Rob Ellis' percussion adding a propulsive urgency.[6] The chords become more open and airy on each chorus, temporarily releasing the listener from the tense undertow of each stanza. Harvey's electric guitar bolsters the fullness of the sound, and she adds a rare solo after the second verse and chorus. Most unusual, however, is how the overall arrangement is given depth by Harvey's darkly hued violin. While the violin remains mostly in the background, it adds an uneasy undercurrent that haunts the song. Harvey's reading of the lyric, especially during the verses, includes inflections and slight coloring that echo her character's anxiety. As a performance, "Dress" captures and portrays feminine anxiety.

The single for "Dress" also features cover art by Maria Mochnacz, an artist who would collaborate on a number of early Harvey singles, albums, and videos. The cover of "Dress" is listed as a photograph, though the black-and-white contrast is so high that the picture looks like a sketch. The content is also difficult to ascertain. A girl or woman wearing a dress is upside down, suspended or held in some way by ropes. There is also a heavy black shadow beside her. On first glance, it appears she could be on a swing set (thus the strange angle) or perhaps jumping rope (in the video for "Dress," it is a circus-style swing). But the rope is anchored in what appears to be a ceiling, and the hanging rope is twisted around the girl's arms and held in her hands. The girl's face/head cannot be seen, and the shadow is out of sync, seeming to fall away from the girl's body. While the combination of high contrast, unusual angle, a body with no head, and suspended ropes creates an unsettling image, it simply lacks the cohesion needed to make its connection with the song convincing.

Harvey released her second single, "Sheela-Na-Gig," in February of 1992, a month before the release of her first album, *Dry*. "Sheela-Na-Gig," like "Dress," was a sonic powerhouse that underpinned an unusual lyric by almost any standard. Sheela-Na-Gigs are ancient statues in Britain and Ireland that feature a feminine figure, frequently laughing, with an exaggerated vulva, which the female figure is pulling open or apart with both hands. In the song, Harvey's persona exhibits her naked body, provocatively asking her man to view her natural sexuality, which includes the ability to procreate. Instead of being enticed or intrigued, however, he repeats the song's title, "Sheela-Na-Gig," as an insult and tells her that she is an exhibitionist. Instead of feeling ashamed of herself, however, the narrator, referencing *South Pacific*, promises to wash the man out of her hair and to take her womanly curves to another man who appreciates them.

As with "Dress," the subtext complicates what may seem like a straightforward lyric. On one level, the narrator of "Sheela-Na-Gig" disrupts feminine stereotypes by asserting her sexuality. But while her naked display may be read as sexually aggressive, the lyric is less concerned with the idea of woman-as-temptress or aggressor than a woman's natural sexuality and her natural state of nakedness. In this simple act of undressing, then, her persona has revealed all that she is in her natural state, a process not unlike baring one's soul. The process has left her vulnerable. Her man, however, finds her natural state vulgar and rejects her.

Sonically, the arrangement for "Sheela-Na-Gig" offers greater nuance than "Dress," with the instrumental backdrop carefully raising and lowering the volume to match both the lyrical content and Harvey's vocal emphasis. The opening vocal of the song is delivered with no instrumental accompaniment, while the remainder of the opening verse is only highlighted by Harvey's electric guitar. Here, "Sheela-Na-Gig" is almost lyrical, singsongy, presented by Harvey in a reserved, sensual voice. The bass and drums, along with Harvey's heavier guitar work and more forceful vocal, only kick in when the man responds on the chorus. Musically, then, the woman's dialogue is accompanied by quieter passages that support her reticence and exposure; the man's dialogue is accompanied by heavier rock, supporting his aggressive and violent response.

A listener might note that this sonic split appears to reflect the traditional soft female/hard male gender division. The listener should remember, however, that the behavior of Harvey's female persona, revealing and reveling in her nakedness along with demanding that the man recognize her feminine body for what it is, is aggressive. The male's anger results from a breakdown in traditional gender relations: by allowing himself to be provoked to anger, he reveals a fault line in the masculine persona. Why, the listener might ask, does he feel threatened in some way?

The cover art of the "Sheela-Na-Gig" single by Mochnacz seems better matched to the material than the cover art for "Dress," though perhaps still falling short of making a direct or symbolic connection to the material. An image of the young woman dominates the album cover, which resembles the mockup of a magazine, though dark smudges and, in one or two places, print type appear on her face. On the left side of the frame, other miscellaneous ink print gives the impression of a magazine cover, perhaps for fashion, with statements like "Over 200 Hair Styles" and "Getting into Films." The color scheme includes black, off-white, and two tones of blue, creating a murky image of a smiling young woman with her eyes glancing upward. If the image is meant to convey the cover of a fashion magazine, then it undercuts, as does "Sheela-Na-Gig," the idea of the beauty myth by presenting a smudged, imperfect—from the contemporary patriarchy's point of view—image. Still, Mochnacz's image basically looks like the cover of an unattractive fashion or movie magazine and is hardly evocative of the song's candid subject matter.

In a sense, "Dress," about the need to socially construct gender, and "Sheela-Na-Gig," about the need to completely deconstruct it, work well as a pair. Many of Harvey's concerns—desire, gender identity, male-female conflicts, and violence—first appeared in "Dress" and "Sheela-Na-Gig," as did her sonically reimagined classic rock. She also showed a willingness to expand her material visually by working with sympathetic collaborators on cover art. All of these elements would come together forcefully on *Dry* in 1992.

Dry

For the listener or potential buyer of *Dry*, the first sensory information received is less likely to be the sound of the music than the visual image of the cover art. As with "Dress" and "Sheela-Na-Gig," Mochnacz completed the art, this time including photographs for the cover, inside, and back of the album. If the cover art of both "Dress" and "Sheela-Na-Gig" had seemed intriguing but only partially successful, Mochnacz's work on *Dry* matched the disturbing candor of Harvey's material. At the same time, the relationship between the material and the photographs was symbolic in the larger sense, suggesting and summarizing Harvey's themes without repeating them.

The disturbing frankness of *Dry*'s cover photograph is startlingly simple and straightforward. The color shot is an extreme close-up of a woman's face (Harvey's, pressed up against glass) that includes her chin, most of her lips, and the edge of her nose against a black backdrop. The color of the photograph is poorly represented with the right-hand portion of the woman's face appearing green instead of flesh tone. Other elements seem equally off-balance. Her red-purple lipstick has been haphazardly smeared, creating a blotched line from her nostril to her chin. The unsmeared section of her lips appears drained of natural color. The out-of-kilter colors, the smudged lipstick, and the extreme close-up give the impression of a Polaroid taken for evidence in a domestic abuse case. Because of the close-up nature of the photograph, it is impossible to judge whether the young woman is lying down, standing up, or sitting in a chair. It is also impossible to tell if she is dead or alive, or, within the scenario of the photo session, *supposed* to be alive or dead.

Inside is another, even simpler color photograph of an open tube of red lipstick with light reflecting from the gold cylinder. The tube of lipstick lies diagonally in the photograph, with the black base positioned in the bottom right-hand corner and the opened red lipstick positioned in the upper left-hand corner. While nothing in the photograph is smeared and the color is properly balanced, the tube of lipstick relates to the smeared lipstick on the woman's face on the cover. The diagonal angle is kinetic, restless, and the movement, from right to left, further suggests instability. Whether intended or not, the golden cylinder resembles a bullet casing both in color and design, and, once again, suggests violence or potential violence.

In comparison, the black-and-white photograph on the back cover of Harvey, from her face to the middle of her uncovered breasts, seems rather straightforward. The light focuses on Harvey's face, leaving her midsection muddy, grainy. The photograph has captured a number of unattractive features that photographers usually attempt to smooth over in black-and-white portraiture, including the exaggerated outline of Harvey's collarbone. As with the earlier image for "Dress," Mochnacz seems to have manipulated the contrast and, in this instance, to have purposely made a technically imperfect photograph. To the left, behind Harvey, a bright light, brighter than her face, blotches the mostly black backdrop. This light also appears in a smaller splotched area on Harvey's right (from the viewer's point of view) shoulder. It is as though the negative had been burned during printing, which gives the photograph a sloppy look, similar to riot grrrl album art: the less-than-perfect image plus nudity seems to offers the viewer Harvey as she is.

Psychologically, these smeared, out-of-kilter, and imperfect photographs prepare the listener for Harvey's smeared, out-of-kilter worldview on Dry, a worldview colored by betrayal, obsession, and violence. Instead of falling in love with one another, men and women suggest strange relationship arrangements ("Oh My Lover"), become fixated ("O Stella"), and attempt to usurp or destroy one another's power ("Hair"). Harvey has more fully complicated and obscured her worldview on Dry by relying on oblique lines and loose connections between verses, leaving dramatic events within her songs ambiguous and/or dependent on understanding her unstated point of view within the song. Her bleakness, along with her willingness to allow the listener to read between the lines and make connections, may remind listeners of loosely stated blues lyrics. Still, as with "Dress" and "Sheela-Na-Gig," the classic rock that Harvey, Ellis, and Vaughan draw from on Dry does evoke liberation.

Dry's opening track, "Oh My Lover," is an instance where these indirect lines and loose connections between verses work very effectively, evoking a sense of dread while never stating the reason for it within the lyric. For those unfamiliar with Harvey's earlier singles, the opening lines may come as a bit of a shock. As the song begins, Harvey's persona tells her lover or perhaps ex-lover that she doesn't mind if he loves two women at once. Is Harvey's persona in love, in lust, desperate, or just obsessed? Is this an attempt to salvage a relationship, or is she simply willing to try something daring, expanding the relationship to include a third person? The first verse allows these questions to remain open, while the performance—Harvey's pleading vocal, the minor key, and the plodding bass line—creates a menacing undertow. What might give the impression of sexual freedom and exploration as a lyric has actually been transformed into a sense of uneasiness, perhaps fear within the sonic palette of the song.

The second verse, with a reference to thighs that are like honey, further focuses the attraction as sexual. The electric guitar, bass, and drums work in restrained unison here, still suggesting an undertow, and Harvey's vocal becomes more passionate. The lyric, as with the first verse, is a sensual plea that spills over into infatuation. On the bridge ("Oh My Lover" lacks a proper chorus), the volume rises again and includes the repeated reassurance that everything is all right. In the third verse, the steady undertow comes to the surface as Harvey's persona describes the color forming around her lover's eyes, signaling, perhaps, that his mood has changed. The volume of Harvey's guitar and vocal rise here, and her persona, who has previously assured her lover that everything is all right, now asks for his assurances that everything is really all right.

What exactly transpires between Harvey's persona and her lover is never made explicit. Instead, the listener is only left with several impressions: that a woman has offered herself to a man she is obsessed with or attracted to, that their relationship is sexual or that she wishes it to be sexual, and that he is uninterested or has grown tired of her or is now angry at her. At a glance, this seems to have little potential for a woman-friendly reading, but Harvey's focus remains aimed at the oblique drama, not the choices made by the song's character. Repeatedly in Harvey's work, desire is dangerous, inciting individuals to put themselves at risk to fulfill it. The obsession within "Oh My Lover" may represent no more than physical attraction and sexual desire, but for a woman to openly request sex is to leave herself vulnerable to rejection—from a man, from society—and perhaps open to danger.

Harvey expands upon this theme in "Hair," a rock-drama built upon the trials and tribulations of one of the Old Testament's best-known pair of lovers, Samson and Delilah. The song, however, is less interested in the story's outcome—Samson losing his sight and destroying the temple along with his enemy—than the drama between a woman and a man over the source of his strength. Harvey's distinct encoding of the song's point of view is likewise intriguing: Delilah narrates the verses, while Samson responds in the choruses, much like the male-female split in "Sheela-Na-Gig." By narrowing her focus, Harvey has distilled the conflict to its basic elements.

The progression of each stanza follows the progression of Delilah's thoughts, which she addresses to Samson. At first she refers to the strength in his arms and imagines what it would be like to be his bride. Next, she refers to his hair, how it glistens, and, instead of only admiring it, wishes that it were hers. In the third stanza she tells him, as she holds his hair in her hands, that she will keep it safe. While she never mentions cutting his hair or the act of cutting his hair in the first three stanzas, Samson's angry response on the first chorus addresses his sheared locks. His response is fairly straightforward, predictable: a woman has betrayed him, and he is angry with her. What is more interesting, however, is Delilah's motivation.

Within Harvey's narrative, there are no Philistines demanding that she subdue the Israelite strongman; here, she seems to be acting on her own. And while Delilah may admire both Samson's strength and beauty, she also desires to possess it or to possess its power. In the final stanza, with Delilah now holding Samson's hair in her hands, her motivation is further clarified. Now, she tells Samson, she holds his strength (his hair) in her hands and he will stay with her: Delilah, by striking at the heart of his masculinity, has turned the tables within the relationship. Author Elizabeth Wurtzel noted, "Perhaps Delilah only wanted to know, just for a little while, what it felt like to hold the weight of the world and the strength of the universe in her arms, at her mercy."[7] With his physical strength and as a man, Samson could decide when to come and go, and if and when to make Delilah his bride. After he has lost the source of his strength, he appears powerless, impotent, even in his anger. She now possesses Samson, and by possessing him possesses his strength; her final words in the last stanza celebrate her victory, repeating that he is her man.

Vaughan and Ellis open "Hair" with a vigorous, rolling rhythm before pulling back for Harvey's vocal. A cross between an entreaty and sensuous admiration, Harvey's vocal relays the nuances of Delilah's desire and calculation during the first two stanzas. On the edge of each chorus, the guitar, bass, and drums explode, and Harvey's vocal, switching from Delilah's to Samson's point of view, turns angry and accusatory. A brief musical interlude intrudes after the second stanza, highlighted by Harvey's subdued electric guitar, extending both the musical and narrative tension. By the third stanza, on the periphery of the unstated act that brings the song to climax, Harvey's vocal grows louder, expressing Delilah's narrative with greater confidence. Her delivery of the final stanza is a combination of her approach on earlier stanzas, both sensuous (like the first two stanzas) and confident (like the third stanza). Although the angry and explosive chorus is repeated, the story has been told: Delilah, assured of her victory, never reacts to Samson's anger.

The complications of vulnerability, rejection, and desire (the desire to be considered attractive, sexual desire, and the desire for power) weave themselves through "Dress," "Sheela-Na-Gig," "Oh My Lover," and "Hair" as well as elsewhere on *Dry*. Sonically, the dynamic arrangements by Harvey, Vaughan, and Ellis allow each instrument—drum, bass, and guitar—to play a dramatic and interactive role in mimicking the lyrical drift. Likewise, Harvey's vocals are expressive of each mood, displaying sensuality, playful mischief, anxiety, and aggression that give voice to each of her characters.

Perhaps the oddest quality of *Dry*'s sonic dimension is the unusual relation between the highs and lows of the recorded music throughout the album. It is an effect that, whether intentional or not, imbues an edgy quality into PJ Harvey's version of classic rock. It is as though the music has not been subjected to studio compressors, leading the listener to turn the volume up at the beginning of a song only to realize that it is much too high as the song reaches the chorus. For those reared on the smoother volume transitions of a rock album like *Led Zeppelin II*, these disruptions may be irritating, pulling one out of the musical moment. But there is also a sense in which the listener is forced to pay attention: *Dry* refuses to fade into the background, even when the listener becomes familiar with it.

While both the anxious lyrical content and edgy soundscape may seem unsettling on *Dry*, PJ Harvey's (the band) performance still falls within the tradition of classic rock, offering the sonic hope of liberation. The rejected lover in "Sheela-Na-Gig" promises to find a new lover who will appreciate her for who she is; Delilah's victory over Samson may be temporary in "Hair," but it is a victory. And while the heroines of "Dress" and "Oh My Lover" are both losers, the music, alternately reeling and menacing, works as a release valve for the pent-up emotion. Harvey's next album would build upon the sonic and lyrical themes of *Dry*, but the salvation of rock with its hope of liberation would quickly fall away.

Rid of Me

If some female artists dream of escaping the cage of the body, others stage a kind of prison riot, a carnal insurrection.

—Simon Reynolds and Joy Press[8]

Issued on May 4, 1993, *Rid of Me* is a powerful, though disturbing, statement, highlighting male-female anxieties, destructive obsessions, and violent fantasies. Driven by desire and obsession, men and women are condemned to enjoin an unwinnable battle. Arguably, the album is less accessible than *Dry*, especially upon first listen. Sonically, Harvey, Vaughan, and Ellis, along with producer Steve Albini, crafted a sound that lunged from quiet empty spaces to grating industrial rock. Lyrically, Harvey had distilled her vision, relying less on mythic archetypes ("Sheela-Na-Gig," "Water") than uncensored testimonials from her tortured characters' deep subjective selves. The album was promoted with two singles, "50 Ft Queenie" and "Man-Size," and was further expanded with the release of *4-Track Demos* in October, which included eight tracks from *Rid of Me* and a number of unreleased demonstration records. Mochnacz completed the cover art for these albums and singles, echoing and expanding Harvey's ideas. *Rid of Me* would become Harvey's first album to chart, reaching number 10 on *Billboard*'s Heatseekers and number 158 on the Billboard 200.

As with the above mentioned "Snake," most of *Rid of Me* is deeply immersed in a blues-like universe, offering little hope of liberation from the struggle between men and women. In one sense, the battle seems eternal, with women following the pattern established by Eve, condemned to desire and need the very men who will betray them. Harvey's vision, however, is a contemporary one where women actively assert themselves, sometimes in highly aggressive and violent ways. The male-female battle, then, may be ancient, but the aggressive female response is new. Harvey even suggests within the worldview of *Rid of Me* that this assertion of female power, confronting and challenging men, may create more tension, anxiety, and violence. *Rid of Me* paints a dire picture of male-female relationships made even more combative by the necessity of women's revolt against a status quo that harms them. On the subject of whether a woman's refusal to be an idle victim will institute real change—in men, masculinity, or society in general—or simply cause more problems in the future, however, Harvey remains mute.

Desire
Embroiled in obsessions and desires, Harvey's male and female characters reveal little perspective about their relationships on *Rid of Me*. In "Me-Jane," an unhappy Jane never reflects about why she is with Tarzan; she just is. In "Rid of Me," Harvey's angry persona never wonders why her lover wishes to leave; only that he does. As with men and women in traditional blues songs, little explanation is offered. No one bothers to scrutinize the conflict at hand; no one bothers to scrutinize either their own or their partner's

motivations very deeply; and no one wonders if they would be better off opting out of male-female relationships. Men and women are simply bound to one another by desire and thus destined to disappoint, hurt, and make one another miserable. It is love as a physical and elemental need, not as a romantic pleasantry.

Within the realm of desire, men and women are much the same. They experience the same appetites and desires, and are both constricted by the needs and limitations of physical bodies. Despite these similarities, Harvey recognizes fundamental differences, differences that complicate these relationships, creating conflict and leading to violence. Within Harvey's world, men desire and become obsessed with ideal women, ignore real women, and leave women behind without explanation. In this sense, her male characters share many of the same shortcomings that feminists have perceived as being part of traditional masculinity. In "Rid of Me," the male character attempts to exit a relationship, seemingly without explanation or his partner's input; in "Hook," a man seduces a bereft woman with the promise that she will feel like a queen, only to imprison her in his home; in "Snake," Eve, in an attempt to free herself from two men (God and Adam), is betrayed by another; in "Me-Jane," Tarzan seems to hardly recognize Jane's existence, even when she is injured; and in "Dry," a man seems incapable of sexually satisfying a woman's desire.

While these failings are significant, they are also recognizable of fairly typical ones committed by men under the patriarchy. Harvey, however, expands her dark vision of masculinity in the contemporary world in "Yuri-G" and "Man-Size." Men, when greeted with indifference, beset by doubt, or obsessed, frequently turn violent.

Similar to "O Stella" from *Dry*, "Yuri-G" relates one man's obsession with the moon (Luna), an ideal incarnation of feminine beauty that he wishes to possess. With the help of doctors, he resorts to a kind of voodoo, sticking needles in a figure in order to draw the moon down.[9] The reality of Luna is immaterial: he sees her, he wants her, and he will do anything to obtain her. Within the song, though, it is unclear whether his magic works. Although he says that he has pulled her down in the second and third verses, he becomes less certain of his accomplishment as the song progresses, undercutting his confidence. In his obsession, it seems, he has become delusional.

The title of the song may refer to the Russian cosmonaut, Yuri Gagarin, the first person in space (1961). With this reference, Harvey complicates the song considerably, changing one man's obsession with the moon/women to a masculine pattern of conquering or wishing to acquire what one has become obsessed with, whether that is a woman or the faraway moon. It also suggests a masculine indifference to both the subject, which is objectified, and anything that might block one's path in obtaining/possessing it.

Once again, noting men's will to power may seem a familiar criticism of traditional masculinity, but Harvey is more concerned with the state of her persona's mind in "Yuri-G." Something, Harvey is not specific, seems to have gone wrong during the process of gaining possession. The man in the song has reached for more than he can obtain, and can offer no more of an excuse than that his memory has been somehow been altered or destroyed by the woman/moon. His failure and doubt reveals an underlying masculine anxiety: what happens, "Yuri-G" asks, when men are no longer able to obtain the object(s) of their desire by traditional means?

"Man-Size" partially answers that question, detailing the anxiety that underlies the gender in the dominant social position. In Western tradition, popular belief frequently accepts masculinity as a natural state of being; a person does not construct masculinity, but, as a man, simply possesses it. In "Man-Size" (and the similar "Man-Size Sextet"), however, Harvey's male persona is deeply troubled; he speaks partly to himself, bolstering and assembling his masculinity, and he speaks to no one in particular, noting that he has the natural accoutrements of masculinity. At the beginning of the song, he has been skinned alive, but he is determined to outfit himself so that he fits within the traditional masculine mold. He does this by wearing leather boots, by being handsome, and by having his girl by his side. But he also plans to complete several abstract tasks, calculating his birthright and measuring both height and time. He repeatedly reminds himself that he does not need to shout—to overemphasize what should be natural—or he might call attention to the nonnatural or socially constructed state of masculinity.

"Man-Size" ends when Harvey's male persona pours gasoline on his hair to silence what he refers to as his lady head. Real and metaphoric violence is common within the sketches and stories of *Rid of Me*, but it is perhaps surprising that it is primarily perpetuated by women against men. In "Man-Size," however, male violence is self-inflicted. Becoming a man means silencing anything that hints at femininity, hardening oneself against all doubts and criticisms regarding one's masculinity.

"Man-Size" forms a central core in Harvey's thought process during this time period. She released three versions of "Man-Size," two on *Rid of Me* and another on the single for "50 Ft Queenie." One version, "Man-Size Sextet," is arranged radically different than the other two and deviates far from the demo, which is somewhat unusual in Harvey's early work (much of her studio work closely follows the outline of her available demos). "Man-Size," then, occupies a large space within Harvey's new world order.

While "Man-Size" reveals the contemporary male as anxious, the song never delves very deeply into this anxiety. Is he reacting against his failure to accomplish a task or gain the object he desires, as in "Yuri-G"? Why does he have to wear certain clothing and why does he have to construct his masculinity? Why does he need to invest effort into something, becoming a man or proving his manhood, that, once upon a time, was seemingly natural? What has happened to prompt this change?

The quick answer is that the change in contemporary men has been initiated or caused by the change in contemporary women. While Harvey's male characters may express anxious masculinities, they nonetheless strive to preserve them. Her female characters, on the other hand, express no anxiety regarding femininity and fully embrace the trappings of being a heterosexual woman. Still, Harvey's female characters embody a contemporary response to male insensitivity, indifference, and irresponsibility, one that refuses to remain silent, is openly angry, and is willing to commit acts of violence to settle a score. A torrent of feminine desire and resentment, long repressed and twisted by an unbalanced gender system, overflows on *Rid of Me*.

In three early songs on *Rid of Me*, "Rid of Me," "Legs," and "Rub 'til It Bleeds," Harvey sketches out her bleak male-female landscape from a female point of view. In "Rid of Me," her persona pointedly tells a lover who wishes to leave her that she will not be easy to get rid of. The lyric ranges between pleading to admonishment: she will hold him by emotional appeals if possible, but if not, by threats and perhaps violence. In a sense, "Legs" is a continuation or fulfillment of "Rid of Me": Harvey's persona physically restrains her lover against his will. In "Rub 'til It Bleeds," Harvey's character entreats a man to allow her to comfort him, only to reveal that she has no intention of doing so. In fact, all she wishes for is revenge, partly fulfilled by the very fact that he believes her when she promises to comfort him.

In each of these lyrics, women alter the traditional rules of engagement between women and men in intimate relationships. When men behave badly, women seek revenge; when men exit relationships, women pursue them; and when all else fails, women hold men against their will. It might be easy, over the course of these three songs, to misinterpret Harvey's female characters: their behavior may seem extreme because the sins committed against these women lie buried beneath the drama of each song. Harvey, however, makes these sins more explicit in "Hook," "Snake," and "Dry."

"Hook" is one of the more disturbing dramas to unfold on *Rid of Me*, a story of one woman's journey from nothing to less than nothing, from blind, lame, and alone to blind, lame, and enslaved (a man's maid). As the lyric begins, Harvey's persona refers to herself as being nothing when she is approached by a man who promises to make her sing as well as feel like a queen. The heroine Kathleen accepts his promises without question, though her faith is short-lived. Dark imagery, including the image of a black halo over the man, precedes her disillusionment in the second stanza: her love now makes her gag. After a noisy musical interlude, with barely audible Italian words buried under the mix (these words are clearer on a second version of "Hook" from *4-Track Demos*), Kathleen relays that she has returned to her original state, blind and lame. Addressing the man, though perhaps her address is an interior monologue, she remarks that all of his promises remain unfulfilled: she cannot sing and she does not feel like a queen. Instead, she has been left stained by his deceit and now serves as his maid.

In a sense, "Hook" is straightforward, a story of a traditional woman, socially conditioned to view herself as incomplete without a man, and socially conditioned to believe his promises of a home that will also be her home. Harvey imbues the song with a dark undercurrent, however, with seduction turning into crippling enslavement. Even the title, "Hook," conjures up the imagery of a fishhook with its barbed edge and, perversely, the idea of catching a woman like a fish. When Kathleen gags in the second stanza and reports that she cannot sing in the third stanza, one may imagine that the hook remains imbedded in her throat.

"Hook" also has structural and lyrical similarities to the nineteenth-century American popular song "I'll Take You Home Again, Kathleen" by Thomas P. Westendorf. In Westendorf's song, a husband sings of his wife's sorrow, a sorrow he attaches to homesickness. He promises to take her back across the ocean, where her friends and family reside, where her "loving heart will cease to yearn." The song is melancholy, with the husband noting that "the roses all have left your cheeks" and calling attention to the "dark'ning shadow on your brow." Kathleen no longer smiles at her husband, hinting at a possible undercurrent of estrangement, though the husband believes it is only homesickness and reassures himself with the refrain "I know you love me, Kathleen, dear." "Hook," then, might be thought of as the same story from Kathleen's point of view: the source of her depression is her husband and her confinement within traditional marriage, not homesickness. In both instances, the suitor and husband express concern and offer to help, assuming happiness will follow their benevolence. The woman's point of view—he never asks her what she would like—is deemed unnecessary.

In "Snake" and "Dry," Harvey adds other nuances to male betrayal. In "Snake," discussed at the beginning of the chapter, the betrayal is fairly straightforward. Satan promises Eve that he can free her from both Adam and God, but instead, has merely seduced her, leaving her to convince Adam of her innocence. "Dry" is one of Harvey's most explicitly sexual songs, similar in its direct language to Liz Phair's "Fuck and Run." The lyric is also deeply subjective, making it difficult to understand what sexual act has or has not transpired between Harvey's persona and the male of the song. On one level the refrain, that the experience has left her dry, is a direct lash against male potency: he has failed to sexually entice or satisfy her sexual desire, and she, in turn, has uttered a stinging insult against his masculinity.

It would be a mistake, however, to only interpret "Dry" as no more than an extended insult about a failed sexual experience. The tryst between the couple seems preplanned—he has traveled a long way; he is immaculately groomed—suggesting (since Harvey's persona describes him) that she is attracted to him. The insult of the lyric, then, also suggests that he has left her desire unfulfilled, that he has proven inadequate and insensitive to her needs. Masculine failure extends beyond performance to an inability to understand and be responsive to the needs and desires of others.

In "Hook," "Snake," and "Dry," then, Harvey outlines the sins of contemporary masculinity against women, identifying the betrayal that prompts her heroines to aggressive acts in "Rid of Me," "Rub 'til It Bleeds," and "Legs." Motivated by an elemental desire for revenge because of unfair treatment, Harvey's heroines either threaten to commit violence or actually commit violence. In response to her belief that her lover is leaving her in "Rid of Me," Harvey's narrator declares that she will tie his legs in order to keep him close to her chest before twisting his head off. She will continue to assault him, she says, until he wishes he had never met her. "Rub 'til It Bleeds" goes further, with Harvey's persona promising to smooth the man's head as he lies against her, fulfilling her traditional role as a woman who reassures the man. Once she has gained his trust, however, she delivers a blow: she will rub his head, as she promised, but she will rub it until it bleeds.

In "Legs" Harvey pushes this theme to its limits. At first, it appears that her narrator is speaking to a corpse, asking it whether it hurt when it bled. As the macabre drama unfolds, a woman has cut off her lover's legs, literally preventing him from leaving. In the last stanza, she asks if he has ever wished her dead, then wonders whether she would be better off dead, but ends the last line by noting that she could kill him instead. Does the narrative swallow itself? Is he already dead and the narrator only retracing her steps? Whatever has transpired, these songs focus on violent acts of revenge mixed with sadomasochistic imagery (tying up and cutting), underlining just how fraught with danger the world of male-female relationships has become.

The extremity of Harvey's language throughout *Rid of Me* may lead one to ask if it is meant to be read metaphorically or literally, as fantasy or reality.

It would be easy, for instance, to understand "Legs," "Rid of Me," and "Rub 'til It Bleeds" as interior monologs by woman imagining their response to indifferent and hurtful men. But one might also juxtapose these songs against the darkly comic "50 Ft Queenie," a song more clearly metaphorical. Like a feminist blues fantasy, Harvey's giant persona brags of her prowess and strength; her ability to sire children, gods, and queens; her gigantic size; and the fact that she is, ironically, the king of the world. In the end, it matters less whether Harvey intends these songs as realistic or fantasy; if Harvey's heroines are not, in reality, ready to rule the world, they are nonetheless ready to assert themselves aggressively within relationships. This desire, one imagines, lies at the root of masculine nervousness in "Man-Size": the rules of engagement between the sexes had been radically altered, opening up an unfamiliar space beneath men's feet.

Industrial Rock

> Harvey, Ellis, and Vaughan invoke classic rock forms (power ballad, three-minute thrash, acid overdrive, postpunk discombobulating), blow them out of proportion, then shred them to pieces.
>
> —Ann Powers[10]

Rid of Me, especially when a listener comes to the album for the first time, may not be as easy to enjoy as Dry. Unlike "Dress" or "Sheela-Na-Gig" from Dry, songs on Rid of Me lack the visceral thrills of a rock band kicking out the jams; unlike "O Stella" and "Hair," there are no sensual pleasures from catchy riffs; and unlike "Happy and Bleeding" and "Plants and Rags," there is no pause for acoustic ballads. Instead, it is as though Harvey, along with Vaughan, Ellis, and producer Steve Albini, has purposely undermined typical listener expectations, extending the sonic disparity of highs and lows on Dry to all aspects of Rid of Me. It is a sonic pattern, however, that matches the ferocity of Harvey's lyrics, and one that sustains and deepens the violence and dissonance of the album. Sonically, then, Rid of Me is bitter medicine meant to be taken straight.

The album opens with the title track, and as with Dry, the volume has to be pushed higher to hear the quieter passages. "Rid of Me" begins softly, forebodingly so, with the thump of the bass and a gentle drum shuffle coming to the forefront of the mix, and extends in a similar manner for over forty-five seconds before Harvey's vocal begins. Still, everything remains submerged, even while Harvey's vocal and the lyric speak of quiet desperation. Other uneasy elements are added into the mix, as when Ellis offers a high-pitched vocal refrain from the left channel of the stereo spectrum, echoing the intensity of the character's desire. It is only halfway through this four-and-a-half-minute song that Harvey pushes her guitar forcefully into the mix; she is joined by the group, which lets loose a barrage of industrial noise, sharp and metallic. The fury of Harvey's persona rises in the vocal, but nonetheless remains buried in a morass of noisy garage rock. If one has turned the stereo volume loud enough to clearly hear the first half of the song, "Rid of Me" now overwhelms the speakers, spilling out like a rude interruption. If Harvey's character appeared desperate on the lyric sheet, the soundscape magnifies her desperation to mythic proportions.

On "Yuri-G" and "Hook" Harvey increased dissonance by running her vocal through an amplifier ("Reeling," on *4-Track Demos*, is even more dissonant, with the entire band channeled and recorded through the amplifier). Here, the amplified voice creates a vocal track that sounds as though it has been oversaturated on the recording tape. The highs take on a harsh edge, especially on "Yuri-G," also allowing Harvey's voice to cut sharply through guitar, bass, and drum, no matter how much noise they generate. Vocal harmony, also by Harvey, is added to both songs in various places, creating a screechy echo of the lead voice.

The most radical experiment on *Rid of Me* is the string arrangement on the first version of "Man-Size," "Man-Size Sextet," arranged by Ellis. At the beginning of the song, the discordant strings seem to be in a different key, or at least out of kilter with Harvey's tortured vocal. Nervous and kinetic, the string arrangement unrolls like the soundtrack of the man's mind coming unraveled. Harvey matches the arrangement with a similarly fragmented vocal, and the entire track stands in stark relief to the remainder of this rock album.

One intricate question pertaining to Harvey's industrial blues-rock is whether it is inherently masculine in its aggressiveness. Deborah Frost noted this quality in *Rolling Stone*: "*Rid of Me* . . . is determined to prove that Harvey's band can rock as fast and as noisily as any bunch of guys whose dynamic creativity is limited to speeding up and slowing down and rolling over and doing it again."[11] Even without the music's aggressiveness, a listener might ask if blues and rock as forms have been imbued with a masculine code, and if so, would any musical vision offered by a woman singer-songwriter within these genres be muted? Should women in rock adopt a different musical language to circumvent male tradition?

The idea of masculine and feminine forms in music, however, seems to rely too heavily on clichés based on traditional ideas of gender. In this scenario, masculine forms exert power, the classic example being an electric guitar solo. Women musicians, on the other hand, are not represented by the three-minute song that works toward a climax, which, in this scenario, just copies the male sexual response pattern. Is it possible, however, that many men and women simply react in the same way to the sound of rock music? That the music helps create a sense of empowerment, heightened ego, and, most simply, a good feeling that transcends gender?

Harvey does rely on rock tradition on *Rid of Me*, but it is a reliance that allows her to appropriate old forms, disassemble them, and then reassemble them in startling configurations. By relying on an industrial soundscape and abrasive delivery, Harvey, Vaughan, Ellis, and Albini have crafted an album that seems more intent on aurally challenging than entertaining the listener. Like *Dry*, *Rid of Me* is not the kind of album that fades easily into the background, but unlike *Dry*, *Rid of Me* never relents. The listener, in the end, will have to meet *Rid of Me* on Harvey's terms, not rock tradition's.

Dressing Up

> *Whatever a woman puts on, it is likely to be a costume, whether it is fur, white lace, a denim skirt or black leather pants.*

—Susan Brownmiller[12]

Mochnacz's cover photograph of Harvey on *Rid of Me* contrasts sharply with the photograph utilized for *Dry*. Whereas the color cover of *Dry* suggested that violence had been committed, perhaps that the very act of becoming feminine (dressing up, wearing lipstick) represented violence, the black-and-white cover of *Rid of Me* imagines Harvey as Medusa, a woman more likely to inflict violence on others.

As with *Dry*, there are many printing flaws on the cover of *Rid of Me* that render the portrait technically imperfect: the lighting is unflattering, the contrast is harsh, and the backdrop looks like a makeshift shower stall. There is a concentrated dynamic, however, that renders the lack of perfection irrelevant: Harvey/Medusa's long, wet hair has been frozen in flight as it whips from left to right, and her concentrated stare is as harsh as the lighting. Her eyes serve as the center of the photograph's focus, but because of the harsh contrast, they have become two dark sockets framed by the arch of each black eyebrow. Harvey/Medusa's stare is difficult to read, partially because her right eye seems to stare directly at the viewer, challenging him, while her left eye seems to glance lazily to the side with indifference. A thick strand of hair has flopped over her right shoulder resembling a snake, while the print contrast has darkened Harvey/Medusa's skin, producing lines that appear like veins across the top part of her chest. If the half portrait of a woman's face on *Dry* speaks of victimization, the full portrait on *Rid of Me* promises revenge.

The back cover is another black-and-white photograph of Harvey, this time a headshot. Her dark, dry hair frames her face, and her eyes are closed; the scene is under lit, and while the contrast is less harsh, it nonetheless appears technically incorrect, rendering the portrait muddy. As with the cover photograph on *Dry*, it is not clear whether the subject has simply closed her eyes, is asleep, or dead. By using the same model (Harvey) and a similar photographic style (i.e., black and white, technically imperfect) on the front and back of *Rid of Me*, one might draw a connection between the two images, guessing that one served as a doppelganger for the other. Is the quiet, tranquil woman on the back cover the acceptable version of femininity? Does the woman on the front cover represent who she becomes in her dreams or fantasy world? Or do these portraits represent both sides of every woman or person, a continuum with multiple modes of expression? Any interpretation, however, leads back to the photograph chosen for the front cover, the image that serves as the face of the album. The dynamic Harvey/Medusa image is intent on revenge and seems indifferent to the violence that will ensue.

Harvey and Mochnacz attempted to undercut the seriousness of these images on the singles for *Rid of Me*, and later with the bizarre color photograph of Harvey in a bathing suit for *4-Track Demos*. On the cover of "Man-Size," a black-and-white photograph shows Harvey wearing a dress that is partly falling from her right shoulder; she is also holding the stem of a flower in her teeth. The inside image of "50 Ft Queenie" shows Harvey wearing sunglasses, a short red dress, a leopard-skin coat, and gold high heels. She has both arms propped on her hips and stands against a backdrop that displays spray-painted letters reading, "Hey I'm One Big Queen." While one could easily offer readings of these photographs, it is unclear how serious they should be taken. In both cases, Harvey seems to be dressing up, playing the dancer with the rose in her teeth in "Man-Size" and the more contemporary, feminine big queen of "50 Ft Queenie." Both, in fact, seem to undercut each song's lyric and suggest, especially with "50 Ft Queenie," that the music is all in good fun (Harvey has said that "50 Ft Queenie" was supposed to be funny). While both photographs might be described as fun or play acting, then, neither adds to the overall vision of *Rid of Me*, nor the understanding of that vision.

The Medusa/Harvey photograph on the cover of *Rid of Me* is finally the image that best prepares the listener for the male-female dramas that form the album's content. Whether a figment of another woman's dream or reality, within the realm of *Rid of Me*, Medusa, the dynamic figure ready to commit acts of violence to even the score, is the dominant figure. More than dressing up, she is a masculine nightmare come to life.

"Ecstasy"

Harvey ends *Rid of Me* with an entrancing, though odd, track titled "Ecstasy." The song is intriguing in that its title, along with its dream-like lyrics of floating and flying, addresses the desire to escape from all that has come before. The song also evokes a drug experience and references ecstasy, whether intentional or not, which had become very popular at raves in England in the early 1990s. In first person, Harvey's persona remarks that she is flying in the heavens and above the sea, though who she is speaking to—at first—is unclear. At the end of the second stanza, she gives the impression that she is speaking to a specific person, telling that person to look at her. By the third stanza, however, her floating and flying have turned to singing, and now she is begging to be noticed.

The lyric of "Ecstasy" could hardly be more open for multiple readings, though the slow, dragging accompaniment, dominated by a bluesy slide guitar, suggests a downward mood. Harvey's vocal likewise unravels in slow motion, as though mimicking the state of one's mind when trapped in a bad drug experience. These elements offer an ironic twist on the title: the word *ecstasy* may express a desire to escape, but Harvey's character remains as bound to the physical world as her sister and brother characters on the remainder of the album.

There is also the curious matter of singing as a replacement for floating and flying in the third verse. With this comparison, singing, like floating and flying, represents escape, which might be considered a familiar idea in art: as the artist creates her work, she finds a temporary respite from her demons. But Harvey adds a catch. Her persona is begging someone to watch her, and this general someone could easily be translated as an audience (Harvey addresses an unspecified "you"). In this case, the singer seems to need the audience for her release, perhaps echoing the symbiotic need between males and females throughout *Rid of Me*.

While the meaning of "Ecstasy" may be difficult to pin down, the song does offer a finale to Harvey's worldview on *Rid of Me*. Simply put, there is no escape. Perhaps, through a drug-induced experience, a sexual encounter, the art of singing, or the adoration of fans, one escapes temporarily. But even wanting to escape, to create art, to connect with other people, is to, once again, be entrapped by desire.

Harvey, Redux

If *Dry* represented classic rock reimagined from a woman's point of view, then *Rid of Me* represented the blues for the late twentieth-century woman. It was as though Harvey had updated Led Zeppelin's rock-blues, providing a point of view from the other side of the bed. If a listener could travel back to the blues-drenched world of *Led Zeppelin I* and *Led Zeppelin II*, what might the women, whom the band's lyrics had complained of, lusted after, bedded, and left behind, have said had they been given a voice? And how might they have responded had they grown up in Harvey's time with expectations that extended beyond being a groupie or the guitar player's "old lady"? What if these women had made, the same way the men in these songs freely do, their own demands? What if they had committed their own acts of violence in response to acts of violence perpetuated against them?

The late twentieth-century women's blues, however, is a dour affair when compared to the easy braggadocio of the classic rock male. His lust is natural and freely expressed, and he can love them and leave them, because above all else, he strives for liberation from all authority. By comparison, most of Harvey's heroines are earthbound, trapped by elemental forces of emotional and physical desire that bind them to men. While a woman's desires may be no different than a man's, she lacks the same freedom to act upon them. Instead, she must wait for a man to come to her ("Hook," "Dry"), and then hope that he is willing or capable of living up to her expectations and desires. Unfortunately for Harvey's characters, this never happens. Women are ensnared in a fatal loop, repeatedly desiring men who will never fulfill their yearning, and desiring men who are perhaps too self-centered to even recognize another person's needs. All Harvey's female characters can do is register their dissent in words and acts of aggression.

Is there a way out of this loop? It would be tempting to say that the male-female discord on *Rid of Me* is a continuation of an eternal struggle that began in the Garden of Eden. That Harvey's worldview of imprisonment by desire is essentialist, and that she is simply calling attention to the genetic encoding that condemns men and women to be lovers and enemies. This is Ann Powers' view of Harvey's work:

> *Rid of Me* exudes too much terror to work as dogma; instead of critiquing or even documenting the struggle to be sexually whole in a misogynist and body-fearing society, Harvey means to create that fight's sonic equivalent. And although Harvey may herself believe in the fight for women's rights, it's not the point of her art. *Rid of Me* envisions a subject between sexes, empowered by the possibilities and entrapped by the limits of both masculine and feminine.[13]

The one aspect, however, that throws this view out of kilter is the actions of Harvey's heroines. While her male characters usually act in predictable masculine ways that meet traditional expectations, her female characters have upset traditional feminine roles in Western cultures, assuming many of the same aggressive traits as men. Openly expressing anger, her female personas demand something much more basic than true love or undying fidelity: to no longer be ignored. In the world of *Rid of Me*, men may continue to disregard, leave behind, and fail women, but they cannot do so with impunity: feminine violence is never far below the surface.

How does this lead to better male-female relationships? Harvey never says that it does. All she does is mark or offer a fantasy of this basic change in the male-female dynamic: as women assert themselves within relationships, the relative stability between the sexes becomes unbalanced, even volatile. And while feminine assertion will potentially lead to more violence, Harvey also imagines that it may plant a seed of doubt within the masculine psyche ("Yuri-G," "Man-Size"). Male self-doubt, then, may represent a starting point toward a new or less constricted masculinity, perhaps creating an opportunity for greater equality within male-female relationships. Until then, however, the idea of true liberation for women will remain a chimera, and women, with little hope of rock salvation, will be left to sing the blues.

Notes

1. Timothy White, "PJ Harvey: A Lover's Musical Musing," *Billboard*, August 15, 1992, 3.

2. Simon Reynolds, "PJ Harvey: What Makes Polly Scream?" *i-D*, October 1993.

3. "Hips. Lips. Tits. Power," *Q*, May 1994.

4. James R. Blanford, *PJ Harvey: Siren Rising* (New York: Omnibus, 2004), 8.

5. Susan Brownmiller, *Femininity* (New York: Linden Press/Simon & Schuster, 1984), 86.

6. According to the liner notes, both Ben Groenevelt (double bass) and Ian Oliver (bass) played bass on the track.

7. Elizabeth Wurtzel, *Bitch: In Praise of Difficult Women* (New York: Anchor Books, 1998), 70.

8. Simon Reynolds and Joy Press, *The Sex Revolts: Gender, Rebellion, and Rock 'n' Roll* (Cambridge, MA: Harvard University Press, 1995), 337.

9. Blanford, *PJ Harvey*, 60.

10. Ann Powers, "Houses of the Holy," *Village Voice*, June 1, 1993; reprinted in *Rock She Wrote: Women Write about Rock, Pop, and Rap*, ed. Evelyn McDonnell and Ann Powers (New York: Delta, 1995), 328.

11. Deborah Frost, "PJ Harvey: Primed and Ticking," *Rolling Stone*, August 19, 1993.

12. Brownmiller, *Femininity*, 101.

13. Powers, "Houses of the Holy"; reprinted in McDonnell and Powers, *Rock She Wrote*, 328.

CHAPTER THREE

Exile in Guyville: Liz Phair

All those bloody records I'd listened to for years and years with the boys—the Rolling Stones' Exile in Main Street and Bob Dylan's "Lay Lady Lay"—I was having a good time, but I always wondered where I fitted into it as a woman. Suddenly, four or five tracks into Exile in Guyville, I knew Liz Phair's songs were on my side, that they were twisted to my viewpoint, my advantage. Lots of women have written like that, but to me it had the edge.

—Gina Birch of the Raincoats[1]

On the sixth track of *Exile in Guyville*, Liz Phair sketches a portrait of a wannabe hero in "Soap Star Joe." Soap Star Joe arrives in town mysteriously, much like the John Wayne hero in a 1940s Western, but dressed as James Dean. Everything about him—his arrival in town, his origins—is cloaked in rumor and mystery. There is a sense that his arrival is pregnant with promise, like the nameless Western hero with no past who has come to make his mark. His arrival portends change.

But for all the mystery surrounding Soap Star Joe's arrival, Phair adds unflattering details that undercut his heroic portrait. She begins by noting that as a hero, he is not unusual; in fact, he is only following in the footsteps of many other heroes. His arrival, then, is more mundane than significant, further suggested by the fact that he arrived on the back of a pickup truck; while the truck may be the modern equivalent of a horse, it does not belong to him. Prefacing Joe's name with "Soap Star" also serves to gut the seriousness of his ambitions, and his goals—such as to appear on a billboard—are equally small. The mystery surrounding Soap Star Joe only works as a smoke screen to hide these unflattering qualities.

There are also fantastical and nonsensical details used to describe Soap Star Joe, and similar details—combined with satire, dark humor, and absurdity—are used on many other Phair songs. The narration of these songs, then, is not meant to be taken literally. The anonymous narrator of "Soap Star Joe" mentions his possible birth from Athena's skull (more rumors) and that Joe feels safe when it is dark. There is also an odd detail, related to the safety of the dark, about glowing dashboard lights. These stray details seem to add a quasi-mystical component to Soap Star Joe, but as with the mystery surrounding him, only serve to obscure the smallness underlying the purpose of his arrival.

Phair's driving guitar and John Casey Awsumb's harmonica propel "Soap Star Joe" forward at a swift rate, creating the impression of the song's hero/ antihero sweeping into town to stake his claim. This contrasts sharply with the character of "Soap Star Joe," whose ambition seems more focused on creating an image than the active pursuit of accomplishments. Phair's vocals and electric guitar seem rhythmically connected at the hip, one a singsongy drone, the other spunky and repetitive. With no bass and only rudimentary percussion, "Soap Star Joe" captures a homemade ambience that's as lonely as the portrait.

The biggest sonic deviation occurs on the two choruses. Here, the arrangement is much busier, with a second voice joining Phair's, adding a ghostly echo. The harmonica becomes more persistent, too. Sonically, the choruses almost sounds oversaturated, adding an edgy, lo-fi energy to the track.

Instead of seeming ambitious, finally, the blue-jean-clad Soap Star Joe only seems on the make, a hustler. He wishes to find something that is attractive to save; he wishes to find action at an affordable price; and he wishes to remain in town until people know his name. The narrator underlines his shallowness, suggesting that someone should make him an offer just to see how he will respond. He is supposed to be famous, but nobody recognizes him. Phair ends her portrait with the cruelest details of the lyric, that Soap Star Joe has thinning hair; furthermore, that he is an American icon or at least what has become of American icons. He is a James Dean grown old, Marlon Brando with a beer gut.

One might even recall another drifter named Joe from America's "Ventura Highway," a hit in 1972. The song offers a romantic portrait of a drifter and evokes the promise of the open road, the next town, and warmer seasons. Joe may be lost in the dreams of the 1960s, and he may have no deeper purpose than to keep moving; but the easy-flowing mood of the lyric and melody never judges Joe's dreamy self-indulgence. "Soap Star Joe" offers a snapshot of the carefree Joe of "Ventura Highway" twenty-odd years later, after the golden glow of California as the Promised Land has faded.

The Mythic Landscape of Guyville

When interpreting *Exile in Guyville*, a number of critics have leaned on the album's connection to the Rolling Stones' *Exile on Main Street* (1972). Phair not only gave her album a similar name, but included the same number of songs, leaving the impression that *Exile in Guyville* is a song-by-song response to *Exile on Main Street*. Phair encouraged this concept, which seemed to be an extension of Pussy Galore's ramshackle rerecording of *Exile in Main Street* in 1986:

> I thought it was a cool structural device, and I wanted to give myself something extra to think about. I come from an academic background, and I got off on going through my little warehouse of songs to find the ones that I thought had the same feel, were of the same type.[2]

The comparison between Phair and the Rolling Stones' work, however, seems to be a loose one, perhaps serving to obscure more than it reveals. As critics have noted, half of the eighteen songs included on *Exile in Guyville* are rerecorded and rewritten versions of songs Phair had already included on the bootlegged *Girly Sound* cassettes from 1991. "Soap Star Joe" is one of those songs, and comparing the story of a washed-up, aging hero wannabe with the drug-fueled references of the Rolling Stones' "Sweet Virginia" seems unpromising.

The reference to the Rolling Stones and *Exile on Main Street*, however, does work in a broader sense. The Rolling Stones remained, even twenty years after *Exile on Main Street*, recognizable as one of the—if not *the*—most infamous and renowned bands in rock history. Unlike their more pop-friendly and cleaner-cut rivals the Beatles, the Rolling Stones romanticized bad boy behavior, from their evocation of universal evil in "Sympathy for the Devil" to the dilapidated despondency of *Exile on Main Street*. Originally based in the blues, the band's songs were steeped in unapologetic sexism that crossed the line—in "Midnight Rambler"—into blatant misogyny. The Rolling Stones, in both the band's music and publicized personal behavior, were the personification of classic rock's lopsided message: the rebellion for liberation was a male rebellion. Worst still, it was a rebellion willing to subjugate women to the sexual and emotional needs of men.

What the listener is left with, then, is not a direct answer to *Exile on Main Street*, but an extended description of a place called Guyville and the inhabitants—like the aging hero of "Soap Star Joe"—who have been exiled there. Soap Star Joe is simply one of the many characters who populate her mythic Guyville. The term *Guyville*, Phair has noted, partly derived from a song by a Chicago alternative band, Urge Overkill. As such, the concept of Guyville works on at least two levels, first describing a music scene (or any small scene) not unlike the scene Phair experienced in Chicago (but not limited to that) while also describing a broader mythic space that cuts a wide swath across the male and female consciousnesses in contemporary America.

In the first sense, Guyville is similar to Sherwood Anderson's *Winesburg, Ohio*, a picture of a place and time, encompassing the lives of Gen X men and women, aging Baby Boomers, and the indie rock community. Phair noted in an interview with Timothy White in *Billboard*, "For me, Guyville is a concept that combines the smalltown mentality of a five-hundred-person Knawbone, Kentucky-type town with the Wicker Park indie music scene in Chicago, plus the isolation of every place I've lived in, from Cincinnati to Winnetka."[3] On this level, "Soap Star Joe" is about another character who wanders into a local Guyville. Even as a stranger—a self-imposed exile—Joe nonetheless has one advantage: he is a man. His nonreflective attitude about the precariousness of his own position (he is older now; no one knows who he is) seems to represent an easy confidence born of privilege (in this case, of being a guy in Guyville). One might even imagine that he has simply traveled from another Guyville to arrive at this one.

As a rock community, Guyville also represents a potentially unfriendly landscape for women. This includes a prejudice against women as musicians, especially in terms of performing on instruments central to rock like the drums and guitar. In *Rockrgrl*, one guitarist noted, "While professional female musicians fight for respect in the horrible sexist music industry, I find myself, as an amateur, fighting for respect in local music stores."[4] A common complaint against the hardcore punk community during the 1980s was the relegation of women to minor characters within the scene. Author Maria Raha noted, "The female presence that was generally lacking in hardcore more likely had more to do with the unfortunate intolerance that festered within the scene than with willingness on the part of women to participate."[5] In the early 1990s, riot grrrl bands frequently underlined this point by excluding men—from mosh pits and from their shows—to help even the playing field on the music scene.

Speaking to Martin Aston in 1993, Phair recalled this imbalance in the Chicago that she grew up in and, more specifically, the imbalance in the local music scene. Growing up, she noted, you could be considered cute or smart, but not both. Part of the sexism on the music scene was generalized, with men ignoring women's opinions. Other responses more directly disparaged women's participation in music. Phair remembered dating musicians and feeling like a band wife more than a participant on the scene, and how other male musicians would be surprised when they learned that she could play guitar.[6] Even a friend whom she considered sympathetic toward women's issues stated his belief that women could not be geniuses.

But Guyville also encompasses an expansive mythic space that permeates male and female consciousnesses in contemporary America. Guyville is a world imbued with masculine myths, habits, and values that have been handed down by cowboys, actors, and rock stars. Soap Star Joe embodies these values without self-awareness; they are simply part of his inner landscape. His blue jeans and aftershave are the standard male costume in Guyville, just as his assumptions and attitudes are part of the standard male thought process. Even on the make, he embodies an easy confidence; even pursuing small goals, he considers his actions heroic; even entering a new town, he gives the impression of being on a mission, of rapidly moving in and staking his claim in a new territory. The myths and territories of Guyville are fleshed out considerably across the expanse of both *Exile in Guyville* and the *Girly Sound* cassettes.

Within its broader definition, the values of Guyville, both within the music industry and everyday life, seem to permeate the world in which women live. In this sense, it remains an open question across the expanse of *Exile in Guyville* whether women can create a free social space to work either within or outside the confines of Guyville. When looking at Guyville in the most specific sense, as a small community that polices and promotes a limited set of values, women may be left with a discomforting realization: the local Guyville may be the only game in town. In order to gain street credentials, women may have to work within this community. Is it possible for women, as musicians, for instance, to stake their claim, to gain street credit, from within Guyville? Or is it possible for women to move beyond Guyville, carve out their own space, and establish their own rules?

Mapping Guyville

If *Exile in Guyville* and the *Girly Sound* cassettes are Phair's own *Winesburg, Ohio*, she relies on many of the same literary devices as Sherwood Anderson to build her portrait. In this way, she grafts a literary background and literary techniques onto the singer-songwriter tradition, and draws from and mixes both forms freely. She is an inhabitant of Guyville and an outsider; she is the confessional poet and the disinterested observer; she is sentimentally sincere and darkly satirical. Even the connection between *Exile in Guyville* and *Exile on Main Street* seems to work as another literary device, drawing from the gritty rock tradition of the Rolling Stones (which, by connection, lends *Exile in Guyville* greater authenticity) and reflecting on the tradition in which it was created (male dominated classic rock). These multiple approaches serve two purposes on *Exile in Guyville*.

This literary approach allows Phair to play against the idea of the confessional singer-songwriter, at one moment seeming to offer the real Phair, at another winking at the listener. This approach also serves to add multiple dimensions to a place and frame of mind called Guyville. Through portraits and confessions, a listener experiences Phair's personal story within a larger social context made up of Guyville's inhabitants while also learning the rules that govern the behavior and relationships of men and women within Guyville.

A Guy in Guyville

As in "Soap Star Joe," "Johnny Sunshine" offers another portrait of the American male on the move across the American landscape. Physically, Phair never describes, as she does with Soap Star Joe, Johnny Sunshine. His movement across the landscape seems hurried and unreflective, as though he is reacting to an atavistic drive instead of a rational response. The course of his flight—to the far-western state of Idaho—also seems more driven by a gut feeling than rational thought processes. Whereas the narrative of "Soap Star Joe" begins with his arrival in a new town, the narrative of "Johnny Sunshine" begins with his desire to escape. Because of this, Johnny Sunshine holds even less potential for heroics than Soap Star Joe. We never learn about the events that precede his escape, only that he has left the woman he was living with, and that he has enacted, before his escape, a scorched-earth campaign.

Another primary difference between the songs is that for all of Soap Star Joe's unflattering qualities, he seems basically benign. Johnny Sunshine's scorched-earth campaign—initiated against the woman he is leaving behind—adds an element of aggression and violence to the male characters that occupy Guyville. Before his flight begins, Johnny seems intent on leaving nothing behind; he is intent on destroying or taking everything of value to her. His most sadistic act is to kill her cat with antifreeze, and then dump her cat in the trunk of the car. He also changes the locks on the door (which forces her to live in a box) even though he, in the process of leaving, would no longer need the house. In an earlier version of the song from *Girly Sound*, Johnny Sunshine also takes the checkered rug from the floor. After committing these acts, he takes her Dodge Dart and drives to Idaho.

"Johnny Sunshine" also has a Western motif that Phair weaves into much of her work. While the origin of the couple's house is never mentioned, Johnny Sunshine's destination—Idaho—is very specific. Other details, some fantastical and absurd, broaden this motif. Johnny Sunshine steals her horse and rides the thoroughbred on the interstate. There is also cattle feed in the trunk of the car where he dumps the cat. His journey, combined with riding the horse on the interstate, seems to be an attempt to go West (as another Phair song, "Go West," states explicitly) and mimic the heroic journey and feats of earlier travelers. While these feats seem designed to elevate or add purpose to his actions, Johnny Sunshine is no more heroic in his flight than Soap Star Joe is in his arrival in town.

The beginning of "Johnny Sunshine" is driven forward by Phair's repetitive, hypnotic guitar and vocals, evoking—as in "Soap Star Joe"—movement. The movement, however, is circular, seeming to go nowhere. Sonically speaking, the arrangement at the beginning of the song is fuller than "Soap Star Joe," with Phair's vocals and guitar parts doubled. Bass and drums fill out the track. Phair complicates this basic pattern considerably in the second half of the song, but the initial impression in "Johnny Sunshine" is one of someone moving rapidly while remaining in place.

In both "Soap Star Joe" and "Johnny Sunshine," Phair has chosen familiar, even cliché, American male names (there is another Johnny in "Dance of the Seven Veils"). The names also evoke the simplicity of 1960s rock 'n' roll titles like "Johnny Angel" (1962). The title itself, "Johnny Sunshine," even seems to suggest an uplifting song (like "Johnny Angel"). The title, then, becomes perversely ironic when Johnny Sunshine reveals himself as vengeful and petty. In general, the title, by connecting itself to "Johnny Angel," also evokes an earlier, more innocent era.

Phair's lyric in "Johnny Sunshine," then, is more disruptive than the title suggests and is reminiscent of another song from 1962, Joanie Sommers' "Johnny Get Angry" (references to this song also appear in Poe's "Angry Johnny" in 1995 and Phair's "Johnny Feelgood" in 1998). In "Johnny Get Angry," the singer/narrator castigates Johnny for his timidity: she wants a more traditional or primitive man who wears his anger on his sleeve. If he really cared for her, he would become upset when she told him that their relationship was over; he would become angry when other guys showed interest in her. Instead, he seems either indifferent or incapable of action. The Johnny of "Johnny Sunshine" has taken Sommers' advice it seems, but only partially: he enacts his anger and violence while she is away, not in her presence. His actions, then, are ultimately cowardly. The two songs—"Johnny Get Angry" from 1962 and "Johnny Sunshine" from 1993—also juxtapose two eras: one, naïve and romantic, and the other, tarnished and cynical.

Phair brings these details together to sketch the brutal underside of traditional masculinity: while Johnny may believe that his actions (driving to Idaho; riding a horse on the interstate) feed into a heroic American tradition (the Wild West; John Ford Westerns), these traditions only provide a prop or ready script for destructive and irresponsible behavior. Johnny Sunshine, like Soap Star Joe, might even use his freedom to reestablish himself as the mysterious stranger who was rumored to have arrived in town in a Dodge Dart. Within Guyville, Joe and Johnny are archetypes: one, the self-deluded man who is unaware of the precariousness of his own position (his time, even in Guyville, is running out); the other, the relationship-phobic man who prefers flight to emotional commitment. If their position (in a relationship, in the local community) becomes overly complicated or difficult, they simply take flight and establish themselves in new locations.

Phair does not merely assume the values of Guyville, but establishes their origins in the American landscape. Two songs from the *Girly Sound* cassettes, "South Dakota" and "Go West," flesh out the lure of the road and the lure of the West in the American male consciousness. "South Dakota" would later appear on the *Juvenilia* single in 1995 and "Go West" as a rerecorded song on *Whip-Smart* in 1994.

"South Dakota" is the equivalent of the kind of tall tale that became popular in nineteenth-century American literature, but with a perverse 1990s twist. Part of this twist, perhaps, has its origins in Phair's contemporary source material: "South Dakota" borrows heavily from Iggy Pop's "Fun Time" from 1977. Phair's lyric is told from the point of view of a prairie man or cowboy who is preparing for a night on the town. While a night on the town seems no more promising for heroics than the actions of Soap Star Joe and Johnnie Sunshine, Phair's male persona adds a mythic element to the song by repeatedly emphasizing the title, "South Dakota": more than the state of his birth, he claims it as a birthright. He also asserts his superiority by insulting people from the city, referring to them as city fucks, and states that "South Dakota" is his—a prairie man's—world. The wide open space of South Dakota is a place for real men.

The prairie man's night on the town, however, is a parody of his larger than life persona. As the lyric begins, he seems to be coming on to a woman, complimenting her pants and her hips. This, like his desire to get drunk or stoned, may seem like normal behavior (traditionally speaking) for a male cowboy spending a night on the town. Phair totally undercuts a normal night on the town, however, when the cowboy states that after visiting a rodeo town and getting drunk, he wants to fuck cows. If anyone has reached this second verse and missed Phair's purpose, her bluntness makes her satire clear. The prairie man's brief, absurd description of his Western landscape extends the joke, identifying masons and lumber chucks (the latter of which conveniently rhymes with city fucks) as his prairie companions.

Phair recorded "South Dakota," like the other songs on the *Girly Sound* cassettes, on a four-track tape player. As it begins, "South Dakota" is spare and poorly recorded, with no more than a quietly strummed electric guitar and an almost spoken lyric. The only real variation with the arrangement is the doubling of Phair's voice/vocal at various places on the track. Whether talking or singing, she delivers much of the lyric in a cool, calm voice, one that imbues her persona with a relaxed confidence befitting her Western character. The pacing of "South Dakota" is equally calm and collected, save for the bridge—the emotional high point of the song—where the cowboy reminds city dwellers that South Dakota is a prairie man's world. Phair also adds a manly grunt in several places, topping off her spare aural portrait.

The music of "Go West" is similarly spare, though the lyric is much more straightforward. Although we are never told why the man leaves (just as in "Johnny Sunshine"), "Go West" is another contemporary tale of flight. Unlike "Johnny Sunshine," however, "Go West" is more melancholy than vengeful. While there is a love interest involved, and Phair's persona believes he will miss her, he follows through with his travel plans nonetheless.

The title itself—"Go West"—also makes a direct connection to the famous saying attributed (wrongly) to newspaper editor Horace Greeley and the idea of manifest destiny. Following the Civil War (1861–1865), westward expansion would be fueled by gold rushes, government land grants, and transcontinental railroads. Large tracts of open land allowed longhorns to roam free on the range, and the cowboy culture of the cattle trail, Dodge City, and ranch hands grew up around it. Thousands of homesteaders and self-made men would build homes and stake their own claim to the American Dream from the prairies of the Midwest to the valleys of California. Any man, alone or with his family, could pick up and start anew in the West, fulfilling his personal destiny as he also built a nation.

The price of manifest destiny, however, was highly problematic and, at least in retrospect, destructive. With a righteous providence, however, little thought seemed to be given to the fact that the original inhabitants—various tribes of Native Americans—would have to be removed. The decimation of the buffalo would work to deprive Native Americans of a food source while also conveniently freeing the ranges for cattle. The heritage of the railroad was equally problematic, from the use of cheap immigrant labor (including Chinese immigrants in the West) to the alteration of the very landscape to make way for the transcontinental tracks. Every heroic move, by the army, cattle ranchers, and individual homesteaders, required a sacrifice of lives, land, and environment.

Even focusing on manifest destiny's romantic side, the era of the wide open West came to an end by the mid- to late 1880s thanks to barbed wire, droughts, and an economic depression. In 1893, Frederick Jackson Turner famously declared that the frontier was closed. The era, however, would continue to live on as a central myth in the American consciousness through dime novels, Owen Wister's *The Virginian* (1902), Zane Grey's novels, singing cowboys in the 1930s (Gene Autry), and, most prominently, the Western movie.

The West, even as a mere shadow of its mythic past, remains an ever-present heritage in the thought processes and actions of the inhabitants of Guyville. Phair's male persona in "Go West" feels safe while driving on the interstate because it gives the impression that he, like his forefathers, is in the process of accomplishing something important; he relies on his gut feeling or the past or the heritage of Guyville, because he does not wish to think for himself. The most telling line in "Go West" details his reason for leaving New York City. He notes that it may seem as though he is trying to prove something by going West; in reality, however, his journey is just something to do.

A Girl in Guyville

> I know what I'm doing when I use the word fuck, but I think it's termed explicit only because I'm a girl. The thrill of it is like, your little sister could be . . . having these thoughts and you wouldn't know it. . . . It makes you look around at all the good girls and wonder what's going on in their heads.
>
> —Liz Phair[7]

Guyville is hostile territory for women who may be considered a friend, a sexual conquest, a temporary safe harbor, or a competitor. In "Fuck and Run," Phair's persona reveals a contemporary landscape of relaxed sexual mores and underlying loneliness; in "Flower," she revels in a frank sexuality that mimics raunchy guy talk; in "Never Said," she wears the mask of the tight-lipped man, defending her honor; and in "Girls! Girls! Girls!" she becomes the female aggressor, bragging that she can, when it comes to men, get away with anything. Ultimately, a girl is only an accessory or inconvenience to the guys of Guyville, a position that forces her to become a chameleon: only by adapting a series of masks can she protect herself and perhaps prosper within the confines of Guyville.

In "Fuck and Run," sex, or hooking up, is portrayed as an activity that attempts, but always fails, to ward off loneliness; in the end, it leaves people even lonelier. Phair never judges sex as morally wrong, only as a poor substitute for real relationships. Her female persona juxtaposes contemporary intimate relationships against an idealized past where girls and boys shared sodas at the local malt shop. She then rhetorically wonders whatever happened to the traditional boyfriend: the kind who gave you his letter jacket, the kind who wanted to make love because he was in love. The lyrics of the song are colored by Phair's plaintive vocal, rendering her character vulnerable, but she undercuts the sentimentally by repeating the harsher words of the title on each chorus, "Fuck and Run." There is a sense of futility in "Fuck and Run," with the narrator realizing that her relationships have always been like this and that they are likely to always be this way.

Phair's persona never accuses the boy of the song of emotional mistreatment (though men and masculinity are negatively singled out through the remainder of *Exile in Guyville*); likewise, there is no obvious focus on a sexual double standard. When her companion wakes up, he makes excuses (he says that he has a lot of work to do), which she knows are untrue. She projects that he feels bad about the encounter, but when he invites her to phone him, she believes that he does not really mean it. While we may accuse her male companion of being insensitive, we might also note that the encounter seems to have been a casual one, probably with little expectations on either side. On an earlier version from the *Girly Sound* tapes, Phair underlines the lack of blame by adding a verse about the boy's desire to have a traditional girlfriend.

Within the context of the song, it finally seems as though contemporary society (the 1990s or Generation X), or something within that society, is somehow to blame. Like the innocent/naïve world that created "Johnny Angel" and "Johnny Get Angry," an earlier era of sock-hops and drive-ins—even if they are idealized within popular culture—may seem preferable to hooking up. It is the era or Generation X that is in some way defective or to blame. In this sense, "Fuck and Run" is a contemporary morality tale.

"Fuck and Run," then, tells the story of a one-night stand in which the woman (any Gen X woman), wakes up in a strange place in a stranger's arms, and is filled with regret. Her regret, however, has less to do with guilt than with the futility of her situation: as she notes later in the song, she has been living like this—waking up in strange places with strange men—since she was twelve. Because of the futility, she repeats that her intentions were not to become involved again. It is easy, however, to gain the impression that this is a promise she has made and broken before. Sexual desire itself plays little part in the song's narrative or her broken promises; instead, she seems driven by a desire for companionship, a desire to no longer be alone. As a contemporary morality tale, "Fuck and Run" reveals the dangers of being lured in by the men of Guyville when there is no chance of emotional commitment.

Phair underlines this emotional distance by noting that the man in "Fuck and Run" almost—but does not quite—feels bad about the one-night stand. But even if he phoned her, there seems little chance that it would lead to anything other than another one-night stand. This point is made even clearer in songs like "Shatter" and "Mesmerizing," where Phair's personas are emotionally broken in the aftermath of relationships with insensitive men.

Personal and direct, Phair's lyrics draw heavily from the traditional idea of the singer-songwriter genre in "Fuck and Run." The lyric is both revelatory and told from a first person point of view, giving the impression that there is little separation between Phair and the words of the song. "Fuck and Run" and Joni Mitchell's "River" (1971) share a deep sadness over disappointment in love, and the only significant difference, lyrically, is that Phair, recording twenty years after Mitchell, uses more forthright language. In isolation, "Fuck and Run" seems to be a fairly straightforward lyric about '90s-style loneliness.

The confessional mode, however, is complicated by appearing within *Exile in Guyville*, where the confessional mode is only one style among many. Like "River," "Fuck and Run" is meant as an honest confession; unlike "River," it is also a reminder of the rules within Guyville: if you allow yourself to become involved emotionally with men (as friends or lovers), you will be disappointed, hurt, and possibly abused. In order to survive and possibly thrive in Guyville, a girl must adopt a series of masks that hide her emotional vulnerability.

"Flower," which has been sequenced four songs after "Fuck and Run," is one of Phair's most sexually frank songs. The entire lyric is made up of a half-sung, half-spoken rap detailing the narrator's sexual fantasies; these fantasies are set in motion each time she sees the face of the boy she lusts after. It is set against a slowly spiraling backdrop of another female voice (also Phair's), which repeats a series of phrases also expressing sexual desire. Both personas state that they have little interest in him other than sexual: within the narrative of "Flower," he has been objectified.

In one sense, "Flower" is a straightforward expression of female sexuality, explicit and unashamed, just as "Fuck and Run" is a straightforward expression of disappointment in love. The lyric is aggressive because Phair allows her female persona to publicly express desire in graphic terms. Instead of fearing public reprisal as a slut or for appearing promiscuous, the narrator boldly embraces her sexuality. She does not, as many girls have been taught, attempt to sugarcoat her sexuality with idealized love for a boy. On the contrary, the boy she has chosen, whose face looks like a flower, is purely an object of her lust.

But she also utilizes two different voices to render the lyric, one offering blunt words in a near-monotone voice, the second providing equally blunt words presented in a demure voice. If it is easy to accept the first voice at face value, as a straightforward rendering of female sexual desire, it is equally easy to accept the second voice as a rendition of idealized female desire from a male point of view (to a casual listener, however, both voices may seem to express, essentially, the same thing.) Read this way, the voices are set at opposite ends of a spectrum of female responses, one (the demure voice) "dirty" but culturally acceptable from a traditional masculine point of view (not unlike objectified women who appear in pornography for men's pleasure); the other "dirty" (the monotone voice) and, because of its aggressiveness, culturally unacceptable from a traditional male point of view (it is okay for women to be sexually available but they should not be sexual aggressors).

There is also the possibility that Phair is parodying both the masculine fantasy of female desire with the demure voice *and* the more aggressive expression of masculine desire in the monotone voice. Phair leaves the lyric of "Flower'"—like many of her lyrics—open to a number of interpretations, and no matter which one you choose, Phair has destabilized traditional ideas of male and female sexual desire.

In "Never Said," Phair's persona goes a step further by assuming a traditional masculine pose when accused of revealing a secret. Although Phair does not signify gender in "Never Said," the lyric portrays masculinity as a set of characteristics, a role that can be adapted by men and women. Instead of signifying gender in "Never Said," then, she suggests it by the fact that her persona actively defends her masculine stance: a male narrator would assume the role and feel no need, or no self-consciousness, in defending it.

In "Never Said," Phair's persona repeatedly denies that she has divulged a secret, and her response mimics masculine behavior: she has her hands in her pockets, offers that she has never uttered a sound, and warns her accuser not to look at her sideways. She is strong and silent, and Phair delivers this tight-lipped portrait at a deeper vocal register. The guitar-heavy arrangement moves deliberately through its progressions, echoing the narrator's masculine stance. By embracing an emotionally clipped silence, the narrator of "Never Said" attempts to pass unnoticed as one of the guys.

Phair reveals her most aggressive strategy for survival in "Girls! Girls! Girls!" Within this song, her characters go one step further, assuming both the masculine characteristics of "Never Said" and the feminine aggression of "Flower." Musically, the slow, steady guitar propulsion provides "Girls! Girls! Girls!" with a brooding undercurrent, though the satirically dry humor of the lyric balances the mood. This balance allows Phair to pass off words like "murder" lightly, while still leaving a residue of female aggression. This aggression of "Girls! Girls! Girls!" also achieves irony by referencing at least two other songs of the same name, Elvis Presley's "Girls, Girls, Girls" from the movie of the same name in 1962, and more recently, Mötley Crüe's "Girls, Girls, Girls" from 1987.

Phair's persona in "Girls! Girls! Girls!" co-opts traditional masculine qualities, refusing to let her emotions sway her behavior and demanding center stage as the most important person in the room. When she wishes to leave a man in a relationship, she threatens that he better let her go; if someone believes that he is important, he better check with her first. The narrator brags that she takes advantage of all men with whom she comes into contact. In essence, she behaves exactly like many of the men who inhabit *Exile in Guyville*, and presents herself as a female version of a man on the make. In "Girls! Girls! Girls!" Phair's persona has usurped masculine prerogative, acting out her aggressive and unsympathetic femininity on unsuspecting men.

When a woman lets down her guard, as in "Fuck and Run," and crosses the line between one of the guys and romance, the emotional terrain of Guyville becomes treacherous for women. Adopting a series of masks, stances, or attitudes, however, provides a protective shield. By remaining aloof and playing by the same rules as the guys as in "Never Said," one might remain unnoticed or at least avoid the emotional pitfalls of being a girl in Guyville. But one other possibility remains. By going one step further and usurping male aggression and ambition as in "Girls! Girls! Girls!" and "Flower," Phair opens up a new possibility: women could do more than merely survive as one of the guys. By pushing back and building a free space to act or create within, women could prosper and even compete within Guyville.

Street Credit in Guyville

Like any singer-songwriter effort, *Exile in Guyville* is a sketch of an enclosed world. But the album—from the inception of many of its songs on the *Girly Sound* cassettes to its release on the independent Matador label—also represented a physical reality in the wider world. Within the world of Guyville, women must follow specific rules in order to fit in or to pass unobserved, and when they ignore or shun these rules, they must be ready to pay the emotional price. Likewise, Phair's *Exile in Guyville* was unleashed within the physical world of indie and punk rock community, a world with its own rules and punishments.

Even though Phair's music never fit comfortably within a given category, (whether one considers other bands from Chicago like Urge Overkill, label mates like Pavement, or riot grrrl bands like Bikini Kill and Bratmobile), her music would be judged on the general principle of quality within the independent music scene, including the DIY (do-it-yourself) aesthetic and a commitment to small labels. Within the world of indie rock, however, the judgment of the new album would also be influenced by Phair's *Girly Sound* tapes, issued in 1991. These three cassettes helped define her as a lo-fi, independent singer-songwriter and—despite the vastly different sonic palettes—a spiritual follower of the DIY and riot grrrl aesthetic. Partly, then, *Exile in Guyville* would be measured against Phair's approach and the results of the *Girly Sound* recordings; partly, she would be judged by punks, riot grrrls, and other purists for following or refusing to follow indie precepts. But her past work and indie standards also presented potential pitfalls: by adhering too strictly to these given set of rules, Phair would be trapped within the same kind of Guyville that her characters seemed to be stuck in on *Exile in Guyville*.

Even the simple act of rerecording nine songs from *Girly Sound* for *Exile in Guyville* was potentially problematic. From a purist's point of view, it would have been better to either (1) reissue the *Girly Sound* cassettes as an official release, or (2) simply record new songs for a new album. Instead, Phair handpicked nine *Girly Sound* songs, rewrote a number of lyrics, bolstered the sound, and then wrote nine more songs that matched the first nine thematically. While this sharpened her vision considerably and made her music more accessible, it also cast aside part of the offbeat charm and humor of the *Girly Sound* cassettes. Phair's impossible challenge was to present an inner vision of her music within the limitations of indie, punk, and riot grrrl aesthetics and, perhaps, to circumvent these restrictions without anyone noticing. Both the cover art and the sound production of *Exile in Guyville* would have to walk that fine line between these restrictions and Phair's broader musical and philosophical vision.

Cover Art

My sexuality was going to be packaged for me, so I did it myself.

—Liz Phair[8]

Yeah, I just took [the photographs]. I took a lot of them that night and [Nate Kado] liked this one a lot. He just pounced on it. He was like, "This is the cover! Lizzy this is the cover!" He probably bought me a double scotch or something. It was really funny.

—Liz Phair[9]

The cover art on Phair's early albums and singles closely resembles that of many riot grrrl albums from the same period, though with a more professional finish. But the purpose of her album artwork is frequently difficult to discern. In the inserts of *Exile in Guyville* and *Whip-Smart* (1994), it is difficult to know whether the designers were attempting to offer in-depth commentary or just fooling around; whether the cover art should be taken seriously or whether it's simply clever. The biggest exception to this, however, is the well-known cover of Phair on *Exile in Guyville*.

The black-and-white photograph on *Exile in Guyville* focuses on a shirtless Phair, thrust forward in the frame, with a dark coat and hood outlining her body. Her partially concealed (by the coat and the shadow of the hood) eyes seem to express surprise, fear, or aggression, while her open mouth seems to be in the process of releasing a shout or perhaps a scream. The stark white in the photograph, from the bridge of Phair's nose to her partially revealed breasts, contrasts starkly with the dark coat and shadow that frames her body. On both sides of her face, her hair fans out widely, though still held within the coat and hood. On her right ear, Phair is wearing an earring; around her neck and falling between her breasts, she is wearing several strands of necklaces.

The photograph of Phair is disorienting, leaving one to puzzle over its relation to the title of the album, *Exile in Guyville*. Why is she moving forward—is she moving toward something or away from it? Is she attempting to shout or scream, or is she simply surprised? Why is Phair wearing a coat and no shirt? Why is she going shirtless, but displaying jewelry?

These questions complicate any straightforward reading of the cover. Perhaps the most central problem in regard to the DIY aesthetic is Phair's eyes: both are in heavy shadow, a shadow created by her hood; her right eye, in fact, is barely visible. Because of this, her expression is difficult to read and remains either ambiguous or purposely multifaceted. Without her eyes in full view she has, in truth, hid the essential attribute that would allow the viewer to know what she is thinking. Other details strengthen this impression. The coat and hood may protect her from the outside world, but they also hide the real her from the world outside. While Phair appears to be wearing nothing beneath her cloak, she displays several strands of necklaces and is—at least on her right ear—wearing earrings.

In offering a portrait that appears to fulfill DIY requirements for honesty but nonetheless refuses to reveal itself, Phair has pulled off a clever sleight of hand. As she gains her street credit in Guyville by fulfilling the DIY requirements of the indie/punk music scene (authentic, no-nonsense cover art), she reinforces her basic stance within *Exile in Guyville*: any girl who reveals herself too quickly within Guyville, any girl who does not learn to use a series of masks for self-protection, will never survive, much less prosper.

Phair's own conception of the cover art relates once again to the Rolling Stones' *Exile on Main Street*. In a documentary DVD marking the fifteenth anniversary of *Exile in Guyville* (the documentary is packaged with the fifteenth-anniversary version of the album), she explains the cover art of *Exile on Main Street* as representing the two sides of the Rolling Stones, one symbolic, the other realistic. On the cover, a group of circus players appear in multiple single frames and are in the process of presenting themselves to the camera as performers; one man has placed three balls in his mouth, while another sits with a ventriloquist's dummy perched on his lap. These frames stand in relief to multiple frames of the Rolling Stones as everyday guys for the most part, hanging out and recording in the studio. In the first series of images, the circus performers are stand-ins for the public persona of the Rolling Stones, a group renowned for its hard-living rock 'n' roll lifestyle; in the second series of images, the members of the Rolling Stones are everyday people following everyday routines.

Phair views *Exile in Guyville* as presenting a similar duality. In the cover photograph, Phair is the energetic public performer, revealing and aggressive; in the snapshot on the back cover, she is just everyday Liz Phair. Speaking to Alyssa Isenstein in *Second Skin*, Phair noted the difference:

> And so to me to have on the cover me in this performance pose, and then on the back have me in my little home staring at the camera like, right, is exactly the same thing. The Liz of the performance, when I go into my performance head, and me on the back just like right in the camera's face, like I want to do when I am myself.[10]

The comparison, however, seems to underplay the front cover's relationship to a place called Guyville.

Like her comparison between the songs on *Exile in Guyville* and *Exile on Main Street*, Phair's reading of her cover art obscures more than it reveals. Framed in this way, Phair's comparison is another effort to establish street credentials (gaining authenticity again by comparing herself to the Rolling Stones) while obscuring (to the guardians of Guyville) the subversive elements within the photograph. The front cover art may have only presented one side of Phair, but it also worked—much like the anonymous figure in Edvard Munch's *The Scream* did in an earlier era—as a broader symbol.

Indeed, Munch's *The Scream* had become a culture icon in the latter half of the twentieth century. Three years after Phair's album, Wes Craven would begin his *Scream* movie series. Before that, however, Munch's anxious figure had been reproduced multiple times in cartoons and art. Cartoon characters from Bugs Bunny to Homer Simpson have been inserted into the painting and, in 1983–1984, pop art legend Andy Warhol made a brightly colored (yellow, pink, and green) silkscreen titled *The Scream*. In 1991 Robert Fishbone created an inflatable version of Munch's figure. Fishbone's original Scream stood four and a half feet tall and, in 1994, was priced at twenty-eight dollars; Scream, Jr. was nineteen inches and priced at ten dollars. Between 1991 and 1994, Fishbone would sell one hundred thousand inflatable dolls. Also, in 1991 Dan Quayle was pictured as The Scream on T-shirts, supposedly expressing Quayle's fear that he might have to be temporarily sworn in as president in relation to a health crisis involving George H. W. Bush. Munch himself painted more than one version of *The Scream*, and in 1895, reproduced the painting as a black-and-white lithograph.

Munch's genderless figure can be broadly interpreted as an every-person assaulted by the changing world on the precipice of the twentieth century. Its scream, then, is one of fear and anxiety in relation to both interpersonal turmoil and the turmoil of the world that surrounds everyone. Paralyzed by fear and anxiety, the figure can do no more than offer a cry of despair. *The Scream* has also been considered from the point of view of the artist facing a blank canvas or blank piece of paper. Faced with creating art out of chaos or nothing, the artist, like the every-person on the edge of modernity, is paralyzed with anxiety and fear.

Both the figure in *The Scream* and Phair's portrait on *Exile in Guyville* share similar emotions. Both figures have opened mouths and both appear to be crying out; to protect oneself from the outside world, one has placed its hands around its face, the other has surrounded herself with a coat and hood. Both seem to be expressing anxiety and fear, and both seem to be—despite their attempts to protect themselves—exposed. These similarities seem even more striking when comparing Phair's black-and-white album cover with Munch's black-and-white lithograph of *The Scream*.

But there are key differences between Munch and Phair's figures. First, *Exile in Guyville* was issued in 1993, one hundred years after *The Scream* (1893), on the edge of the twenty-first century. Next, while Munch's protagonist is genderless, Phair, with her styled hair, jewelry, and partially exposed breasts, is clearly a woman. Phair's portrait, then, is perhaps more specific, working expressly as a symbol for young women in the 1990s. In this sense, Phair's scream is one of frustration and aggression emanating from her long captivity within Guyville. Unlike Munch's painting, there is no need to depict the outside world: the songs on *Exile in Guyville* detail the broader world that oppresses her and all women.

Phair's multifaceted facial expression on the cover of *Exile in Guyville* also holds one possibility never evident in *The Scream*. Phair's contemporary woman is not standing still with her hands around her head, merely reacting subjectively to the weight of the world. Instead, she may—as she moves forward in the frame—be aggressively asserting her own femininity within Guyville. Like PJ Harvey's version of Medusa on the cover of *Rid of Me*, Phair also leaves the impression that this figure may be ready to defend herself or even commit acts of violence against the forces that hem her in, hold her back, or seek to do her harm. The scream against the oppressive world as depicted on *Exile in Guyville*, then, might also be the scream of liberation. Phair's expressive figure is the girl that Guyville never prepared for; the girl who entered the inner sanctum and publicly revealed its interior workings; and the girl who used Guyville as a launching pad to create a free space for other women.

Bedroom Lo-Fi vs. Studio Lo-Fi

> The songs were amazing. [Girly Sound] was a fairly primitive recording, especially compared to the resulting [Exile in Guyville].
>
> —Gerard Cosloy of Matador[11]

> While Phair's sketchy "Girlysound" recordings do indeed sound as if they were taped in her bedroom, "Exile" is an impressive and varied soundscape with many different moods and atmospheres.
>
> —Jim DeRogatis[12]

For most listeners and critics, it is easy and accurate to categorize *Exile in Guyville* as lo-fi, DIY, or folk-punk. The album shares similar production values with many riot grrrl albums of the time, simple arrangements recorded by small labels on a shoestring budget with a minimum of studio trickery, though Phair's basic sound is quieter than the punk-fueled recordings by most riot grrrl bands. Phair's mostly stripped-down arrangements mesh comfortably with the DIY punk aesthetic, and as a solo artist who sometimes played all the instruments on a given track, Phair's approach may be seen as even more reductive. Phair's bare bones aesthetic was most evident when you compared *Exile in Guyville* to other albums on major labels in 1993. In regard to the work of other women singer-songwriters, the production and arrangements of *Exile in Guyville* would never be mistaken for Sheryl Crow's *Tuesday Night Music Club* or Sarah McLachlan's *Fumbling towards Ecstasy.*

Still, while the songs on *Exile in Guyville* may appear off the cuff—recorded in a basement or bedroom on a four-track tape machine—they are in fact the results of professional sessions, recorded at a studio, and overseen by a producer, Brad Wood. This becomes more evident when one compares *Exile in Guyville* to the *Girly Sound* cassettes recorded earlier.

Recorded on a four-track tape machine, the *Girly Sound* cassettes possess an off-the-cuff innocence and charm, and gain authenticity through a lack of perfection. Recorded in Phair's bedroom in her parents' home, it is easy to gain the impression that each song was a diary entry or perhaps the social equivalent of a girl zine. But if authenticity is considered off the cuff, or close to live performance, the very idea of one person recording with a four-track tape machine is problematic. A four-track tape machine allowed a performer like Phair to record each track—a vocal (track one), a guitar part (track two), another vocal (track three), and a second guitar part (track four)—separately, building the final take piecemeal. Even if one accepts that live recording is an impossible idea and that even punk bands, in the studio, require overdubs, the idea of one person recording all parts meant that the track would be less live than the average punk band. Still, the songs from the *Girly Sound* cassettes are raw and basic, complete with tape hiss and poorly recorded vocals, fitting the inexact requirements of DIY and punk/indie authenticity.

Phair complicated her relationship with the DIY aesthetic, however, when she chose to rerecord nine of *Girly Sound's* songs for *Exile in Guyville.*[13] While it was not unusual for punks or riot grrrls to rerecord their work—Bikini Kill recorded "Rebel Girl" at least three times—a number of factors would complicate Phair's choice. Phair not only chose to rerecord old material, but she chose to change lyrics, arrangements, and the very method of recording the songs. While none of the changes made the new versions of the songs unrecognizable, they did transform the meaning and aesthetic quality of many of these songs in significant ways, expanding the sonic quality of her music and sharpening her feminist critique of Guyville. In essence, Phair treated each of the nine *Girly Sound* recordings as though they were demos, basic ideas that could be expanded in the studio. Over the course of her career, she has continued to recycle older material: "I'm constantly changing and rewriting my songs. I constantly pilfer my old material."[14] The distance between the two sets of recordings, the first completed in 1991, the latter completed in 1993, had allowed time for Phair's ideas to gestate and evolve.

Changing the songs, however, would be a balancing act between the requirements of DIY and her own artistic sensibility. There was also the chance that her producer, Wood, might be given credit for the results (this would be a repeated theme throughout the women singer-songwriters' movement). Phair's talent in recording *Exile in Guyville*, once again, lay in her ability to split the difference philosophically, offering recordings that gave the impression of meeting the aesthetic requirements of riot grrrl/DIY/punk within Guyville, but that nonetheless subverted and superseded these requirements; of maintaining artistic control, but nonetheless utilizing the talents of others to broaden her vision.

"Fuck and Run" received one of the more noticeable transformations between the *Girly Sound* and *Exile in Guyville* versions. The arrangement on the original version is simple, just Phair's vocal backed by an acoustic guitar and perhaps a rudimentary bass line; her progressive strumming drives this four-and-a-half-minute version forward, generating a song structure that resembles an odd marriage between 1950s rock 'n' roll and bolero. On *Exile in Guyville*, the arrangement is much bigger, with electric guitar, bass, drums, and what sounds like bells at one point, creating a full rock sound. The performance and vocal are brighter, more upbeat, and this version of "Fuck and Run" is over a minute shorter. A removed verse accounts for the shorter running time. On the original, Phair included the boy's point of view, detailing that he, like the girl of the song, also wished to return to an earlier time and the idea of old-fashioned romance. By cutting the verse, Phair minimizes sympathy for the boy and sharpens her critique of masculinity within Guyville.

Phair accomplished a similar though less radical transformation in the arrangement and lyrics of "Flower." In the original version, the electric guitar provides a steady thump-thump backdrop, perceptible but low in the mix. The pacing is lethargic, and the original version, at around two minutes and forty seconds, seems at a standstill. On the *Exile in Guyville* version, Phair quickened her vocal delivery and inserted a simple though sonically insistent guitar part, and as a result, "Flower" is thirty seconds shorter and has the propulsive feel of a playground taunt or game. She also changes her persona's promise to have sex with his girlfriends in the first version to a promise to have sex with his minions. Again, all of these sonic and lyrical changes enrich the track and offer a shift in meaning. By removing the reference to girlfriends, Phair remains focused on the male/female dynamic within Guyville; by increasing the pacing and adding a more prominent second guitar, she creates a track with a richer sonic palette.

In other songs Phair follows this pattern, either removing or adding elements to strengthen the overall structure of the song. In both "Shatter" and "Stratford-On-Guy," Phair removes extra background vocals that are either unnecessary or annoying. In "Shatter," a voice repeats "sha-doobie" and "shatter" in the background, creating the feel of 1950s doo-wop; in "Stratford-On-Guy," a waitress, acting as a travel guide, invites the passengers to look at the sights below. While the repeated "shatter" helps to underline the emotional state of Phair's narrator in the first song, it also seems busy within the song's languid pacing; the waitress in "Stratford-On-Guy," on the other hand, simply breaks the mood of the narrator's Zen-like moment. In "Johnny Sunshine," however, Phair adds a new background vocal to the *Exile in Guyville* version, helping smooth over the clunky transition between the song's two parts in the original version.

"Girls! Girls! Girls!" received the most truncated treatment from *Girly Sound* to *Exile in Guyville*. The original is nearly seven minutes long, and consists of three sections. While these divisions are fairly cohesive, with similar structures and chord patterns, the length is unwieldy. Phair's acoustic guitar work, alternating between a low, steady thump-thump to full, energetic strumming, also demarks the different sections. The length and the multiple sections, however, do not expand or improve the basic theme/satire of "Girls! Girls! Girls!" The version from *Exile in Guyville* retains only the first section of the song, and structurally, nearly matches the *Girly Sound* version. But while the second version retains a similar, simple arrangement, an electric guitar and better overall recording quality invest the song with a greater sonic impact.

In each case Phair enriches the new version sonically, improves her vocal(s), and shapes the song to fit within the overall philosophical matrix of *Exile in Guyville*. In each case, the demo has been transformed into a richer, more cohesive track. While certain elements—an off-the-cuff charm, quirkiness, and immediacy—are left behind, Phair exchanges these items for an album that maintains a tighter focus and sounds better. As a result, the rerecorded songs on *Exile in Guyville* achieved, musically and thematically, a much greater force than those on the *Girly Sound* cassettes.

Did Phair's balancing act between lo-fi and studio aesthetics work? Did her cross blending of styles satisfy fans of her *Girly Sound* recordings and other purists? Not everyone, it seems, was completely convinced. Fans would wonder whether the *Girly Sound* recordings would ever be officially released, and purists would ask Phair whether she might return to her *Girly Sound* style one day. But any censure was rendered mute when *Exile in Guyville* was met with an overwhelming critical response from a broader musical community.

The *Girly Sound* recordings, after all, were not a commercial product, and it seems likely that many people—critics and listeners—judged *Exile in Guyville* on its own merits. In a write-up of *Exile in Guyville* in *Billboard*, the album would be described in much the same way that many had described the *Girly Sound* recordings:

> That the vast range of prurient psalms in *Exile in Guyville* truly adheres is due to the austere recording recipe employed by Phair and [Brad] Wood, the album's ingredients so close to the basic household acoustics of instrumental/vocal rumination that listeners may wonder if the songs aren't demos of their own soul-kitchen subconscious.[15]

Recording in an "austere" style for an indie label, Phair managed to leave her sonic mark on *Exile in Guyville* while leaving the impression that she had never left Guyville.

Escaping Guyville

Phair had the distinction of generating some hometown backlash before her album was even released. But as bootleg tapes, and ultimately the record, made the rounds, her detractors found themselves eating crow.

—Bill Wyman[16]

In her early 20s Phair played guitar and wrote to prove she was not their groupie but an equal. At 26, having just completed her first album, she has come to define herself against the norms of the club.

—Sue Cummings[17]

In "Stratford-On-Guy," the next to last song on *Exile in Guyville*, one of Phair's personas engages in a fantasy of escape from Guyville as she looks out of her airplane window. As the plane is arriving in Chicago at twilight, the lake below turns the sky a smoky blue-green, while the orange glow of the setting sun reflects inside the airplane's cabin. The ground below, as the airplane enters the grid of the city, reminds her of an electrical ball, and everyone on the plane seems frozen in stillness while the ground rushes beneath them. The moment is less surreal than ethereal, and Phair's narrator captures the minute details of an unfolding, Zen-like moment: she is conscious of suspended time, but unaware how long the moment has stretched out.

It is a serene moment, far away from the realities that have defined the outer limits of *Exile in Guyville*, and during that moment—suspended in the sky and suspended in time—she seems to have left Guyville behind. Is her escape real, or is it only a temporary fantasy that she indulges in before her plane lands in the midst of an even more real Guyville in Chicago? Is her Zen-like experience a temporary time-out, only possible when she is isolated from a particular physical Guyville, or is her experience a state of mind or free space that one can claim within the midst of Guyville? Or is it finally a vision, suggesting the possibility of building a space of one's own outside of Guyville, a space where women can make up and live by their own rules?

More than any other song on *Exile in Guyville*, "Stratford-On-Guy" suggests another way of seeing and living in the world, one free from traditions and preset rules, one outside the influence of Guyville. It also serves as a vision of artistic possibilities, unhampered by the need to navigate a hostile environment. The vision of "Stratford-On-Guy," however, is not completely isolated within the album. Near the beginning of *Exile in Guyville*, Phair leaves a couple of important clues that seem to connect, or build up, to "Stratford-On-Guy." More than a fantasy, then, "Stratford-On-Guy" offers a real possibility for the smart, ambitious woman.

Phair drops one clue in "Help Me Mary," relating one woman's experience with male roommates, a microcosm of Guyville. It's never clear why Phair's persona has chosen to live with male roommates, only that living with these roommates, like exile itself, seems more like an imprisonment than a living arrangement. The housemates test and harass her, and attempt to provoke a response. Their behavior seems more ritualized than calculated, a gut-level response to all things female. She disciplines herself against their rude remarks and taunts, and locks her door each night to protect herself. She also prays to Mary to temper her hatred, though her motivation is less concerned with survival than one-upmanship: if she can transform her repulsion of her housemates into ambition and fame, then she will place herself above them and above Guyville.

Here, one might imagine Guyville in the smaller sense, as a music scene filled with a cast of characters who are on the make. Some are living off the glory of the past ("Glory"), while some are too old to compete ("Soap Star Joe"); others, like the roommates in "Help Me Mary," would form part of a current music scene. A woman entering the scene would probably be no different than many of her housemates; she, too, is on the make, wishing to be successful on the music scene (start a band, get a recording contract, record an album, etc.). In order to compete, however, she has to have more than talent; she has to navigate Guyville successfully, keeping an eye on her surroundings while trying to rise above them.

But Phair's personas need something more than this to succeed. The competitive music scene requires more than a competitive spirit: a girl within Guyville needs to be ruthless. One of Phair's personas takes that next step in "Dance of the Seven Veils." Here, she is a contemporary Salome, vying for the head of a contemporary John the Baptist, who, like Johnny Sunshine, is over-the-hill but doesn't know it. With her shiny platter in hand, a new threat, though never explicit, enters the world of Guyville: Salome is more than a pawn depicted in the New Testament who only asks for John the Baptist's head to fulfill her mother's request. As the Johnny of "Dance of the Seven Veils" realizes too late, Salome wishes to take his place as a prophet, as a rock singer, or both. Aggression, mixed with ruthless ambition, offers a girl in Guyville potential for more than survival as one of the guys: she could also compete with and eventually replace them.

Exile in Guyville became ironic after the fact: to be accepted in Guyville, Phair would have to record a solid indie album like *Exile in Guyville*. In a sense, then, she used her hostility to the parameters and occupants of Guyville to fuel her art, creating an album that critiqued her oppressors and put her beyond them. As depressing as many of *Exile in Guyville's* lyrics may have been concerning male/female relationships, Phair's vision of aggressive femininity wins the day. In the very act of recording these songs, she transforms her position against her oppressors. She has survived Guyville, even escaped from it, and the album establishes her independence.

By recording *Exile in Guyville*, Phair outlined the new terrain for contemporary women. The album uncovered the boundaries of Guyville, detailing every woman's multifaceted existence and the nightmare of living within an openly hostile, masculine environment. Guyville was a self-enclosed system, seemingly un-self-conscious of itself and incapable and uninterested in change. A woman might try to conform or prosper within Guyville's confines, but the system itself was stacked against her. More important than defining the parameters of Guyville, *Exile in Guyville* provided directions, by the very fact that Phair wrote and recorded it, of a way out. Women in the 1990s may have remained mired in a hostile masculine culture that included a backlash, but they were also beginning to realize other possibilities. Phair's portrait on the cover of *Exile in Guyville*, then, is ultimately one of contemporary women in motion, moving away from the limitations of the past toward the unknown. In motion, the contemporary women would create new free spaces by the simple fact of moving into them. As Phair told *Rolling Stone* following the release of *Exile in Guyville* in 1993, "This is the call to young girls who have the ability to compete. Get out there and slug it out. There's not enough female voices in popular culture. It's a fucking crime."[18]

Notes

1. Amy Raphael, *Grrrls: Viva Rock Divas* (New York: St. Martin's Griffin, 1995), 219.

2. Greg Kot, "Gal in 'Guyville,'" *Chicago Tribune*, May 2, 1993.

3. Timothy White, "Liz's 'Guyville': All Is Phair in Love," *Billboard*, May 8, 1993; reprinted in *Music to My Ears: The Billboard Essays* (New York: Henry Holt, 1996), 131.

4. Amy Wilson, "Exile in Guyville," *Rockrgrl*, March–April 1996, 20.

5. Maria Raha, *Cinderella's Big Score: Women of the Punk and Indie Underground* (Emeryville, CA: Seal Press, 2005), 115.

6. Martin Aston, "Liz Phair," *Independent Catalog*, September 1993.

7. Lorraine Ali, "Liz Phair," in *The Rolling Stone Book of Women in Rock*, ed. Barbara O'Dair (New York: Random House, 1997), 537.

8. Chris Mundy, "Liz Phair: Last Train to Guyville," *Rolling Stone*, October 14, 1993.

9. Alyssa Isenstein, "Liz Phair," *Second Skin* 5 (circa 1993), Mesmerizing: Another Liz Phair Website, www.geocities.com/SunsetStrip/club/2471/00000049.html.

10. Isenstein, "Liz Phair."

11. Tom Herman, "It's a Fucking Debut Album," *Chicago's Subnation* 1, no. 6 (December 1993): 16.

12. Jim DeRogatis, "Rock-Solid Response to a Stones Classic," *Chicago Sun-Times*, October 20, 2002, 19.

13. The songs are "Divorce Song," "Johnny Sunshine," "Fuck and Run," "Soap Star Joe," "Girls! Girls! Girls!," "Clean"/ "Never Said" (retitled for *Exile in Guyville*), "Shatter," "Flower," and "Stratford-on-Guy."

14. Gail O'Hara, "Girly Chat with Liz Phair," *Chickfactor* 3 (Spring 1993), Mesmerizing: Another Liz Phair Website, www.geocities.com/SunsetStrip/club/2471/00000300 .html.

15. White, "Liz's 'Guyville'"; reprinted in *Music to My Ears*, 131.

16. Bill Wyman, "Liz Phair's Suburban Blues," *Option*, September–October 1993, 60.

17. Sue Cummings, "Liz Phair Explodes the Cannon," *L.A. Weekly*, July 16–22, 1993, 27.

18. Chris Mundy, "Liz Phair: Last Train to Guyville," *Rolling Stone*, October 14, 1993.

CHAPTER FOUR

Live through This:
Hole/Courtney Love

*Not since Yoko Ono's marriage to John Lennon has a woman's personal life
and exploits within the rock arena been so analyzed and dissected.*

—Nick Wise[1]

Two photographs enclose the content of Hole's *Live through This*, working
as a parameter that simultaneously poses a question and offers a declaration.
On the front, a color photograph focuses on a beauty contest winner who
is wrapping both of her arms around a bouquet of flowers and pulling them
to her as though she were holding on tightly to a child or one she loved.
The contestant's mouth, outlined by lipstick, is opened wide (a "hole"),
exposing her mouth and teeth; her eyes, surrounded by smeared mascara and
purple eyeliner, are equally wide open. Her big, stylized hair appears frozen
in movement, flushed out on one side and spilling over into the bouquet on
the other. She is surrounded by a black backdrop, and appears to be moving
forward in the frame.

On the back cover, a girl on the edge of adolescence wears a flannel shirt
and no make-up; her unstylized, straight hair falls over both shoulders. Her
shirt is partially unbuttoned (creating a white V), both of her sleeves are
loose, and the checkered flannel shirt is too big for her. She holds herself
straight but not rigid, holding one hand in the other and looking directly
at the camera. The legs of her dark pants extend to the top of her bare feet,
and she is standing on gravel (perhaps a road), which forms the immediate
foreground; further back, there is grass and a small rise.

In one image, traditional femininity seems to have been taken to its logical extremity where it receives its just reward (fame, fortune, and adulation); in the other, femininity appears in a more natural state, unaware of itself. In one, a woman seems teetering on the edge of ecstasy, her features elated and overwhelmed by her victory; the other, the bright face and alert body of a child, perhaps holding her intensity in (her straight posture, clasped hands) as she pauses from her play for a snapshot. The beauty contestant, although no older than her early twenties, has reached a pinnacle of social acceptance and recognition for her feminine attributes; the young girl is teetering on the precipice of adolescence, soon to begin her journey toward social acceptance (or rejection) and recognition (or nonrecognition).

The question that the photographs pose is a simple one on the surface: how does the girl on the back cover become the woman on the front cover? The question, however, is a loaded one. Even though she has received social recognition for her perceived beauty (flowers, a crown, and first place), the beauty pageant winner on the front cover is disheveled. Her ecstasy seems closer to hysteria or a breakdown of some kind, leaving the impression that everything that went into attaining this moment is quickly coming unwound. Within the realm of ideal beauty, she seems to have lost everything at the very moment it has been socially confirmed. Colloquially speaking, she is a mess. Love said of the image,

> What I want to capture is the look on a woman's face as she's being crowned. The sort of ecstatic, um, blue eyeliner running, kind of . . . "I am—I am—I won! . . . I have hemorrhoid cream under my eyes and adhesive tape on my butt and I had to scratch and claw . . . to the top, but I won Miss Congeniality!" And that's the essence of sickness in this culture that I'd like to capture.[2]

The girl on the back, however, is an image of innocence, and is seemingly in a natural state. She is attentive, but not overly so; her clothes are thrown together, but she appears comfortable. She seems un-self-conscious of her appearance and looks at the camera as though unconcerned about how it will capture her. One might easily be impressed by the vitality of her image and describe her as a healthy kid with dirty feet. With her lack of effort, her ability to simply appear as she is, she becomes the antithesis of the contest winner on the cover. The young girl, then, seems to represent femininity in its natural state, before the fall of adolescence.

The question, however—how does the girl on the back cover become the girl on the cover?—is more complicated than this: even the contest winner was once a preadolescent girl, perhaps no different than the young girl on the back cover. Even before adolescence, the young girl will start to worry about how she appears and, if she has not already, internalize social expectations from family, television, women's magazines, and schoolmates. Over time, as she will cast aside her flannel shirts for more feminine attire, she will learn to regulate her body (her weight, her sexuality) and her demeanor (how to hold herself, when to be quiet). With these expectations will come rewards and punishments, depending on how well she plays the game. Joan Jacob Bromberg wrote in *The Body Project*, "Until puberty, girls really are the stronger sex in terms of standard measures of physical and mental health; they are hardier, less likely to injure themselves, and more competent in social relations. But as soon as the body begins to change, a girl's advantage starts to evaporate."[3]

Even after learning that there may be heavy prices to pay for social approval, the young girl may nonetheless choose such a path or feel that it's the only socially acceptable one. Becoming a beauty queen may not be her first choice in life, but it is nonetheless an acceptable avenue that promises social rewards. Even if the role proved ultimately less than she had hoped, she will have attained status and a degree of power. The young girl may even choose to embody the role and play it with passion, embracing its power despite its limited view of femininity.

The question—how did the girl on the back cover of *Live through This* become the woman on the front cover?—evolves once again when the viewer realizes that the girl on the back cover is a young Courtney Love. At the time of *Live through This'* release, this young version of Love has moved from the private world of girlhood to public life as a rock singer, as Kurt Cobain of Nirvana's spouse, and as mother of Frances Bean Cobain. She was also well known publicly and was frequently covered and critiqued in the tabloids and rock press. The anonymous cover image of the beauty contestant, then, also works as a stand-in for Love. Love, playing Yoko Ono to Cobain's John Lennon, offers an image of herself as imagined in the tabloids. In this scenario, Love plays the role of rock star and, later, the grieving widow. Instead of sinking back into her private world in the face of criticism, she plays the assigned roles (heroin addict, irresponsible mother, and rock royalty) with relish, crowning herself Miss World.

Another photograph in the *Live through This* booklet underlines this point. The image frames the members of Hole against a trashy, indoor backdrop, perhaps the aftermath of a performance. Everyone looks drained, tired, and indifferent. Love, wearing a white fur coat, white stockings, and tiara, holds the center; she is surrounded by the band, with band mates Kristen Pfaff and Patty Schemel dressed in darker clothing, and Eric Erlandson, though wearing a white T-shirt, partly out of the frame. Love, then, is clearly the focus, dressed like a princess and surrounded by squalor. Her lazy posture, her closed eyes, and the cigarette she is in the process of lighting lessen her glamour. She is Miss World, the godmother of grunge, and this is what life looks like at the top. This may or may not be the life she wished for as a child (like the beauty contest winner), but she will embrace it nonetheless.

In this scenario, the title—*Live through This*—is a dare, a confrontation to anyone who wishes to take her crown or remove her from the podium. Here, Love offers herself as an iconic bad girl and grunge queen, making up her own rules and living out the rock fantasy usually reserved for men. As with Love's life in the tabloids, she offers her life and the songs on *Live through This* as public theater, either, depending on one's point of view, giving her detractors and the curious what they want (a chance to watch her crash and burn) or openly defying feminine expectations and limitations (living the life of a male rock star; telling the world to fuck off). The title itself is a continuation of Love's autobiographical quarrel with her detractors, the media, and all public authority.

Live through This also serves as a public challenge and perhaps even an assault, with Love asking if anyone can survive what she (like the beauty contest winner) has; whether anyone could experience everything that she has experienced and remain sane; and whether anyone could withstand the social criticism that all women face in the public eye and remain a whole person.

And finally, at the most basic level, the title reminds one (whether intended or not) that her husband, Kurt Cobain, is dead, that he did not "live through this." While this last connotation may have not been the intended effect of the title, the fact that the album was released four days after Cobain's body was found underlines this point. The title would take on further unintended irony when bass player Kristen Pfaff died of an overdose two months after the release of *Live through This*.

Within her challenge, however, Love has also planted one more suggestion that slowly unveils itself across the span of *Live through This*: beneath her tiara and moxie, beneath her role as a punk truth teller, part of Love remains the vulnerable girl on the back cover. One may adapt the persona of a witch or ball breaker, but it is merely a mask one uses in order to survive. Underneath, the traumas of childhood and adolescence remain. The public life she has embraced may have brought her fame and notoriety, but it has also robbed her of a private life and perhaps the possibility of love and a family. Within the grooves of *Live through This*, Love measures out the spaces between childhood and motherhood, love and fame; between what one wishes for and that for which one is willing to settle. The dare, then, is more than a bruising punk assault: it is an attempt to purge the emotional turmoil that engulfs any woman as she grows from a young girl to a beauty contest winner or punk rock princess.

"Asking for It"

Whether you love Courtney or hate her, Hole was the highest-profile female-fronted band of the '90s to openly and directly sing about feminism.

—Maria Raha[4]

There's a part of me that wants to have a grindcore band and another that wants to have a Raspberries-type pop band.

—Courtney Love[5]

Over the length of Hole's history, the band would switch styles rapidly with only its name to remind listeners that it was the same band with the same singer (Love) and guitarist (Eric Erlandson).

Early Hole (1990–1991) created a noisy, aggressive punk sound closer to grindcore (slow, hard rock) and was comparable in style to other riot grrrl and riot grrrl–associated bands of the early 1990s. The first Hole album, *Pretty on the Inside*, was similar in content and approach to early Babes in Toyland albums (*To Mother* EP in 1990 and *Fontanelle* in 1992). Unlike many riot grrrl bands, though once again like Babes in Toyland, Hole relied on poetic lyrics that left impressionistic traces of anger but little in terms of a definable subject matter. Even on a song like "Teenage Whore" where the feminist intent seemed obvious, the lyrics added little depth to the title. To complete the soundscape of Hole's early recordings, Love growled and twisted the lyrics, and often her words were buried under the grinding of electric guitars. *Pretty on the Inside* had many of the bad tendencies of riot grrrl (nonoriginal punk) and few of its virtues (politically inspired lyrics). Simon Reynolds and Joy Press noted of the album, "Love rasps out an unclassifiable alloy of growling defiance and retching disgust, while Hole's tortuous music grinds out her humiliation and hatred with a creakiness that betrays how long this howl has been lurking in the back of the throat."[6]

This sound and approach shifted quickly at the end of 1992 when a changing band recorded three songs for the "Beautiful Son" single: the title song, "20 Years in the Dakota," and the band's first version of "Old Age." At this point, bassist Jill Emery and drummer Caroline Rue had left the band, replaced by drummer Patty Schemel and bassist Leslie Hardy (soon to be replaced by Kristen Pfaff). Love's vocals were more audible, and while Hole still qualified as punk, the band had added more melody and hooks (pop-punk). Love had also begun to clarify her themes and, within her lyrics, dramatize her standing within the indie music world. On one side, she explored the same issues that many of her peers such as Tori Amos, PJ Harvey, and Liz Phair were exploring: childhood trauma, heterosexual relationships, femininity/masculinity, and family; on the other side, her explorations of her own life, or her life as it appeared in the tabloids, imbued her music and cover art with the drama of public theater.

While "Beautiful Son" tackled the gender politics of clothing (the narrator's beautiful son looks good in her dresses), "20 Years in the Dakota" unashamedly drew a line from Yoko Ono to Love. She would also be the first of her peers to write extensively about motherhood. The "Beautiful Son" single, then, served as a brief introduction to the pop-punk, feminist assault, and personal politics of Live through This. Love had found her subject matter and an effective way to deliver it.

Perhaps surprisingly, Love lined her pop-punk assault with an emotional vulnerability seldom associated with hard rock. With Hole, she would borrow grunge's signature style, alternating between quiet rock verses and noisy metal-laced choruses, but with an expressive difference. The alternation allowed her to match the extremes of her own emotional turmoil within a single song, first expressing the vulnerability of a child or a woman in love, and then delivering an angry assault against lovers, fans, and straight society. In this fashion, she created a rich, expressive tapestry that moved beyond the rage of punk and grunge.

This method also played against a backdrop of Love's public persona. By the time Live through This had been released, she had gained a reputation for destructive behavior, kinder-whore dresses (ripped up, little girl dresses), and a basic "fuck you" attitude. She gave the impression of saying and doing as she pleased. The emotional turmoil expressed within the musical structures of Live through This, however, offered vulnerability that was at odds with Love's public persona. This space between Love's public and private life allowed Love and the band to shift between different personas in different songs and between different moods within individual songs. Adding a mixture of pop to punk also softened the group's sound, adding strong melodies and chord progressions that broadened the music's emotional depth.

Not surprisingly, however, her pop-punk style opened Love and the band to accusations of selling out by the hardcore punk community. Rumors would also attempt to detract from Love's songwriting skills by suggesting that many of the songs on *Live through This* had been written by or cowritten with Co-bain. For the audience the album reached, however, these criticisms seemed less important. Love's marriage of pop and punk allowed Hole to reach more listeners than other riot grrrl and riot grrrl–related bands while simultane-ously garnering broad critical approval. Maria Raha noted in *Cinderella's Big Score: Women of the Punk and Indie Underground*, "Hole . . . used pop, punk, and metal in equal doses, making *Live Through This* a thoroughly accessible rock album, even for Top 40 fans."[7]

The Camera's Eye
If one finds it difficult to imagine the young girl on the back cover of *Live through This* as a future beauty contestant, the young girl on the cover of the "Miss World" single is a recognizable fit. The black-and-white photograph of a small girl (four or five perhaps) seems to originate from an earlier era (pre-1960s perhaps). She is placing a tiara on her head with both hands and looking straight ahead (though not at the camera; the camera has caught her at a slight angle); her lips are pursed together in a straight line. This photo-graph from the first *Live through This* single expanded on the idea presented by the album's front and back cover: the corruption of girls actually begins in preadolescence.

But the younger version of "Miss World" lacks the exuberance of her older self. Instead of hyperenergetic, she appears to be sleepwalking through her victory: her stare is blank and her pursed lips are emotionally void. She places the tiara on her head automatically. It is easy to gain the impression that the younger contest winner is frozen in place, her face lifeless save for her opened eyes. Her dazed stare is an inverted version of the hysteria ex-pressed by the older beauty contest winner; the childlike candy hearts that spell out the band's name (Hole) stand in contrast to a child with no child-ish qualities. Even at an early age, the requirements and pressures relating to femininity begin to exact their toll, draining a girl's natural resilience.

The photograph on the "Miss World" single, then, reveals a young girl passing through a series of motions without feeling, following a path designed by others. On the back cover, a second black-and-white photograph offers commentary on the front-cover portrait. Here, Miss World is shown from her skirt to her shoes. Her white, almost knee-length socks stand out against her polished black shoes, and her skirt seems to be bunched up.

The point of view is odd, leaving the impression that the original pho-tograph was divided into two halves. Separated, the second image looks improper, more like a peep shot than a portrait. What is true of the improper emphasis, however, is also true of the portrait on the front cover and the photograph of the young Courtney Love on the back cover of *Live through This*: the camera's gaze reminds the viewer that even young girls fall under public scrutiny in both socially acceptable and unacceptable ways. Feminist Susan Brownmiller wrote,

> At what age does a girl child begin to review her assets and count her deficient parts? . . . When is she allowed to forget that her anatomy is being monitored by others, that there is a standard of desirable beauty, of individual parts, that she is measured against by boyfriends, loved ones, acquaintances at work, competitors, enemies and strangers?[8]

In other *Live through This*–era artwork, Love's vision of childhood and of motherhood's impact on childhood is much darker.

A black-and-white image from the *Live through This* booklet shows a doll's body and its separated head lying against a bedraggled teddy bear and another stuffed animal with a chunk of its head missing. These childhood toys are lying on a grate, outside among vegetation, and the stuffed animals look as though they have been left out in the rain. From the baby doll's feet in the bottom right-hand corner to the missing section of the stuffed animal's head in the upper left-hand corner, the trio—teddy bear, doll, and stuffed animal—form a kinetic line. Only the baby doll's decapitated head seems to offset the line, falling into the upper right-hand corner of the picture.

Just at a glance, the headless baby doll and matted stuffed animals evoke the feeling that something is amiss. Clearly these are items that belong inside a home with children and, when found in the trash or outdoors, have been carelessly cast aside. The overall image might be interpreted in a number of ways, but read within the context of *Live through This*' cover art—the beauty contestant on the cover and the young girl on the back cover—the image offers a causal link. These symbols of childhood innocence have been discarded and subjected to violence. Together, they leave a negative impression, suggesting that even the idea of childhood innocence is a fantasy.

The vintage black-and-white photograph for the "Violet" single may be the most disturbing of all of these images. The photograph focuses on a young girl with bruised eyelids lying with her doll at her side. Before the viewer even studies the photograph closely, a number of questions intrude. Why are her eyelids bruised? Is she simply asleep or perhaps dead? And if she is, in fact, dead, then why is she lying on the couch with her doll and why, if she is dead, would anyone take her photograph?

The photograph was taken from *Sleeping Beauty: Memorial Photography in America* (1990) by Stanley B. Burns. The book featured a series of postmortem photographs taken between 1840 and 1930, and Burns reminds readers that these images were quite common in nineteenth-century America. "Young Girl on Couch with Her Doll" was taken circa 1895, one hundred years before the release of "Violet" as a single in January of 1995. Burns notes that an anonymous photographer had taken this postmortem image during a time period when the deceased were often posed as though still alive:

> This view of a "sleeping child" with her doll illustrates the turn-of-the century desire to make the dead appear alive. There are no visible signs of the child's death except for her classic pose. There are no flowers, no casket. The dress, however, is a funeral dress. Although the child's eyes are closed, the doll's eyes are wide open.[9]

The child's style of dress is formal, and even her doll is wearing a white dress. Her hair has been carefully styled, with ringlets hanging from each side of her face along with a white ribbon or bow that rests on top of her hair. Her puffy white dress is decorated with frilly sleeves and a frilly border at the hem, which ends at her knees. She also appears to be wearing some kind of necklace plus a ring on the middle finger of her left hand.

Without the context of Burns' *Sleeping Beauty*, the young girl becomes an eerie symbol of childhood trauma, unrelated to the actual cause of the girl's death (the cause of death is not listed in the photograph's credits). Furthermore, the image itself reminds us that even in death she has not escaped the public eye of the camera.

These images connect and interlock with repeated lyrical themes expressed across the expanse of *Live through This*. In "Plump," Love's first verse offers a vision of childcare that borders on horror story. The lyric, delivered by the child's mother, complains of his rattle and spittle; instead of washing the dishes, she throws them into the child's crib. In "She Walks over Me," Love details a different scenario suggesting sexual abuse. Here, a young girl shouts at her father, telling him not to touch her. In "Plump" and "She Walks over Me," children are at the mercy of adults who may not want them, may not know how to care for them, and who may sexually or emotionally abuse them.

Much of Love's criticism singles out mothers. If fathers receive less criticism, it may simply be because they are absent. In the most extreme scenarios on *Live through This*, mothers are unable to provide for their children's basic needs, are abusive toward them, and are unable to locate them at all. In "I Think That I Would Die," Love's persona repeats over and over that she has no milk, and while she calls out for her baby, she seems unable to find her.

Love underlines the failure of mothers most clearly in "Softer, Softest." Love has created a complex persona by inserting an older woman's experience into a young girl's point of view. As "Softer, Softest" begins, the young girl promises to confide in her mother; her trust, however, is betrayed. The lyric then refers to pee-girl, seemingly a reference to the young girl wetting her pants, which leads to a belt whipping, causing her to cry and recoil. The young girl also hints at other abuse, noting that she has blisters. She realizes, with the wisdom of a grown woman looking back, that her mother, not her, has all the power, and she associates her mother's milk with discipline, anger, and poison. Near the end of the lyric, she expresses a desire for her mother's death.

It may seem common knowledge now that girls, from an early age, are vulnerable to violence and sexual threats. It is also common knowledge that psychological damage from abuse follows a child into adulthood. Love seems to understand this on *Live through This*, but she adds another twist. After saying that her persona has received a blister from touching everything she sees in "Softer, Softest," she adds that the abuse also opens up an abyss within her, robbing her of everything. What is "everything"? On *Live through This*, everything signifies a profound emptiness, an existential crisis of meaninglessness. The abuse, then, introduces the child to more than emotional or physical trauma. Without a stable home or family support, Love suggests, the child is introduced to a void or emptiness, robbing her of basic needs like safety and emotional warmth. One arrives at adulthood, then, handicapped, searching for a way to fill the abyss, searching for a way to replace what one was never given as a child.

Love would later recall her own childhood and the photograph of herself on the back of *Live through This*:

> It was basic Freudian narcissism to put a picture of myself on the back of *Live through This*—I did it because we were living in a teepee and I always smelt like piss and that day I went to school wearing sandals. My ride down the hippie lane was pretty gross. That's who I was and if you look carefully at that picture, it looks like someone who doesn't talk a lot. It's kind of a clue to who I am. Cryptic. It is also atypical of the rock star image: look at me as a child, my inner child, I'm trying to fix it. Ha.[10]

Doll Parts

Virtually a personal diary of the day-to-day trials and tribulations of the "Kurt And Courtney" soap opera, the [Live through This] songs mirror the unfolding episodes in their lives, present and possible future.

—Nick Wise[11]

We had a relationship where we would thrive back and forth creatively. The
relationship only deteriorated around the idea of maternity/paternity.

—Courtney Love[12]

Within the multiple photographs that make up the cover art for *Live through*
This, three include or feature Courtney Love. The photography on the back
cover pictures Love as a preadolescent; the photograph at the back of the
booklet shows her wearing a white fur coat and tiara; and a third black-
and-white photograph pictures Love dressed in tight shorts and a halter
top, drinking a Diet Coke. In a sense the viewer has three versions of Love,
one rooted in childhood, the second as a grunge princess, and the third as
an everyday person; the first of past innocence, the second of corrupt fame,
and the third of the person one never reads about in the tabloids. If part of
Live through This explores the ravages of childhood, an even greater part of it
focuses on the public persona and private loves of a grunge queen not unlike
Love.

Between the time of her romance with and marriage to Kurt Cobain in
1992 through the aftermath of his death in 1995, Love became a public icon
who was regularly scrutinized by the media. Many in the media considered
her public behavior erratic, and she was disliked fiercely by many Nirvana
fans who interpreted her as a contemporary Yoko Ono. After learning Love
was pregnant, the couple married; a daughter, Frances Bean, was born six
months later. Love was accused of using heroin and smoking during her
pregnancy, and she and Cobain temporarily lost custody of Frances Bean
shortly after her birth. During her marriage to Cobain, there was at least one
accusation of domestic abuse, though Love later denied it. A short time after
Cobain's death, Love returned to performing, completing her grieving on
stage and in the tabloids.

This side of Love's public life—hard drugs, Cobain's and grunge's nihil-
ism, and Love's exhibitionist, aggressive, and self-destructive behavior—has
helped hide another, perhaps more important side of her life: Love, despite
her public reputation as a feminist icon, troublemaker, and star fucker, chose
to get married, have a child, and be part of a family. Despite her bruised and
battered childhood and despite the drug-addled world she supposedly lived
in, Love nonetheless sought refuge in an updated version of wife and mother.
As Love later noted of herself,

It's so weird that people's personas are so opposite; like I'm so "Fuck you! Kiss
my ass," and in my personal life I'm such a big pussy, I'm so passive. Like: "Can I

cook you breakfast? Do you need your morning blowjob?" I'm such a good wife. It must be some whacky rebellion against my mother's militant 70s persona. I wanted to be a "good wife" in the most Brady Bunch way. It was really great as well.[13]

Within the grooves of *Live through This*, Love recognized her public role as the queen of grunge on songs like "Miss World," and on kiss-offs like "Gutless" and "Rock Star" (aka "Olympia"); and she recognized this position gave her a platform to launch an assault against a mainstream society that she frequently seemed to despise. But she also recognized on *Live through This* that this role, while satisfying in some aspects, would never provide the redemption that she wanted. The idea of romantic love, motherhood, and a family, however, offered the *possibility* of redemption, even if partly played out in the public realm of tabloids and the rock press.

Love also recognized this possibility within the world of *Live through This*—that adult relationships, parenthood, and family offered the hope of filling in the missing pieces, of removing the vacuum or void that lay beneath fame and her public persona. While a fan might note the existential image of a "hole"—a void or abyss representing despair and meaninglessness—Love brings the image down to earth, interpreting it as a psychic wound created in a childhood bereft of love, trust, and even the feeling of safety. In "Softer, Softest," the trust of a young girl is betrayed by her mother; as an adult, the girl attempts to fill the void left by these experiences, to relearn trust and intimacy through intimate adult relationships. There is also the hope that by having one's own children, there may be a chance to relive or undo the damage of one's own childhood. This hope, however, may be no more than that: within the world of *Live through This*, Love seems to indicate that the space between the hope and reality of these desires may be impossible to bridge.

Even in an emotionally barren childhood, Love suggests, one learns to believe in the idea of romance just as one picks up other social cues as a child and adolescent from popular culture (girls' magazines, television, movies, and music). On the color cover of the single "Doll Parts," there is a wedding dress for a doll, a necklace, a bouquet of flowers, shoes, a crown, a ring, and a plastic dove. Inside the single, another color photograph features doll accoutrements—dresses, shoes, a headband, telephone, and lollipops. Printed on the single CD itself, in black and white, are shoes, a handbag or shopping bag, a gavel, a cake, a record player, and what looks like a single Hostess cupcake.

Another item or symbol that has formed an intricate part of a girl/woman's life appears on the single "Softer, Softest." On the cover, the fingers of one hand (the male; no painted fingernails) hold a wedding ring upward toward another hand (the female, with painted fingernails) that is reaching downward toward the ring. The male hand holding the ring appears stationary; four fingers of the female hand are stretched out, reaching for the ring. Both hands are positioned at a slight angle, and the nearly touching fingers vaguely recall the detail of God creating Adam in Michelangelo's Sistine Chapel. Only part of each hand is visible, and the hands are framed by a circular outline (three rough lines that look as though they were drawn by a gold-colored crayon) against a background of deep blue. Inside the single, there is another photograph of a glass slipper, and on the single itself, printed in color, a drawn silver diamond ring with emanating sparks (as though it shines) surrounded by pale blue.

By focusing on these symbols, an emphasis has been placed on their cultural value in a girl/woman's life. This emphasis also indicates that while these items may set up unrealistic expectations—that traditional femininity will be rewarded with true love and happiness ever after—they also offer a rich fantasy world in a young girl's life. Within this world, a young girl is deemed special despite her position or seeming insignificance within her own family or peer group; the prince will arrive, recognize her special qualities, and turn her into a princess. All of the wrongs committed by her family in her childhood will be made right. And while everyone cannot find a prince, most any woman can find a man (true love) and a wedding dress (glamour), exchanging her childhood home for a new one with her husband.

In "Violet," the opening track on *Live through This*, Love's persona is speaking—alternately—to her lover and to no one in particular. To her lover, she questions the depth of his feelings for her: his feelings may only last a short time, she tells him, but hers will last forever. To no one in particular, she repeats a well-known cliché: when a man gets what he wants, he will not want it anymore. She demands that he, her lover, take everything, and later dares him to take everything; the specifics of her dare, however, remain vague: what, exactly, does she want him to take, and from whom, exactly, does she want him to take everything? Near the end of the lyric, she offers an ironic twist; she tells him that she knew from the beginning how their relationship would end: when she gets what *she* wants, she will never want it again. The lyric ends with her, once again, asking him to take everything.

A similar scenario develops in "Asking for It" and "Doll Parts." In "Asking for It," Love's persona alternately speaks to her lover, herself, and to no one in particular. The lyric begins with a confession, that every time she sells herself to him, she feels cheap. The exact meaning of this phrase—selling herself— remains as vague as her dare for her lover to take everything in "Violet."

She then refers to tearing petals from her lover, as though she were playing a game of "he loves me, he loves me not," as a method of making him tell the truth. The phrasing seems awkward, though, because Love's persona appears to be tearing the petals directly from her lover, not from a flower. As in "Violet," she seems to accuse her lover of an undefined infraction, perhaps involving another woman. Within the lyric, she makes a number of cryptic promises to her lover, that she will rock him until the end and, repeating the title of the album, that if they live through an undefined "this," then she will die for him.

Finally, there is "Doll Parts," the third song that forms a trilogy of troubled love songs on *Live through This*. Here, Love's persona describes herself as a doll, though she has added several oddities: she has doll veins and describes herself as dog bait; later, she adds that she has bad skin and a doll's heart. As in "Asking for It," the narrator switches between speaking to her lover, to herself, and to no one in particular. She tells her lover that an undefined "they" really want him, but that she also wants him; she wants, however, to mean more to him than all of the others. She also says that she is so good at faking it and that she is beyond faking it, before telling him that one day he will feel pain like she does. Finally, she tells him that he only loves the things that he does love because he enjoys watching them break.

In each of these lyrics, Love, while remaining enigmatic, offers two types of information, one describing her personas' lovers, the other describing her personas. In these songs, each persona questions the depth of her lover's affections for her, his faithfulness, and his ability to care for her, while describing herself as faithful, image conscious, and fragile. Through questions and dares, each of her personas seems determined to provoke her lover, while each lover seems unwilling to clarify his feelings, make commitments, or react to provocation. Over the course of these three songs, Love sketches the dynamic of fragile relationships that seem threatened by insecurity and assailed by undefined, outside forces.

In all three songs, Love either relies on clichés (asking for it) or phrases that sound like they should be clichés (wishing to be the girl with the most cake). In each instance, however, the context of these clichés changes the expected meaning of the phrase. While "asking for it" has often seemed to imply asking for trouble of some kind, within the song Love's persona seems more concerned with the presence of another woman in relation to her lover than violence. In the instance of losing interest once one has obtained what one desires, the listener might take the meaning as sexual, but once again, Love's persona's reflection is more concerned with her emotional well-being than sex: once he has won her affections, she seems to say, he will no longer be interested in her. And finally, wishing to be the girl who has the most cake is not a general statement of self-importance or an expression that she desires to be more important than other people in general, but is centered on her affection for her lover and her wish to be seen as more important than others in his eyes.

While "Violet," "Asking for It," and "Doll Parts" are musically rich, they are also cryptic and difficult to interpret. The curiosity, as mentioned above, is that each lyric seems to be delivering similar information about Love's persona(s) and her persona(s)' lover(s), though the information needed to unlock the underlying meaning of these songs seems to be missing. It is only when we return to the idea of the singer-songwriter as a confessor who publicly reveals her private life that we discover this missing information, adding a new dimension to the songs and lyrics on *Live through This*. Because Love and Cobain were well-known public figures, it is easy for the listener to imagine the pair or a version of the pair as the male and female personas of "Violet," "Asking for It," and "Doll Parts." Working within the singer-songwriter tradition, Love leaves the impression that the drama of the Mr. and Miss World is unveiling itself as we listen to these songs. Love, then, seems to use public knowledge of the couple's relationship as a springboard for the themes of *Live through This*.

Within this scenario, Love has rewritten her life script, drawing equally from her life as imagined in tabloid images, her image as a public rock star married to another rock star, and her private life as a wife and mother. In this way, *Live through This* offers Love a chance for self-portrayal and self-parody, a chance to tell her own story and a chance to live up to her reputation, and a chance for revelation and a chance for self-myth.

In this fashion, "Violet," "Asking for It," and "Doll Parts" are conversations between Mr. and Miss World supplemented by diary entries and public outbursts. "Violet," then, becomes a mini-drama between lasting love and temporary fame. His fame (Mr. World), Love (Miss World) tells him, might only last a day, whereas what she has to offer (true love) will last forever. In this reading, it is the public that becomes bored after it receives what it wants; soon, they will want something else or someone new. When she tells him to take everything, she is referring to fame: she is daring him to push things as far as he can, to take whatever there is to take. Her own admission, that once she receives what she wants she will never want it again, is only an ironic reversal. Unlike the lover's fans, she is not fickle: once she has his love, she does not need fame. She implies by her tone, however, that the battle has already been lost: he does not understand, when it comes to fame, how to say no.

The same struggle is repeated in "Doll Parts," with Love, made of doll parts, expressing her flesh and blood vulnerability. She knows that everyone desires him, just as she does, but she wants to be the most important person in his eyes. Her frustrated love, however, turns to hate, though it seems unclear in the lyric whether that hate is more focused on him or herself. While the immediate meaning of people who are able to fake it so well that they are beyond fake may be empirically tangled, the phrase seems to refer to Love's own critics: they have frequently accused her of fakery and insincerity. Her doll features, however, offer a different version of Love behind her more aggressive public persona: her doll heart will always leave her vulnerable. Her threat, that some day he will ache like she does, seems idle. If he loves to see the things he loves break, as she says in the lyric, then perhaps he also loves seeing her break.

Within relationships in Love's songs, then, women may seek to fill the void with love, but they must compete with the outer world (a man's job, his rock band). Furthermore, they must live with the threat of violence (emotional and physical), even from those who claim to love them. This is suggested more clearly in "Jennifer's Body," both by the violence of the boyfriend's actions (he hits Jennifer) and the more symbolic violence of keeping pieces of her by his bed. Violence may not be specifically a male providence, but within heterosexual relationships, Love suggests that it is a male prerogative. The idea of romance filling the void, then, is illusive, not necessarily because it was falsely sold through childhood dolls and other symbols, but because of the failure of men or masculinity to embrace the possibility. Since this closes off the possibility of filling the void with love, then, women are left to find alternative pursuits to fill the childhood void. In Love's case, this means playing the rock star (competing in the masculine arena), even while realizing that playing the role, compared to experiencing love (a nonrole), will never fill the "hole."

As is true of many songs on *Live through This*, Love expands punk's emotional and sonic palette considerably on "Violet," "Asking for It," and "Doll Parts." In "Violet," the arrangement is similar to "Miss World," veering between the softer verses and harsher choruses, between emotionally vulnerable and angry. "Doll Parts," however, works primarily as a rock or punk ballad. Here, acoustic guitar and, in the choruses, vocal harmony garner a softer edge, with Love only returning to her angrier, punk vocal assault toward the end of the song. "Asking for It" is more pop influenced, floating along at a medium tempo, though Love continues to alternate her vocal parts between vulnerable and angry. Musically, "Violet," "Asking for It," and

"Doll Parts" offer broad variations on Hole's pop-punk, with Love's vocals and themes tying the three songs together. Although the mood is similar in all three songs, the basic arrangement—electric guitar, acoustic guitar, bass, drums, and vocals—allows the band a great deal of versatility in delivering and building it.

It is interesting that despite her reputation as a punk rocker and hell-raiser, Love delivers mostly pathos on "Violet," "Asking for It," and "Doll Parts." These female narrators experience outbursts of anger, but it is anger generated by frustrated love. Love's persona or personas are victims of their own feelings, their personal "void"; victims who wish for no more than the same love they freely give to another. The myth of love has left each of them vulnerable to the promise of a new start, while the reality of the dream has failed to fill the void of childhood and adolescence.

Mother's Milk

The other possibility, that of finding salvation through motherhood, proves just as shortsighted within the world of *Live through This*. This, if we return to the beginning of the chapter, is the flip side of being a child, with Love's personas attempting to successfully fulfill a role at which their parents failed.

In songs like "Softer, Softest" and "Plump," mothers are abusive, while in "I Think That I Would Die," the mother begs for her baby that is not—for undisclosed reasons—present. In "Softer, Softest," a mother repays a young girl's trust with physical abuse; in "Plump," a mother's physical obsessions with her own body eclipse her concern for her baby's well-being. In "I Think That I Would Die," it is difficult not to read Love's own temporary loss of custody of her own child due to accusations of drug use during her pregnancy into the lyric. Instead of finding salvation in motherhood, then, these characters seem to repeat some of the same mistakes that their parents made. The idea of the traditional family, a heterosexual couple and a child who build a life together as family, proves hollow.

As mentioned earlier, "Plump" reveals parents as incapable of caring for children. Unlike "Softer, Softest," which is narrated by a young girl who is abused by her mother, "Plump" is delivered from the mother's point of view. In "Softer, Softest," then, Love imagines her persona as a child; in "Plump," as a mother. While the end results may be similar—in both cases children are improperly cared for or abused—the point of view is nonetheless important. In one, Love imagines her persona as a child and delivers an unsympathetic portrait of an uncaring mother. In the other, Love imagines her persona as an adult, and while the portrait is still unsympathetic, we understand that the mother has unresolved problems that complicate her ability to care for even herself.

In "Plump" and "I Think That I Would Die," Love focuses on the impossibility of resolving one's childhood problems through motherhood. In "Plump," the mother has (or had) an eating disorder and complains that people have called her plump. Far from resolving her problems, however, motherhood has only made her more indignant. She throws the dirty dishes in the baby's crib, seemingly resentful of her household chores, the baby's noisiness (rattle), and his messiness (spittle on bib). Her anger also stems from the fact that the baby relies on her for breast milk, and she offers a portrait of a baby as a parasite. Instead of providing a release from her own body obsessions and childhood trauma, then, motherhood has only complicated matters.

Both "Plump" and "I Think That I Would Die," which is also from the mother's point of view, seem to focus on Love's personal drama around her own child. Because of accusations of heroin use during her pregnancy in a *Vanity Fair* article, Love and Cobain's child (Frances Bean) was taken into custody by authorities in Washington State following her birth. In the last verse of "Plump," Love's persona complains that her baby is in someone else's arms; she accuses the person of being like a liar at a witch trial. In "I Think That I Would Die," there is a continued lament by Love's narrator that she wants her baby; she follows this by asking who took her baby. She also complains that she has lost her breast milk. In both songs, then, Love's personas are failures at motherhood, as much so, perhaps, as their own mothers.

In these songs, and in the songs from *Live through This* that focus on romance, Love finally paints a damning portrait of the traditional family. It might seem ironic that Love, with her reputation in the tabloids, would have ever considered love, marriage, and motherhood as salvation to her own childhood trauma; that she would consider the family unit as a possibility for redemption for the things that she had missed in her own childhood; that she would place hope in the same idea of family that, within her songs, sets men against women and women against children; and that she would place faith in the same family that had failed to nurture girls like her because it prefers sons. But Love's vision is one of realization on *Live through This*, one noting that her attempt to replace her original family with another one was perhaps doomed from the start. It is almost as though the recorded words and music on *Live through This* are capturing Love's realizations—the breakdown of her dream—in the present tense.

In these songs, Love underlines that even as an adult, one's self-created family fails to provide an emotional safe harbor. Girls turn into their mothers and marry people like their fathers, and motherhood becomes a burden; family itself is a burden, not a safe harbor. Patterns are repeated because the faulty structure of the patriarchal family guarantees that power and frustration is always passed to the person below in the hierarchy (father to mother to daughter). Love underlines this point on the bridge of "Softer, Softest," noting how dangerous the entire cycle is. Her persona complains that her mother's milk is mean, then says that her mother's milk turns into *her* milk, and then ends by saying that her mother's milk turns to cream. The lyric is somewhat cryptic. How can a mother's milk, after all she has done to her daughter, turn to cream? It turns to cream simply because as an adult, the young girl also becomes a mother (her mother's milk turns to her milk); and while she would like to imagine that her milk is cream, unlike her mother's milk, it is literally her mother's milk. The legacy has come full circle.

"Gutless"

The photograph on the cover of *Ask for It* (1995) would have been disturbing even without both Cobain's suicide and Pfaff's accidental overdose the year before. But with both deaths as a backdrop, the color photograph focusing on two arms with slit wrists is even more disturbing. While there is no blood and the scars appear to be healing, the lacerations are prominent and provocative. The title, *Ask for It*, seems to express little sympathy for the victim. Through the photograph and title, Love seems to be taunting both detractors and fans.

Love brings *Live through This* to a closing point with "Gutless" and "Rock Star" ("Rock Star" is also called "Olympia"), two songs that, perhaps strangely, seem to open a new theme at the end of the album. A skeptic might suggest that since these songs fail to fit in with the other material on the album, Hole and producers/engineers Paul Q. Kolderie and Sean Slade decided to dump them at the end of the album. Regardless of the reasons the tracks were placed at the end of the album, they nonetheless serve as a perfect dovetail to the story that unfolds within *Live through This*.

Despite all of the pathos and personal drama on *Live through This*, then, "Gutless" and "Rock Star" open a new and more familiar chapter in the Courtney Love story. In both songs, she delivers unabashed kiss-offs aimed at both detractors and hangers-on, as if to live up to her reputation as a social misfit and deviant. Here, she has returned to her riot grrrl roots, first with "Gutless," a song in which the title has summed up the totality of its content, and second with "Olympia," an angry letter to anyone who believes that they, just because they happened to be from Olympia (an important city in the development of grunge), are somehow revolutionary.

Delivered in first person, the lyric of "Gutless" is less a narrative than scattered observations and nonsensical details. The song begins with Love's persona defining her friends in various ways: in the first verse, they are embryonic or undeveloped; in the second, dead and missing; in the third, microscopic; and finally, in the fourth verse, they wake up alone. Revolutions, she says, come and go, dismissing them just as Liz Phair dismisses heroes in "Soap Star Joe." Speaking to a broad "you" that serves as a stand-in for her fans, she tells them that even though they may try to suck her dry, they will fail because there is—already—nothing left for them. She dares them to try to hold her down and shut her up. She makes a reference to step and fetch (being servile), before saying that she does not miss God, but that she does miss Santa Claus. Each chorus centers on the title of the song, with only one change, replacing "gutless" with "undressed" twice at the very end of the lyric.

"Olympia" is the last song on *Live through This*, referencing one of the cities that gave birth to the grunge revolution in the early 1990s. The lyric is extremely simple, with the narrator saying that she went to school in Olympia, where everyone is the same—everyone looks the same, talks the same, and has sex the same way. Then, much like "Gutless," Love delivers the final assault on the chorus: everyone in Olympia disgusts her, and she follows this with an unceremonious "fuck you." At the end of the lyric, she delivers the slogan "Do it for the kids," which seems rather odd, following her lengthy insult against the town, the school she attended, and everyone who attended it.

Musically, the real aggression arrives on the choruses of "Gutless" and "Olympia," as wild and unadorned—and as punk—as anything on *Live through This*. Here, Love laces her lyrics with venom, and isolated from the album's other material, both songs easily correlate to riot grrrl and what was considered the angry women in rock movement. Both songs identify the grunge movement as a joke and over, and all the hangers-on as posers. These posers still fear girl germs in the guise of the riot grrrls or Love herself, and as Love underlines in "Gutless," getting rid of God was one thing, but Santa Claus, representing consumer wealth and goods, was another. Grunge, then, was no more than a movement of disgruntled middle class males who borrowed their identities from bands that they liked. By adding, "Do it for the kids," Love is mocking the sanctimoniousness of a popular slogan and the society that dreamed it up. The kids, from Love's point of view, are beyond help. Overall, these songs are a kiss-off to Nirvana and Pearl Jam fans, and a kiss-off to nongenuine, white male revolutions.

Rehearsals for Retirement

I got worse press than her.

—Courtney Love, referring to Yoko Ono[14]

The black-and-white photograph of Love on the inside of *Live through This* is a rare shot in which she seems to be neither looking at nor posing for the camera. One might unkindly describe her casual wear—tight terry cloth shorts, a halter top, and messy hair—as white trash. But unlike the more stylized photograph of the band on the inside cover of the "Violet" single, this photograph seems to be offering Love as she is, a candid shot that captures the queen of grunge as a normal person lost in reflection. Another black-and-white photograph, printed in 1998 on the cover of the compilation *My Body, the Hand Grenade*, showed one of Love's baby doll dresses hanging in a glass case of a museum. During the early to mid-1990s, Love helped develop the kinder-whore look, one that featured little girl dresses, frequently torn, giving the impression that she had been attacked. One image showed Love as an everyday person, the other as willing to shed her role as grunge queen.

If both "Gutless" and "Rock Star" (aka "Olympia") serve as the final kiss-offs on *Live through This*, then "Old Age," a song recorded for the album but not used, serves as Love's epitaph. While bitter, "Old Age" offers a mellower, more self-reflective finale than "Gutless" and "Olympia." On "Olympia," Love uses her prominent position on the stage to insult her detractors along with self-righteous punk fans; on "Old Age," she realizes that one day, no matter who you are, no one will remember you or care who you *were*. If "Olympia" is a poison-pen letter to the world, then "Old Age" is a poison-pen letter to herself.

"Old Age" works as a bookend to Love's muse between 1993 and 1995, one that manages to both affirm her status as queen of grunge and undercut it at the same time. The song was initially written by Nirvana, but Love rewrote the lyrics. In this sense, "Old Age," like "20 Years in the Dakota" from the "Beautiful Son" single, is an anonymous portrait of an undefined someone who is now no one. She is now unloved and unlovable. She has become so unattractive, she no longer needs to dress up for Halloween; on Valentine's Day, she is a forgotten concubine. Whenever she dies, her death will mean nothing to no one. The distant narrator elaborates on the older woman's physical and mental decay, and offers ironic asides: it is okay to kill one's rivals, the narrator says, before noting that Jesus saves. The bitter older woman spits at mirrors, the narrator notes, because she has reached a point where worrying about her beauty seems to be a moot point. While the woman in the song's portrait is both angry and forlorn (everything that once glittered is now sour), Love's narrator compares her to martyrs: Hester Prynne and, less directly, Anne Boleyn. Like Yoko Ono in "20 Years in the Dakota," she has paid the price for her martyrdom, and now she is simply forgotten.

At the end of the lyric, Love's narrator underlines the older woman's bitterness by revealing that this anonymous portrait is really a self-portrait. This, the narrator says, in a short time, will happen to her. Here, Love removes the paper thin veil that separated herself, the narrator, and the older woman. Love knows that whatever the revolutionary quality of her work or of her lifestyle, it will be short-lived, a brief fifteen minutes of infamous fame. And while living out the decline of one's fame unknown, friendless, and alone may seem like a depressing proposition, Love does hold out one strand of hope. In one's declining years, it is no longer romantic love or family or fame that promises to fill the void. Instead, she can dream of reaching a point (old age) where she can live without worrying about appearances or the need to embrace a role or public face. She will no longer, as she sang in "Doll Parts," have to fake it; when she has grown old and no longer needs to pretend, the very act of living will be enough. She will not even ask to live well; the simplicity of life without the expectation of others will be sacred. Here, Love understands that part of her craves the spotlight, but looks forward to the day when she will no longer care.

Love's life cycle, then, begins in childhood, where one must obey or follow the precepts of selfish and abusive adults. This maltreatment leaves a void that she attempts to fill with romance, family, and fame, but the attempt to fill the void only leaves her more hollowed out. After these disappointments, her only satisfaction in life might be asserting her own agency, even if that means no more than telling everyone else to fuck off. Still, by acting out, by *needing* to tell the world to fuck off, she remains ensnared in the same childhood traps: she continues to react to what she has already rejected, perhaps out of revenge. Only upon reaching old age, Love imagines, can she truly get beyond the need to react, allowing her to discover her own wants and needs or at least be free from needing to respond. No longer concerned about her attractiveness, no longer needing to prove anything, she can simply live, whatever that involves. With "Old Age," the turmoil of *Live through This* quietly resolves in negation, allowing Love to imagine the end of her own life story before anyone else had the chance to do so.

Notes

1. Nick Wise, *Courtney Love* (New York: Omnibus Press, 1995).

2. Katherine Dieckmann, "Courtney Love," in *The Rolling Stone Book of Women in Rock*, Ed. Barbara O'Dair (New York: Random House, 1997), 465.

3. Joan Jacob Brumburg, *The Body Project: An Intimate History of American Girls* (New York: Random House, 1997), xxiii.

4. Maria Raha, *Cinderella's Big Score: Women of the Punk and Indie Underground* (Emeryville, CA: Seal Press, 2005), 179.

5. Courtney Love, "Liner Notes," *My Body, The Hand Grenade* (City Slag, 1998).

6. Simon Reynolds and Joy Press, *The Sex Revolts: Gender, Rebellion, and Rock 'n' Roll* (Cambridge, MA: Harvard University Press, 1995), 261.

7. Raha, *Cinderella's Big Score*, 179.

8. Susan Brownmiller, *Femininity* (New York: Linden Press/Simon & Schuster, 1984), 25.

9. Stanley B. Burns, *Sleeping Beauty: Memorial Photography in America* (Altadena, CA: Twelvetrees Press, 1990).

10. Amy Raphael, *Grrrls: Viva Rock Divas* (New York: St. Martin's Griffin, 1995), 6.

11. Nick Wise, *Courtney Love* (New York: Omnibus Press, 1995).

12. Amy Raphael, *Grrrls: Viva Rock Divas* (New York: St. Martin's Griffin, 1995), 23.

13. Raphael, *Grrrls*, 9.

14. Jim DeRogatis, *Milk It: Collected Musings on the Alternative Music Explosion of the '90s* (Cambridge, MA: Da Capo, 2003), 47.

CHAPTER FIVE

Blurring the Edges: From Riot Grrrl to Lilith Fair

We want to make the connection very quickly between "Bitch" and Meredith Brooks, because we think we have a very reactive song. We want people to know by the time this record comes out that, when they hear "Bitch" on the radio, it's Meredith Brooks.

—Steve Rosenbalt, Capital Records[1]

We were talking about being a bitch or not a bitch, and [the conversation went] "God, I had a bad morning this morning," "Yeah, me too," and "How do [men] put up with us when we're like that?" The point was that when we honor that place, it's not a bad place.

—Meredith Brooks, relating a conversation with
songwriting partner Shelly Peiken[2]

In the late spring, early summer of 1997, Meredith Brooks' "Bitch" became a staple of both FM radio and MTV. The song's lyrics describes Brooks' persona as a disparate woman, capable of traditional feminine softness (innocence), but also filled with anger and aggression, both a sinner and a saint, a bitch and a lover. Most of the lyric seems to be addressed to a love interest, with Brooks' narrator explaining, though never apologizing for, her many contradictions. Speaking to him, she emphasizes that he misunderstands her, believing that underneath her inconsistencies she is an angel. Although she admits to having a softer side (she admits to crying, for instance), this is only one of many sides of her personality. On the chorus, she describes these multiple roles: bitch, lover, child, mother, sinner, and saint, and tells him that he would not wish her to be any different. The remainder of the lyric adds further complications and contradictions (she can be a tease, but also an undercover angel). She tells him not to try to change or save her, and at the end of the song, admits that she would not want to be any other way.

Like Alanis Morissette's "You Oughta Know" in 1995 and Tracy Bonham's "Mother, Mother" in 1996, "Bitch" also generated controversy. While "Bitch" was fairly tame lyrically compared to Liz Phair's "Fuck and Run" and PJ Harvey's "Dry," the song, like "You Oughta Know" and "Mother, Mother," received wider exposure. "Bitch" was neither riot grrrl nor indie, but *mainstream*. Early, some disc jockeys simply announced the song as the Meredith Brooks' single, and the title was later removed from the sleeve of the single version of the song.[3] When "Bitch" was first played on radio, some listeners believed that it was a new track by Alanis Morissette, and later, the media would frequently pigeonhole Brooks as another singer-songwriter in the Morissette mold. The popularity of "Bitch" also helped assure Brooks high placement on the Lilith Fair tour during the summer of 1997.

Along with a second track from *Blurring the Edges* (1997), "I Need," "Bitch" seemed to capture the spirit of third wave or lipstick feminism. Working against the cliché of the second wave feminist (a man-hating lesbian who refused to shave her underarms), the third wave feminist wished to embrace both traditional femininity and contemporary feminist ideas without, perhaps, ever calling herself a feminist; to embrace both the traditionally negative feminine stereotypes (a bitch, a tease) and positive ones (a mother, a daughter); and to embrace her whims and desires, whether they center on true love, a diet, her sexuality, or consumer goods.

Likewise, the third wave feminist could—if she chose—embrace traditional roles when she wished to and view these roles as temporary, not a permanent identity; she could be a traditional mother providing for children and preparing home-cooked meals, and sexually available (a goddess on her knees, to paraphrase "Bitch"). In all of these ways, "Bitch" and "I Need" represented the quintessential lipstick feminist. *Newsweek* even claimed that Brooks made the same use of appropriation as had the riot grrrls: "She hopes the song—a postfeminist celebration of moodiness—[will] strip the word of 'its negative meaning by owning it.'"[4]

But while it was easy for some listeners to confuse Brooks' style with Morissette's, lyrically they were far apart. In one sense, Brooks, as a solo artist who wrote or cowrote her material, seemed a natural fit for third wave feminism and the new Morissette role. But the lyrics of "Bitch" and "I Need" were problematic in a number of ways. First, they were nonspecific, with each lyric more closely resembling an anonymous pop song than a confessional such as Morissette's "You Oughta Know." This general quality was complimented by vagueness, meaning that these lyrics were open to contradictory readings.

It was just as easy, for instance, to read Brooks' lyric as a postfeminist defense of female stereotypes. In this reading, "Bitch" is regressive, praising women's moodiness and reassuring men that they are correct in seeing women as sometimes contradictory. In an interview, Brooks expressed her belief that men needed this reassurance: "Men completely get ["Bitch"] and are so relieved that somebody's saying it; all they want us to do is admit that we can be irrational and illogical sometimes, and then it's their job to put up with it."[5]

Brooks' approach on "I Need" further complicates her split between more culturally grounded expressions within third wave feminism and more conservative ones in postfeminism. In "I Need," Brooks' persona makes a wish list of all the things that she would need to make her happy. Like "Bitch," the lyric is open to multiple readings, and it is difficult to know whether the lyric should be read as straight or tongue in cheek. Is Brooks winking at the listener when her persona in "I Need" wishes for outrageous things? Or is she celebrating her persona's voracious need for new experiences and products? Does the lyric condemn consumerism or celebrate women's agency?

The legacy of the culture wars around feminism during the 1990s may remain too close for us to properly sort out. One of the bigger problems was the sheer variety of viewpoints. Women who held culturally conservative views, like Christina Hoff Sommers in *Who Stole Feminism* (1995), would claim to be carrying the banner of feminism's true, self-reliant legacy. Second wave feminists had opened many doors and leveled the playing field, these writers noted; now it was a woman's responsibility to make her place in the world. This position was complicated by the shifting politics of key figures like Naomi Wolf during the 1990s (from the critically left *Beauty Myth* in 1991 to the more cautious memoir *Promiscuities* in 1997) and the many strands of third wave feminism itself. Writers and editors like Rebecca Walker in *To Be Real* (1995) attempt to reveal a movement that continued to be grounded in politics while magazines like *Bust* offered a more irreverent take on popular culture. Author Camille Paglia seemed to purposely court controversy while the continued presence of second wave feminists like Gloria Steinem overlapped with the contemporary scene.

Because of these many strands, third wave often only seemed like a movement in the loosest sense of the word. Because Brooks' "I Need" and "Bitch" could be read as embracing female stereotypes (conservative) and celebrating women's agency (progressive), the songs were as muddled as the culture wars themselves.

While Brooks' music did represent a shift toward middle ground, however, it was a less dire sell-out of women's issues to the mainstream music industry and postfeminism than critics might claim. It was easy to notice, for example, that the cover art of more commercial women singer-songwriters like Brooks was not radically different from other cover art by other women singer-song-writers. While Brooks' portrait on the single for "Bitch" might be described as sultry or sassy, it was not the typical male fantasy parading as cover art. Un-like PJ Harvey, Brooks seemed to intend her photograph on "Bitch" and her photograph on *Blurring the Edges* to represent her (as opposed to working as a symbol); and unlike Tori Amos, she did not seem to be suggesting any deeper meaning or symbolism with her portraits. Still, her clothing is conservative on both photographs as is her appearance in the video of "Bitch." Compared to the cover art of Mariah Carey's *Butterfly* (1997) or Lil' Kim's *Hard Core* (1996), the album covers of mainstream singer-songwriters like Brooks were much closer to those of Harvey and Amos.

Even if record labels intended to sell Brooks as an image (like Carey), they still had to sell her image within the context of "singer-songwriter as a serious artist."

Brooks, like Morissette, Tori Amos, and Sarah McLachlan, also consid-ered herself an artist and treated her music as serious. She did not try to hide her marital status, her lack of anger, or the fact that her general philosophy was more conservative than the average woman singer-songwriter in the mid-1990s. The music that Brooks generated may have seemed more in line with commercial considerations and sympathetic with the backlash against feminism, but her music still fell within the recognizable realm of woman singer-songwriter.

Questions revolving around these issues—selling-out and watering down the music for mainstream acceptance—were nonetheless relevant. Was it possible for a singer-songwriter's music to become too pretty or beautiful, too immersed in the mainstream aesthetic, for its message (if a lyric continued to have one) to stand out? Could a listener separate a third wave feminist point of view that offered an in-depth exploration of women's issues from a postfeminist point of view that espoused a more regressive stance toward women's issues? And could one draw a line between criticism from rock journalists and others that addressed the limitations of the music crafted by women singer-songwriters and criticism that simply served as a smoke screen for the continuing backlash against women? All of these questions would coexist within the growing women singer-songwriters' movement in the mid-1990s, generating an ongoing dialogue that simultaneously celebrated the movement and attempted to hold it back.

Songbirds, Pop Divas, and the Mainstream, 1995–1997

If 1995 had brought Alanis Morissette and many other women singer-songwriters to the forefront of the mainstream music scene, then 1996–1997 solidified the movement as a popular phenomenon. In 1989–1990, it would have been difficult to argue that the singer-songwriters of 1987–1988 still formed a cohesive movement; in 1994–1995, it would have been difficult to identify the riot grrrls of 1991–1993 as a continuing vital underground phenomenon. The new women singer-songwriters' movement that announced itself loudly in 1995, however, was solidified in 1996–1997 by albums like Sheryl Crow's self-titled release, Paula Cole's *This Fire*, and Sarah McLachlan's *Surfacing*. The success of these and other releases also helped remind listeners of earlier recordings by the same artists (which also served to reintroduce some of these albums back onto the popular charts), pinpointing the beginning of the mainstream womens singer-songwriters' movement.

The roots of the women singer-songwriters' in rock movement dated back to 1991, though popularity would have to wait for two or three more years. Both Sarah McLachlan's *Fumbling towards Ecstasy* and Sheryl Crow's *Tuesday Night Music Club* were issued in 1993, though neither was an immediate hit. *Fumbling towards Ecstasy* sold well, but never reached higher than number 50 on the Billboard 200 (and that was in 1994). Two songs, "Good Enough" and "Possession," reached the charts in 1994, and "Hold On" reached the Modern Rock chart in 1995 ("Possession" also appeared on the Hot Dance Club Play chart in 1995). "Good Enough" also reached the Billboard 100, Billboard's most representative popular music chart, but only climbed to number 77. Crow's debut also peaked in 1994, following the success of "All I Wanna Do" nearly a year after the album's release. Another single, "Leaving Las Vegas," charted in 1994 and "Strong Enough" and "Can't Cry Anymore" charted in 1995. In retrospect, both of these albums were successful, but both were slow growers that took time to reach a broader audience.

Between 1995 and 1997, the overall chart success of women singer-songwriters continued to grow. Some of the biggest successes, Morissette, McLachlan, and Crow, would place albums in the top ten of Billboard's 200 and receive Grammys for their work between 1995 and 1997. Jewel's *Pieces of You* (1995) reached number 2 on the Billboard 200, Fiona Apple's *Tidal* (1996) reached number 15, Brooks' *Blurring the Edges* (1997) number 22, and Paula Cole's *This Fire* (1996) number 20; each of these albums had hit singles, and Apple won a Grammy for "Criminal" in 1997. Other solo singer-songwriters—Joan Osborne, Poe, Patti Rothberg, Tracy Bonham, Lisa Loeb, Alana Davis, Natalie Merchant, and Heather Nova—also charted with albums and singles, while bands with female singer-songwriters, like Garbage, No Doubt, and the Cardigans, also found success. With high artistic quality and a focus on women's roles in contemporary society, these women offered a broad but cohesive vision.

Even with this success, these women continued to be far outnumbered on the popular charts by men, even if one added non-singer-songwriters like Mariah Carey, Celine Dion, and Whitney Houston; popular groups like the Spice Girls; and the explosion of women performers within country music. As a cohesive movement, however, the women singer-songwriters' movement had an extensive impact on the popular consciousness of the mid-1990s. It was easy to draw a line between Morissette's "You Oughta Know," Garbage's "Stupid Girl," Natalie Merchant's "Carnival," and Cole's "Where Have All the Cowboys Gone?" These songs frequently found themselves side by side on the same *Billboard* charts and, as a minority, formed an identifiable group on MTV.

What remained to be seen was how the overall character of the women singer-songwriters' movement would evolve as it reached the mainstream. Would Harvey and Hole's harder rock and punk, or Liz Phair's indie rock, be as welcomed on mainstream radio and MTV as Morissette's pop-rock? And how would the music of women singer-songwriters who had released albums early in the movement continue to develop? Would the new artists maintain the radical musical and lyrical edges of Harvey, Hole, and Phair, or would these qualities evolve into a more socially acceptable mainstream version of pop-rock and more predictable ideas on women's issues? And finally, would the movement be able, whatever the strength of its feminism and musical vision, to maintain its artistic integrity? All of the questions would be answered between 1995 and 1998.

When attempting to understand these questions, even the idea of the mainstream is a complex conception. While the music of an artist may be identified as more commercial for mimicking the current mainstream sound, many musicians bring new sounds to the commercial arena and help redefine or expand what is considered mainstream. Even releasing an album on a mainstream recording label has never been a guarantee that the resultant sound would be commercial or become mainstream. The mainstream, then, is fluid. Alanis Morissette's label greatly underestimated the number of copies that *Jagged Little Pill* would sell, and a number of albums—Jewel's *Pieces of You*, Crow's *Tuesday Night Music Club*, and No Doubt's *Tragic Kingdom*—were slow starters. Because of these factors, it seems as careless to automatically dismiss the music of all singer-songwriters who became mainstream as vapid as it would be to automatically praise all underground bands as artistic.

There were also new possibilities for women singer-songwriters like Brooks within the mainstream during the 1990s. If the mainstream lyric, traditionally, had frequently focused on romantic relationships, singer-songwriters like Morissette revealed that it also had the potential to address the social underpinnings of those relationships. If the mainstream lyric, traditionally, had frequently focused on a more generalized and less personal point of view, singer-songwriters like Morissette revealed that it had the potential to address relationships in a personal way and still reach a wide, sympathetic audience. Within the mainstream, the new women singer-songwriters seemed to promise that substance and popularity were not mutually exclusive, and by doing so, offered women who wrote their material a broader range of expression.

Even within a cohesive movement, women singer-songwriters in the mainstream covered a wide-ranging musical spectrum. By mid-decade, women, as soloists and in bands, could be found in classic rock (Sheryl Crow), ska-punk (No Doubt), alternative rock (Garbage, Veruca Salt), confectionary pop (the Cardigans), alternative (Tracy Bonham, Patti Rothberg, Poe), mainstream pop-rock (Brooks, Morissette, Paula Cole, Joan Osborne, Lisa Loeb, Heather Nova), soul (Alana Davis), ambient pop (McLachlan, Poe), and as the traditional singer-songwriter (Jewel, Fiona Apple, Natalie Merchant, Shawn Colvin). Many women who formed the short-lived singer-songwriter movement of 1987–1988 (the Indigo Girls, Tracy Chapman, Sinéad O'Connor, Suzanne Vega, Melissa Etheridge, kd lang) also continued to be active. It was a broad movement, even without taking into account other women who worked within rap, R&B, and country.

Songbirds

One of the predominant strains within the women singer-songwriters' movement was a return of more traditionally minded singer-songwriters. New artists like Jewel and Fiona Apple, and women who had left bands to form solo acts like Natalie Merchant (10,000 Maniacs), seemed more interested in introspective and carefully crafted lyrics that focused on traditional relationship concerns and self-reflection than in innovation and feminism. Occasionally, they focused on political issues. But the music was generally quieter, featuring piano (Apple), acoustic guitar (Jewel), and gentle folk-rock (Merchant). Each of these artists fell within the tradition of Joan Baez, Carole King, early Joni Mitchell, Suzanne Vega, and Tracy Chapman. Overall, it was a conservative trend, less expansive musically and lyrically, and perhaps more reassuring to listeners intimidated or put off by the anger and emotional fury of PJ Harvey, Courtney Love, and Alanis Morissette.

Jewel's "You Were Meant for Me" was issued in the winter of 1996, the second single from *Pieces of You* (1995). "You Were Meant for Me" covers the subject of unrequited love, and, whatever the reason for the couple's breakup within the song (the reason is never stated), Jewel's persona expresses neither anger nor rancor toward her love interest. Instead, the dominant mood of the song is melancholy, a mood developed by the saccharine lyric and the sorrowful ache in Jewel's vocal. The song is structured around a full day, from breakfast (with eggs and pancakes) to putting on her pajamas before bedtime, emphasizing her loneliness (she is unable to even reach her mother on the telephone): everything she does only reminds her that her love interest is no longer there. Backed by a folk guitar and a sturdier underpinning of bass and drums, the lyric reminds one of a sad/depressing James Taylor or Don McLean lyric from the early 1970s.

Similar problems were present with Fiona Apple's first single from *Tidal* in 1996, "Shadowboxer." In the lyric, two lovers have now become friends, but Apple's persona maintains a watchful eye: she is still tempted by him, and he seems to be playing games with her. While critics have explained perceived shortcomings in Apple's early work by noting how young she was at the time (nineteen in 1996), the lyrics, while more obviously poetic than many of her peers, were not unusual in the singer-songwriter field: attempting to say too much, sounding self-important, and leaving the impression of self-absorption were common hazards of working as a singer-songwriter. The real problem with "Shadowboxer," then, had less to do with the immaturity of the lyric than the fact that its music and lyric were simply overly familiar and thus, safe.

Overall, Merchant on *Tigerlily* (1995) proved to be a more literate songwriter than either Jewel or Apple at this point in each of their musical careers, and her subject matter was much broader. In "Beloved Wife," Merchant takes the point of view of a grieving husband who cannot imagine continuing after the death of his wife. While the song's point of view is unusual (a woman singing from an older man's point of view), and while the listener may view the lyric as emotionally moving, "Beloved Wife" also seems to argue for a male fidelity that borders on veneration; his continued love may be admirable, but he places his idealized spouse on the traditional pedestal. For the most part, Merchant's subject matter frequently sidesteps women's issues at this point of her career. Instead, she often presented herself as a wise mother figure, offering her observations on the world around her including River Phoenix in "River," a virgin birth in "Wonder," and fame in "San Andreas Fault." She also presented her material in an attractive but familiar folk-rock setting, similar to earlier singer-songwriters like Tracy Chapman. While Merchant was a careful craftsperson, her vision frequently seemed more tied to a literary than musical tradition.

The evolution of cover art within the women singer-songwriters' movement was also intriguing. Each album cover of Jewel, Apple, and Merchant features either close-ups (Apple, *Tidal*) or headshots (Jewel's *Pieces of You*, Merchant's *Tigerlily*), offering the singer-songwriter as an image of herself. It is as though the concept of album covers had returned to 1987 and 1988, presenting straight shots of pensive (Jewel, Merchant) and vulnerable (Apple) women singer-songwriters. Each offers a mental shortcut, allowing the potential buyer of each album to understand the singer-songwriter as thoughtful, introspective, and sensitive. Each returns the gaze of the camera, promising honest confessions to the listener. First and foremost, the music on *Pieces of You*, *Tigerlily*, and *Tidal* represents reflections by and about the person on the cover. Like the cover art of Chapman on her self-titled (1988) album and Vega on *Solitude Standing* (1987), these mid-1990s singer-songwriters would deliver observations about life, love, and, occasionally, politics, in the tradition of Joan Baez and Joni Mitchell.

While the quality of the writing could have been better (Jewel, Apple), there is nothing wrong with the chosen subject matter of these songwriters per se: a singer-songwriter does not have to cover feminist subject matter to be a good lyricist. Merchant, in fact, cuts a wider swath on *Tigerlily* than many singer-songwriters. The problems, however, are similar to the problems with the music by women singer-songwriters in the mid- to late 1980s. Even when literate, the overly familiar musical forms allow many of these songs to fade into the background or fold into one another across the expanse of an album. Also, by default, the content frequently (especially with Apple and Jewel) takes a prefeminist approach to relationships. While Apple may have worked hard to write poetically, the sentiments of "Shadowboxer" have nothing substantial to add to many similar songs that had come before it. In essence, each of these albums have little new to offer in terms of aesthetics, presentation, or content.

Alternative Rock Grrrls

One of the more exciting developments during the mid-1990s was the emergence of bands fronted by women who also wrote. Shirley Manson (Garbage), Gwen Stefani (No Doubt), and Nina Persson (the Cardigans) all wrote or cowrote lyrics, bringing a woman's point of view to their respective band's songs. Even if male band members wrote and cowrote material, it is doubtful that songs like "Stupid Girl" (Garbage), "Just a Girl" ("No Doubt), or "Love Fool" (the Cardigans) would have retained the same edge with male singers. Lyrically, however, the words were frequently less confessional and less personal than those by a typical woman singer-songwriter. In this sense, the lyrics assumed a more general quality, somewhere between singer-songwriter and the traditional rock lyric. At the same time, the choice of material along with the fact that women were interpreting the lyrics still imbued the material with a social edge.

Garbage, the Cardigans, and No Doubt also offered a rich combination of pop-rock arrangements, wrapping lyrics in intriguing, attractive, and louder musical packages. While one might have complained that the lyrics lacked the social edge of a lyric by Harvey or Love, these bands represented an intriguing hybrid: musically sophisticated groups that wanted to offer quality content. Stylistically, these bands generated a bigger sound than most women singer-songwriters, an approach that fit well within the alternative rock scene of the mid-1990s. Because they were bands associated with alternative rock and pop, the writers within them escaped being labeled as singer-songwriters. This may have allowed a certain cushioning effect that depersonalized the lyrics. "Don't Speak" by No Doubt, for instance, may have been about the end of one of Stefani's relationships, but the single and video were by a band called "No Doubt." Publicly, then, an individual's connection to the lyric was partially obscured by the group.

But while all of these factors rendered the role of the songwriter less visible within a band, these women nonetheless performed a similar function by appearing as the public voice and face of the band. Even if the singer had not written a particular lyric, the fact that she sang it may be interpreted—by the listener—as significant. Many listeners may not even inquire as to who wrote the lyrics, music, and so on, but assume that the songs that popular singers record more or less represent their lives and philosophy. The lyrics sung by Manson, Stefani, and Persson, then, become part of the persona that each singer presents within the context of a band.

Like Brooks' "Bitch," No Doubt's "Just a Girl" works as a third wave anthem but, unlike Brooks' song, retains its political edge. Delivered in first person, Stefani's tone is mocking throughout the lyric. She is only a girl she repeats, and the world has forced her to rely on men who will hold her hand and keep an eye on her. Once she has removed the pink ribbon from her eyes, the world is a frightening place where she is held in captivity, where she is not allowed to go out at night, and where others stare at her as though she were a freak. In case one misses Stefani's irony, she repeats that she has had her fill of being treated like just a girl. Still, when Stefani sang "Just a Girl," the lyric—even if written by Stefani—seemed more general and less personal than Morissette's "You Oughta Know." Nonetheless, the lyric retains its political edge because of its content and because it is delivered by a woman.

"Just a Girl" also benefits from a bright, bouncy, and full-bodied arrangement with changes in tempo. In the slower tempo of the verses, the ironic and mocking lyric is playful and emotions are kept at a distance; on the quicker tempo of the choruses, the emotions pour forth and the playful mood turns darker. The bigger pop-rock arrangement also allows Stefani the cushioning needed to deliver her vocal without restraint. Her vocal attack, alternately demure and angry, suggests a similar split in women: even though she may adapt the socially acceptable passivity of femininity, part of her is disgusted by her second-tier status.

The generalized lyric of Garbage's "Only Happy When It Rains" offers a more cynical view of life for a contemporary woman. In the lyric, Manson's persona seems to be explaining her behavior to another person, perhaps a love interest. She tells him that she is only happy when she feels bad, and that she enjoys complications, the dark of night, and bad weather. On the bridge, she asks for more misery. While the lyric may seem simple and straightforward, with no obvious irony to undercut the cynicism, it nonetheless possesses a self-reflective complication. She tells her love interest that her revelations are not accidental, and that by the time she is finished, he will understand her message: he can only remain with her as long as he accepts her dark disposition.

The lyric is surrounded by a full alternative rock arrangement undergirded by propulsive rhythm, alternative rock to which one might dance. Manson's vocals serve a dual purpose, working as the de facto lead voice (because she is delivering the lyric) and as another sound within the instrumental mix. This latter effect is accomplished by mixing the vocal at a lower level than would be considered normal in mainstream pop music; as opposed to serving as a backdrop, then, the instrumental mix maintains a strong presence even during vocal passages. With Manson's icy tone evoking the same distance as the electronic-rock arrangement, voice, guitar, and percussion merge into a synchronized soundscape. Even while the song is infused by an energetic rhythm, the soundscape itself suggests a dark and perhaps aggressive mood in "Only Happy When It Rains."

Interpreting "Only Happy When It Rains," however, is much more complicated than "Just a Girl." The generalized lyric of "Only Happy When It Rains" can easily be taken at face value, that Manson's persona is depressed, enjoys being depressed, and that she does not want to have a relationship with anyone who does not accept this. But the aggressive sound and Manson's cool reading of the lyric suggest any number of interpretations. Is Manson offering an ironic take on the cliché of the dark, seductive woman? Or is she simply celebrating the darker side as erotic and socially transgressive? While one could build an argument that within the context of the album the lyrics are ironic, out of context and in the form of a video they are open for each of these interpretations.

The problem of interpretation becomes even more difficult with the Cardigans' "Lovefool." While the Cardigans relied on a bigger band sound like Garbage and No Doubt, the style of music was clearly within the pop tradition. And while *First Band on the Moon*, the album that produced "Lovefool," was much more musically sophisticated than the average pop album, the surface of the music mimicked pop trappings. Set in the minor key, "Lovefool" maintains a bright, bouncy quality even while evoking melancholy. The full arrangement of keyboards, guitar, bass, and percussion is similar to Garbage's "Only Happy When It Rains," but overall, the feel of "Lovefool" is light pop, not alternative rock. Persson's confectionary vocal is both sad and airy, complementing the lighter touch of the production.

As a radio track separated from *First Band on the Moon*, the song gave the impression of a woman forlorn over her failed love life. Although her love interest no longer cares for her, she begs him to stay; she believes that regardless of his stated feelings, he still needs her. On the surface, the trite expressions of Persson's persona are no different than thousands of other popular lyrics about love difficulties. And there is little within the lyric of "Lovefool," or even within the title itself, that would cause a listener to question the intent of the song. Though one might note that Persson's vocal is overly sweet, and that her tone may suggest that her reading is over the top, it remains difficult to separate her delivery from that of the typical popular singer with similar lyrics.

Within the structure of *First Band on the Moon*, however, the listener quickly realizes that "Lovefool," when taken out of context, means exactly the opposite of what it was intended to mean. The song follows the equally sweet "Step on Me," in which Persson's character tells her lover that she does not mind if he is stepping on (and hurting) her foot: if he breaks her foot, she will simply hop around on the other. If her persona in "Lovefool" truly believes the lyrics she is singing, then, she is deluded and meant to be seen as such. Love, within the context of *First Band on the Moon*, is built out of false promises that eventually reveal themselves, leading to disillusionment. Anyone who falls in love, especially with someone who may have never cared for her, is a fool.

While the looseness of the lyrics and isolation of individual tracks complicates interpretation, No Doubt, Garbage, and the Cardigans offered a musical complexity that once again expanded the way in which women singer-songwriters were able to present their work. These bands generated a big sound, one that required a distinctive singer who could stand out in the sound mix. Broadly speaking, these bands were alternative rock with band members working on equal terms to create a rich sound behind the lead voice of the singer. If lyrics had traditionally been seen as more important than music within the confessional singer-songwriter genre, these bands would weigh music and lyrics equally. And, as mentioned previously, even the singer's distinctive sound would have to meld with the instrumental mix. With both *Garbage* and *Tragic Kingdom*, the band members would record and produce or help produce the album. More than solo artists with one person providing a template for the process, these albums were group efforts, allowing a number of people to contribute to the vision of the music.

Gorilla Grrrls

In the mid-1990s, innovative women singer-songwriters like Poe, Tracey Bonham, and Patti Rothberg continued to push boundaries in terms of music and words. Like the bands already mentioned, these artists frequently relied on more progressive and sometimes louder sounds (Poe, Bonham) while maintaining the personal lyrics associated with singer-songwriters (Bonham, Rothberg). Although critics would continue to compare these women singer-songwriters to Morissette and others, each of these artists was able to carve out a singular sound and generate a solid album that ran much deeper than the featured radio cuts. If each of these artists' impact on the singer-songwriters' movement of the 1990s seems minimal in retrospect, this is partly due to the fact that they (1) were active only after the movement had already gotten under way, and (2) only produced one album within the lifespan of the movement. Rothberg, Bonham, and Poe, however, would produce albums that pushed the sonic and lyrical possibilities for the woman singer-songwriter in 1995–1996.

Rothberg's *Between the 9 and the 1* most closely resembled the mainstream version of the woman singer-songwriter of the mid-1990s, relying on various combinations of pop and rock mixed with personal confessions. Her lyrics straddle issues regarding relationships, offering songs that criticize men ("Flicker," "Looking for a Girl," "Treat Me Like Dirt") and songs that ask a lover to take her back ("Forgive Me"). Rothberg's lyrics, however, are both more personal and specific than those of mainstream singer-songwriters like Brooks, never leaving the impression of vagueness. She also distinguishes herself with a solid sense of pop craft on "Looking for a Girl" and "Remembering Tonight," a lively mix of folk-rock on "Treat Me Like Dirt" and "Inside," and solid straight-ahead rock on "Flicker" and "Up against the Wall." If *Between the 9 and the 1* may have been less innovative than earlier work by Harvey or Phair, it was nonetheless a smart example of what women singersongwriters were capable of within the mainstream.

Displaying Rothberg's pop side, "Looking for a Girl" is filled with lovely hooks that, on the surface, hide a more critical lyrical undercurrent. In the lyric, her persona is repeating the words that her noncommittal boyfriend has told her. His desires are contradictory: he wants a girl who will be faithful, but also wants a girl who will allow him the freedom to do as he pleases. Rothberg adds to her persona's emotional vulnerability by singing the lyric at the higher end of her vocal range. Her persona seems to understand that she is being used, taken advantage of, but she remains in relationship limbo, even while her description of her love interest is completely negative. Acoustic guitar is prevalent in the contemporary folk-rock mix, though strings bolster the choruses, adding to the emotional current of the lyric.

In one sense, the criticism within the lyric of "Looking for a Girl" is straightforward: men are noncommittal and this noncommitment negatively impacts women. What is perhaps more interesting, however, is that Rothberg is presenting this information within a pop tradition that, typically, has been perceived as sacrificing content for melody. The presence of content and melody creates an intriguing juxtaposition in "Looking for a Girl," with the happy melody working against the questioning lyric. Instead of the familiar two- to three-minute love song or love gone wrong song, "Looking for a Girl" offers a damning critique of masculine behavior wrapped in an attractive, tuneful package. On first listen, the male's longing as expressed through Rothberg's persona—that he is looking for a girl—seems no more than a heartfelt desire for romance. In a sense, then, the beauty of the melody and vocal pulls the listener in, and only later, on repeated listens, does the harsher content reveal itself. On songs like "Looking for a Girl" and others, Rothberg offers an attractive balance between the traditional singer-songwriter and her contemporary counterparts.

Bonham's *The Burdens of Being Upright* (1996) is an intense, focused effort, bolstered by full-throated vocals and loud rock. If Rothberg's painted cover portrait offers a variation on the portraits offered by Jewel, Apple, and Merchant, the dark cover photograph on *The Burdens of Being Upright* reveals a sour-faced Bonham with her back against a brick wall. Her arms are partly raised, gripping a board that appears to be imbedded in the bricks. On the back cover the bricks have become a pile of rubble, and while Bonham seems to be no longer present, a single-shoed foot is exiting the scene. Bonham continues to create symbolic piles of rubble across the sonic spaces of *The Burdens of Being Upright.*

In "Mother, Mother," a phone call by a young woman reveals the cracks in the fissure of mother-daughter relationships, between tradition and the third wave woman; in "Sharks Can't Sleep," the narrator lays bare the competitive nature of the world in which we live with short, symbol driven verses. When Bonham unleashes her anger vocally against a cascade of electric guitar, both in words and in pure sound, the sonic effect is piercing.

"Sharks Can't Sleep" demonstrates how a simple metaphor and powerful vocal can bring a fresh point of view to a familiar subject. In the first verse, a shark eats a man; in the second, a snake eats another snake. Following these verses, the narrator repeats that neither thing was okay. During these two verses, the music, a creeping electric guitar backed by bass and light percussion, offers a quiet backdrop for Bonham's restrained delivery. On the choruses, the band explodes in volume against this calm surface, with Bonham's wordless vocal assault unleashing the rage and disgust that rests beneath the surface of the verses. Only at the end of the chorus does she repeat her earlier refrain, that none of these happenings are okay.

The third verse offers a lyrical variation on the first two, with Bonham's persona describing an emaciated star with bad teeth. In the final verse, she returns to the structure of the first two verses, but this time her persona eats a man and walks away, emulating the behavior of the shark in the first verse. As before, she repeats that this kind of thing is not okay. Here her persona, perhaps a female rock star on the make like Bonham herself, has become no different than everyone and everything she despises. Like sharks who must continue swimming to survive, a competitive system, whether international banking or the music business, requires continual vigilance. Bonham's lyric suggests that without a deeper critique of the concept of competition, women, even if they become equals within the music business, were contributing to a corrupt system.

Poe generated a complex and eclectic sound on *Hello,* and had much in common with other female-led alternative rock bands. She mixed alternative rock with electronica, and while her lyrics frequently touched on women's issues, her approach was more generalized like Garbage, No Doubt, and the Cardigans. Her sound, however, was even more diverse than these bands, drawing from a broad range of genres and brought to bear on aggressive rock ("Trigger Happy Jack," "Choking the Cherry"), frothy pop ("Hello," "Another World," "Fingertips"), and tender ballads ("Fly Away," "Beautiful Girl"). The lyrics addressed male anger ("Angry Johnny," "Trigger Happy

Jack"), female sexuality ("Fingertips"), and femininity ("Beautiful Girl"). This eclecticism also worked as a musically sophisticated way of presenting multiple personas or characters, much like an urbane version of Phair's *Exile in Guyville*.

Like Bonham's songs, "Angry Johnny" also deals with rage, but unlike Bonham, Poe chose her soundscape from a cooler sonic palette and added an equally distant vocal. The cool palette and distant vocal also match the remote point of view of her persona, who identifies herself as Jezebel. She alludes to Johnny's pain late in the lyric, but the listener never learns why he is angry or what has made him angry. Instead of focusing on the title itself, then, most of the lyric is focused on the ways in which, physically and metaphorically, Poe's persona plans to kill him. These methods are mentioned as matter of fact, without emotion. Johnny is angry, and Jezebel will quiet his rage by killing him. The lyric, finally, tells us more about the resolve of Poe's persona than Johnny's anger: even her delivery of the lyric, addressed directly to Johnny, reveals her as someone willing to openly challenge his anger. Like many of Poe's songs on *Hello*, "Angry Johnny" is composed of multiple layers of voices and underpinned by a slowly pulsating rhythm.

In "Angry Johnny," Poe treats male anger as a given that does not require explanation. Whether one considers killing Johnny as a symbolic or representative act within the song or not, Poe's persona offers no moral qualms about the task. Puzzling, however, is her choice to identify herself as Jezebel who now resides in hell. A listener might guess that her hell is created by Johnny's anger, but still, traditional portraits of Jezebel have almost always carried negative connotations. In third wave feminist fashion, however, Poe's use of Jezebel may serve as an act of appropriation: Jezebel, like Brooks' Bitch, is a woman who refuses passivity.

It is also interesting that Poe, like Phair, chose to name the angry man of the song "Johnny" (not John), a common name, perhaps, but also one associated with early rock songs like Joanie Sommers' "Johnny Get Angry" (1962). In "Johnny Get Angry," the female narrator implores Johnny to show that he cares for her by openly expressing his anger. Poe's persona, however, challenges the idea that male anger is either natural or a sign of affection.

Of the women singer-songwriters who emerged in 1995–1997, these gorilla grrrls perhaps charted the clearest path. In each of these songs, a woman singer-songwriter offered an innovative soundscape and lyrics that addressed women's issues. Furthermore, unlike the women singer-songwriters who were in bands, these lyrics represented nonambiguous positions on women's issues and, often, they were more personalized. Also, the fact that Rothberg, Bonham, and Poe all found at least partial popular success suggests that innovation and solid content, even as the woman singer-songwriter phenomenon spread to the mainstream, could remain central to an artist's vision. Even within the mainstream, art, politics, and popularity could coexist.

The Backlash, Part 2

Looking at the "angry women in rock" phenomenon, it is clearly an example of the incorporation of a radical movement.[6]

CNN: What do you think of the women in rock today? They're angry and opinionated, traits you guys pioneered 10 years ago.

[Donna] Sparks [of L7]: We don't like many of those singers or very much of their music, because they seem to be very mainstream with a fake edge. They're not from our school of rock.[7]

Because so many women had entered the popular music field by the mid-1990s, it was easy to argue that the backlash against women during the 1980s had either ended or at least lessened to a significant degree. While women may have remained a minority in the music business, major labels were signing women and these women were reaching broad markets. Women produced their own music, played their own guitars, and called the shots, following their individual visions even as they created a commercial product within the corporate rock world. Within the singer-songwriter genre, substantive women's issues were being addressed publicly. These triumphs, along with the initiation of Lilith Fair in 1997, seemed to signal that the times had changed and that anything was possible for women in the world of music in the mid-1990s. "McLachlan's brainchild is as mainstream as it gets," *Entertainment Weekly* noted of Lilith Fair, "reflecting the first period in rock history in which female performers face little conscious marginalization."[8]

But this rosy scenario overlooked a number of less benign developments in regard to women's marginalization during the 1990s. First, a number of postfeminist writers continued to defend more conservative positions for women within popular culture. Writers like Christina Hoff Sommers offered antifeminist critiques that were labeled as feminist, confusing the lines between post- and third wave feminism during the mid-1990s. For many, there was also the realization that the liberalism of the Clinton administration was lukewarm and perhaps, with the administration's support of free trade and its promise to end welfare as we know it, conservative. More importantly and immediate for women within the music world, however, was an ongoing hostility expressed by a number of media sources and writers during the mid-1990s as the visibility of women increased. This was especially true as the women singer-songwriters' movement reached mainstream. The musical style including folk, folk-pop, and light pop-rock was seen as lacking authenticity, and the social and political content was seen as lacking substance. While a great deal of coverage was positive, a minority of voices expressed harsh views that went beyond accusations of musical and political blandness. Even seemingly liberal voices, including ones with feminist associations, would inadvertently add to the backlash against women within the popular culture.

Lilith Fair

> Lilith Fair's musical style was a banal hybrid of coffeehouse introspection and the little-girl-lament style that currently passes for "adult contemporary."

—Joe Woodard[9]

The opening of Lilith Fair in 1997 seems to have produced several general opinions during that time and in retrospect. For the people who participated or attended in 1997, Lilith Fair was a resounding success, placing women performers in the spotlight, and offering women a forum to celebrate all things feminine, however they chose to define *feminine*. Arriving two full years after the massive success of *Jagged Little Pill*, Lilith Fair served as a public party to show just how far women had come within the popular music scene. Each year the concept of the festival broadened, growing by including a wider and more eclectic variety of styles and performers. Financially, Lilith Fair was successful, and would eventually spawn a book, three CD packages (one for each year), and a movie. Sarah McLachlan, the architect of the festival, had overwhelmingly proven that a festival could support more than one female performer on the bill. Furthermore, while most Lilith Fair performers were much less overtly political than the riot grrrls had been (though this statement would have also been true of Harvey, Love, and Phair), the event supported a number of women-friendly political causes, both by incorporating them into Lilith Fair (Planned Parenthood booths) and by donating a dollar per ticket to women's charities (including RAINN, the Rape, Abuse & Incest National Network).

Despite a great deal of positive coverage in 1997, however, Lilith Fair faced criticism on two fronts with some crossover. First, there was the general complaint that the music was bland, representing a narrow group of mellow and mostly white singer-songwriters. On the second front, Lilith Fair was criticized for sidestepping political issues, both in how the event was represented to the popular press by McLachlan and in the singer-songwriters chosen to perform. Surprising, however, was the fact that part of the criticism on both fronts originated from the supposedly liberal rock press, sometimes written by women and feminists. In these critical pieces, the perceived musical and political compromises of Lilith Fair created an event predestined for mediocrity.

The narrow range of the musicians chosen to participate was perhaps the most common complaint leveled against Lilith Fair; that, according to Jane Stevenson in the *Toronto Sun*, "the event was in serious need of some female rockers."[10] In *Newsweek*, Karen Schoemer wrote, "If Lilith Fair has a flaw, it's too much yin. Despite the enormous revolving cast of performers, there's virtually no R&B and a shortage of soul."[11] The argument was simple: many of the women singer-songwriters performed quiet, coffeehouse folk like the traditional singer-songwriter. Jim Sullivan noted, "Mostly, these were the figurative daughters of James Taylor and Carly Simon, nieces of Jackson Brown and Bonnie Raitt, grandchildren of Joan Baez."[12] Critics also opined that these singer-songwriters reflected McLachlan's taste and that they sounded surprisingly like McLachlan. Noting but not criticizing this phenomenon, Jon Pareles wrote in the *New York Times*, "The Lilith shows don't try to represent a comprehensive survey of women making music. They reflect Ms. McLachlan's taste, concentrating on guitar-strumming, melody-loving songwriters rooted in folk, pop, and country music."[13]

This blandness was underlined by references to the second stage, Stage B, where less-exposed performers engaged smaller audiences. Here, the sonic variety stretched further, allowing for the soul-jazz of Cassandra Wilson and the alternative rock of Juliana Hatfield. "Hatfield," wrote Jim Sullivan in the *Boston Globe*, "churned up the edgiest, most agitated set of the night."[14]

The accusation of musical blandness was matched by accusations of political blandness, underpinned by a number of McLachlan's statements including, "This tour isn't about politics."[15] *Ms.* magazine would take McLachlan to task for this, noting, "Although the Lilith Fair is steeped in feminist sensibilities, McLachlan seems to be uncomfortable with the 'f' word. She stresses that this 'isn't a soapbox for extremist feminism' (whatever that means)."[16] McLachlan was also accused of having no sense of history when creating Lilith Fair. In 2000, Jennifer Baumgardner and Amy Richards complained in *Manifesta: Young Women, Feminism, and the Future* that Lilith Fair had failed to have a significant impact in part because of McLachlan's lack of knowledge of previous women-based music festivals and recording labels: "Shining a light on the long line of women who continue to transform the male-run music industry would have gotten Lilith closer to its implied goal of equal treatment for women."[17] For these critics, Lilith Fair was no more than a poor copy of earlier efforts to promote women performers. Noting the nonoriginality of Lilith Fair, Urvashi Vaid wrote in the *Advocate*, "The Lilith Fair tour? Olivia Records and Roadwork began that in 1978 with the Varied Voices of Black Women tour. The Michigan Womyn's Music Festival has averaged 9,000 lesbians a year for 22 years."[18] If the "angry women" like Morissette and Bonham had borrowed and watered down riot grrrl content, then the women of Lilith Fair had reverted back to a time when a singer-songwriter offered little more than sophomore philosophy and details of the singer's love life. To these critics, the Lilith Fair experience gave the impression that women's music and riot grrrl had never happened.

One of the legitimate critiques focused on commercial skincare products that were being promoted on the grounds of Lilith Fair. Biore Pore Perfect deep cleansing strips by Jergens was "placed across the bridge of the nose like a Band-Aid. The goal: to clean clogged pores."[19] Within third wave feminism, the idea of merging skincare products and feminism was not mutually exclusive. At the same time, the fact that McLachlan and others had approved the promotion of a commercial skincare product in the midst of the woman-friendly festival seemed to offer mixed messages. In one sense, Lilith Fair was viewed as a safe space for women, and a number of reports noted that women worried little about make-up and hair during the festival. During thirty Lilith Fair dates, however, 1.5 million samples of the Biore were handed out to Lilith Fair attendees, reminding these women that despite the casual atmosphere, a woman still needed to be aware of her blocked pores.

It would be easy to debate both the criticism of the music and the politics, and to offer counterexamples: Sheryl Crow and Meredith Brooks, in fact, did use full bands and create a bigger sound on the tour in 1997; coverage of these performances would later be included in *Lilith Fair: A Celebration of Women in Music*. It would also be easy to note the flaw in the argument that many of the artists sounded too similar: could fans really not tell the difference between the musical styles of McLachlan and Paula Cole? Furthermore, one could argue that the presence of the Indigo Girls and the support of organizations like Planned Parenthood clearly added a political dimension to the festival.

But the roots of the expressed critical responses regarding Lilith Fair seemed to extend beyond mere criticism. The available responses of Lilith Fair attendees, after all, are primarily positive. A great deal of criticism, in fact, seemed less interested in what the festival actually offered than what individual critics believed it should have offered musically and politically.

Many critical stances, then, revealed more about the prejudices of the writers in regards to pop music and women's issues than a defect in Lilith Fair. These critical responses also had the misfortune, in some instances, of adding to the ongoing backlash against women within the popular culture.

In regard to the criticism of Lilith Fair's music, there was continued belief that mainstream music by women, whether categorized as folk, pop-folk, or soft rock, was bland. And within this belief, that light or pop music was incapable of offering anything more than radio fodder for the adult contemporary market. Sarah Vowell wrote in *Salon*, "Lilith Fair isn't a picture of solidarity so much as a picture of uniformity. McLachlan . . . has chosen singer-songwriters in her own image: pretty, polite, folksy moderates with sensible hair and more melody than message."[20] Under this rubric, there was no difference between McLachlan's aural soundscapes, Jewel's more traditional singer-songwriter style, and Crow's classic-derived rock. In a sense, it was the same binary that had frequently separated rock from pop music since the 1950s: rock was substantive as an authentic product that connected to real life (passion, emotion), while pop music was ear candy that focused on love won and lost (sentimentality).

In regards to politics, debating the fairness of Lilith Fair coverage is an inexact undertaking. It is important to underline, however, that the harshness of part of the criticism denigrated not only the music but the women who performed the music. In other words, the criticism became very personal, working within the mind-set of the backlash, whether intentional or not. L7, a riot grrrl–associated band, defined all mainstream women singer-songwriters as "PMS fraud rock."[21] Referencing an article in the *New York Times* that noted that Lilith Fair's audience ratio was three-to-one women to men, Vowell said that she was surprised, "because these performers strike me as just the sort of women most men seem to like: They're cute, nice and not extravagantly smart."[22] In her *Rolling Stone* piece on Lilith Fair, Lorraine Ali reserved a great deal of space to mock Jewel. "Then there's Jewel's set, during which she tells the audience how great it is not to be a waitress anymore."[23] Ali ended her piece by describing the end of one Lilith Fair performance:

> But as the show draws to a close, all is serene and calm, just like womanhood should be. McLachlan brings out her female dog, Rex, who sits on a Persian carpet; her husband, drummer Ashwin Sood, is by her side. As the band stands in a warm circle and performs McLachlan's closing song, Rex lifts her leg, licks her crotch and falls asleep. And like the setting moon on a Celestial Seasoning box, Lilith Fair is done for the evening.[24]

These backlash positions regarding music quality and politics would solidify following Lilith Fair's last shows in 1999.[25] In general, a postcritique of Lilith Fair, and of much of the mid-1990s mainstream women singer-songwriters' movement, regarded the Lilith events as failures. Kristin Schilt wrote in 2003, "The only difference between Mariah Carey and these new stars was that their lyrics addressed sex and other taboo subjects. They had inherited the legacy of Riot Grrrl and 'improved' upon it by setting shocking lyrics to familiar pop music."[26] Maria Raha concurred in 2005, "Lilith Fair, for all its good intentions, reinforced the idea of women writing, singing, performing, and appearing in a traditionally feminine way, without the angrier voices present to balance out the picture (and sound)."[27] Once again, even though many media stories were positive, and while most attendees seemed to enjoy the experience of Lilith Fair, a negative consensus has formed around the event. Critically, the popular media and academics have relegated Lilith Fair as a failed experiment.

Epilogue

The record industry was once pathologically dismissive of female artists, but in the late '90s, cutthroat music biz types, hungry for what they saw as a lucrative niche, jumped on any girl with a handful of tunes and a decent voice.

—Sarah Liss[28]

Every bit of half-baked pop fodder by a female artist—No Doubt's "Just a Girl," Meredith Brooks's "Bitch"—became culturally significant, even if the actual songs were inept or unoriginal.

—Karen Schomer[29]

In 1997 Brooks and Lilith Fair represented the phenomenon of the commercial singer-songwriter in its broadest sense. Whereas earlier performers like Sarah McLachlan and Sheryl Crow had seemed to sprout up in isolation in 1993, by the mid-1990s—as women singer-songwriters saturated radio, MTV, and CD bins at music stores—the phenomenon had begun to seem more calculated. It was easy for observers to suspect that each label was searching for its own Sheryl, Sarah, or Alanis, and that they were less concerned about duplicating the quality of the originals. Building on these suspicions, the cynic could easily point out that Lilith Fair coincided with the release of McLachlan's *Surfacing*, characterizing the festival as little more than an extended advertisement for her new album.

In the mid-1990s, the singer-songwriter phenomenon had actually become what many had predicted it would become in 1987–1988: the movement had established itself as an important player within the popular music scene and seemed likely to continue growing. The question, however, remained whether or not the movement would continue to address questions focusing on women's issues in a forceful manner as had Love, Harvey, and Phair, and whether the movement, with an influx of singers like Brooks, would become watered down and more like the short-lived movement of 1987–1988.

The women singer-songwriters' movement, then, faced both practical problems and problems of perception once it became part of the mainstream in the mid-1990s. As the movement reached a mass audience, with singer-songwriters like Brooks and festivals like Lilith Fair, it was easy for those who advocated more radical personal politics to cry sell-out.

Many of these criticisms were warranted. Musically and politically, Jewel's "I Was Meant for You" was a clearly a step back for women who had rocked out to Morissette's "You Oughta Know"; and while Brooks proved apt at updating the singer-songwriter's musical style, "Bitch" unleashed a muddle of positions that were impossible to sort out. A viewer may also opine, watching *Lilith Fair: A Celebration of Women in Music* (1997), that it was unfortunate that bands with a harder edge like Garbage were unable to attend the festival. It was also easy to suspect if difficult to prove that labels were offering watered-down versions of angry women in order to cash in on the phenomenon as the women singer-songwriters' movement reached mainstream. For many, this reached the height of absurdity with the Spice Girls: there seemed to be no separation between girl power as revolution and girl power as commodity culture.

But the fact that the woman singer-songwriter had reached the mainstream did not necessarily equal a sell-out: women singer-songwriters continued to deliver musical innovation and push women's issues in 1996–1997. As new voices entered the mix, however, weighing these various complications became more difficult. Becoming mainstream has often suggested that compromises—musically and lyrically—would be necessary, even if not consciously planned. But how did one measure these real or imagined compromises without making the assumption that noncommercial was better than commercial, or that indie recording labels produced better results than major labels? Was the explosive music of Garbage and Bonham as uncompromised as the the jagged edges of Harvey's *Rid of Me*? Were the personal politics of No Doubt's "Just a Girl" as personal and political as those of Love's "Doll Parts"? Did Rothberg's tuneful pop-rock dig as deeply into women's issues as Phair's more straightforward rock on *Exile in Guyville*? Exploring these musical and lyrical spaces offers a productive approach to understanding the musical vision of mainstream women singer-songwriters during the mid-1990s.

The question, then, is not whether mainstream women singer-songwriters were capable of musical innovation and addressing women's issues: a number of examples given attest to the fact that they were. The question more clearly focuses on what shape and form these visions would take within the mainstream. How much of the earlier vision of Love, Phair, and Harvey would survive—in the music of new women singer-songwriters as well as in their own work—as the movement reached mainstream? Did the shift in musical styles, a mingling of pop and rock, create a hybrid that was too easily associated with mainstream pop? Did the shift in lyrical content, as mainstream singer-songwriters focused more on relationships, lose essential qualities in regard to women's issues? And in spite of assumed compromises as the movement reached mainstream, were a number of women singer-songwriters nonetheless able to bring something new, lyrically and musically, to the genre? These are questions that we will now turn to in the second half of the book as we look at the work of Tori Amos, Sarah McLachlan, and Sheryl Crow.

Notes

1. Chris Morris, "With a Hot New Cut, Capitol's Brooks Makes Radio Connection," *Billboard*, April 12, 1997, 12 (2).

2. Morris, "With a Hot New Cut," 12.

3. Brooks responded by saying, "What do I care? The song's still the song. I don't care if it says 'Bitch' on the cover or not." "Daily News," *Rolling Stone*, July 8, 1997, www.rollingstone.com/.

4. Yahlin Chang, "Blurring the Edges," *Newsweek*, May 26, 1997, 79.

5. Chris William, "Meredith, She Rolls Along," *Entertainment Weekly*, June 13, 1997, 65.

6. Kristen Schilt, "'A Little Too Ironic': The Appropriation and Packaging of the Riot Grrrl Politics by Mainstream Female Musicians," *Popular Music and Society* 26, no. 1 (February 2003): 5–16.

7. Donna Freydkin, "Fierce Feminists L7 Rant on with Live Album," *CNN*, December 11, 1998, www.cnn.com/SHOWBIZ/Music/9812/11/l7/.

8. "Lilith Fair," *Entertainment Weekly*, May 9, 1997, 44 (4).

9. Joe Woodard, "Mellow-Sounding Demon: Feminist Neo-Paganism Goes Mainstream at Lilith," *Alberta Report*, September 8, 1997, 39, 43.

10. Jane Stevenson, "Beautiful Women, Beautiful Day: Lilith Fair Off to Noticeably Non-Rocky Start," *Toronto Sun*, July 7, 1997, 38.

11. Karen Schoemer, "Quiet Girls," *Newsweek*, June 30, 1997, 72 (2).

12. Jim Sullivan, "Chapman, Hatfield Shine at Lilith Fair," *Boston Globe*, July 23, 1997, D1.

13. Jon Pareles, "Cheers for Self-Determination (and Dumping Bad Partners) at All-Female Festival," *New York Times*, 7 July 1997, C11.

14. Sullivan, "Chapman, Hatfield Shine at Lilith Fair," D1.

15. Mark Lepage, "The Women Have It: No Bills on the Bill?" *Gazette*, August 16, 1997, G1.

16. Dylan Siegler, "Lilith Fair: A New Women's Festival," *Ms.*, July/August 1997, 79.

17. Jennifer Baumgardner and Amy Richards, *Manifesta: Young Women, Feminism, and the Future* (New York: Farrar, Straus and Giroux, 2000), 64.

18. Urvashi Vaid, "Calling All Lesbians," *Advocate*, September 16, 1997, 88.

19. Ann Oldenburg and Karen Thomas, "Nose for Promotion Brings Skin Care to Lilith," *USA Today*, August 1, 1997, D1.

20. Sarah Vowell, "Throwing Ovaries: The Second-Grade Sensibility of the Pseudo-Feminist Lilith Fair," *Salon*, July 11, 1997, www.salon.com/july97/columnists/vowell970711.html.

21. Freydkin, "Fierce Feminists L7 Rant on With Live Album."

22. Vowell, "Throwing Ovaries."

23. Lorraine Ali, "Backstage at Lilith," *Rolling Stone*, September 4, 1997, 30.

24. Ali, "Backstage at Lilith," *Rolling Stone*, 35.

25. In 2007, the festival Estrojam billed itself as the "anti-Lilith Fair."

26. Schilt, "'A Little Too Ironic,'" 5–16.

27. Maria Raha, *Cinderella's Big Score: Women of the Punk and Indie Underground* (Emeryville, CA: Seal Press, 2005), 224.

28. Sarah Liss, "The Gender Curse," *CBC News*, February 7, 2008, www.cbc.ca/arts/music/womensongs.html.

29. Karen Schoemer, "The Selling of Girl Power," *Newsweek*, December 29, 1997, 90.

CHAPTER SIX

Little Earthquakes: Tori Amos

The diaries girls keep are active attempts to construct the self to an imagined reader. There is always an imagined audience to a secret diary, and maybe even an audience to the secret thoughts of a young girl, even if only in her head.

—Sharon Lamb[1]

When Tori Amos chose a metaphor to emphasize the difficulty of contemporary women's lives, she chose an extreme one: crucifixion. In "Crucify" (1992), she leaves no doubt that her persona's crucifixion will require nails, not ropes. She shows none of Christ's fortitude or forgiveness, however, and wishes that she had the courage to spit in the faces of the people who are pointing fingers at her. While angry and wishing to strike out, however, she nonetheless blames herself as responsible for her suffering: her crucifixion is a voluntary sacrifice. Her repeated question—why do she and other women crucify themselves?—seems to be open ended.

Like many Amos songs, "Crucify" is both personal and imprecise, at first leaving the impression of intimate revelation only to dissolve into a surreal and fragmented narrative. The lyric, each song suggests, may be drawn from Amos' own life . . . but it might also be a page taken from any contemporary woman's diary. Spiritual images and words—guilt, angels, and God—are mixed with physical ones—dirty streets and dirty sheets in "Crucify." There are other paradoxes, with Amos' persona placing the blame on women themselves, while also suggesting the sins of others—authority figures, family members, and men—play a role. And finally, there is the paradox of one woman's vulnerability and silence against her oppressors compared to Amos'—the singer-songwriter—dramatization of that silence and vulnerability in music and voice. Amos and Amos' persona are both willing victims and angry accusers, chained to old habits but searching for possible solutions.

"Crucify" is further complicated by the pronouns—I, my, you, and their—that keep shifting beneath the narrative. On each verse, Amos' persona relates the story of her own crucifixion; on each chorus, she equates her experience with a broader "we" that can be read as all women. These shifts, and Amos' impreciseness, are reflected throughout the song. Who, for instance, are the people who are pointing fingers at her persona in the first verse? Also, is her reference to mistreatment in love in the second verse meant to be specific—the mistreatment by one man—or general—the mistreatment of all women by all men? Perhaps most at odds is the use of "you" on each chorus; she repeats that nothing that she does is worthy for an unidentifiable "you." The listener can never be sure whether the "you" is supposed to be a boyfriend, her parents, a blanket pronoun for all authority figures, or perhaps even God.

If Amos' lyric fails to unify her subject in a traditional fashion, her performance unfolds with clarity and conviction that maintains dramatic tension for nearly five minutes. "Crucify," like many of Amos' songs, is delivered as an expressive confessional born of a deep conviction that, despite the obvious irony, one might call religious. As a daughter of a minister, she understands the sacrilege she commits by borrowing Christian imagery, and she plays her role as a heretic to its limit. The arrangement of "Crucify" is oversized, filled with swelling background vocals, cascading piano, persistent heavy percussion, and Amos' emotionally drenched voice. The saturated echo, applied to Amos' vocal and the drums, also loosely imitates gospel music while seemingly inverting its message by underlining the torment of crucifixion and neglecting the gospel of salvation. The end result is exhaustive, both for Amos and her listeners, as though the confessional has left her temporarily spent.

In Amos' early work, her use of musical expression and intense imagery was often unexpected and shocking. For instance, her songs are filled with supernatural and startling images that register sharply, such as the Eternal Footman buying a bicycle, God playing a game of golf, a young girl masturbating upstairs as her family prays downstairs, and the appearance—for no particular reason—of the Antichrist in a woman's kitchen. She likewise delivers acutely etched lines and couplets, and occasionally one of these will come to the foreground of the song/lyric, a practice that may overemphasize one part of the lyric at the expense of the whole. In "Precious Things"

(1992), her persona reminds the beautiful boys that they may be able to give her orgasms, but that this ability does not make them Jesus; in "Waitress" (1994), her persona begins the song by stating that she wants to kill one of her fellow waitresses. The fact that Amos' persona expresses a desire to kill the waitress may continue to stand out, even if she admits, later in the song, that this desire may not be a healthy one. Amos also frequently uses humor, at turns dryly ironic, whimsical, and, on occasion, cutting and dark, to enrich and amplify the intensity of her lyrics.

Many of these qualities come into play with "Crucify." Images, such as her persona describing her emotional fear as a bowling ball in her stomach, are extreme, pushing beyond the expected or typical. In the second verse, she notes that she was kicked—just like a dog—because she wanted love. The most shocking imagery, however, is crucifixion itself, an image that equates the suffering of women with the death of Christ. Amos' persona lifts her own hands, asking those who stand against her to drive the nails into them.

It would be easy to read "Crucify" as overly critical of women: they are ultimately responsible for their own suffering. Taken at face value, Amos seems to be suggesting that if women are criticized by society, they are cowards for failing to react; if they beg for love, they have set themselves up for abusive treatment. Amos' narrator even admits that she enjoys suffering, and, within the lyric, elevates her suffering to sacrifice.

Amos, however, has planted numerous clues that undercut this straightforward reading. Why, for instance, does the narrator of "Crucify" hold her anger in on the first verse, afraid of the possible repercussions from those who are pointing fingers at her? And why, in the second verse, does she plead for love? In both cases, Amos' persona is only acting out a script of socialized femininity. The fingers pointing at her represent both private authority figures (parents, teachers, and peers) and civil ones (the courts, the churches, and the state). Her fear, that a reaction on her part (spitting in their faces) will bring repercussions, is a reasonable one. They hold most of the power. Likewise, women have been taught to actively seek love and to sacrifice themselves to the ideal of love. In both cases, holding her tongue and seeking love, she is only behaving as society has taught her to behave. Women sacrifice themselves every day because that is what they have been taught to do.

Also, if the message of "Crucify" was perceived as weak because it viewed a woman or women at an impasse, it is an impasse that Amos is in the process of comprehending as she has written and performed the song. In other words, she was revealing what she had learned within the song. If *Little Earthquakes* (1992) found Amos trying to uncover layers of nonauthentic selves that had accumulated for years, songs like "Crucify" revealed where she stood when she finished unpeeling these layers. It may have been a weak position, and it may have generalized women's position as the same, but it would be difficult to imagine moving beyond this position without first realizing where one stood. While Amos is sympathetic to the reasons why women follow social scripts, her personal realization that women—as the ones who read and follow the script—play a part in their own crucifixion is only part of the confessional process. Recognizing what she and other women were doing to themselves, and recognizing the emptiness of their own sacrifice, was the first step for her and other women to comprehend and imagine stopping the cycle.

As with many of Amos' songs, "Crucify" works as a fragmented gospel or fairy tale for the contemporary woman coming of age. Fantastic, passionate, and perverse, "Crucify" publicly asks why women willingly participate in the divine fulfillment of a cultural dictate that harms them. Through blasphemy, she names the unnamable, leaving listeners to squirm with discomfort or self-recognition; through primitive symbols, she dredges up the demons of waking nightmares. In this gospel ("Crucify"), Amos seeks the truth through emotional nudism, peeling off each layer until all is exposed; in this fairy tale, Amos dresses the innocence of female adolescence and young adulthood with ugly details and violent imagery. In choosing the image of crucifixion as the central metaphor for contemporary women's lives, then, Amos seeks no more than to reveal what has remained hidden.

Fragmented Fairy Tales

The cover of the single for "Crucify" nearly resembles a typical photograph for singer-songwriter cover art until a viewer notices the circle of onions that have been placed around Amos like a necklace. Otherwise, Amos, from her head to the top of her breasts, is not wearing any clothing, and her eyes are focused straight ahead at the viewer. Her deep auburn hair and the blacked-out background frame her pale face and body. Her facial expression is seemingly neutral: neither her eyes nor the straight line of her deep red lips reveal a trace of her thoughts. Still, however, there is the odd necklace, with the roots seeming to grow from and around Amos' neck, and the green stalks form a partial semicircle from her shoulder to her breast to her shoulder.

Other cover photographs from the same period offer similar mixed messages. On the "Winter" single, the photograph shows Amos dressed in a silver coat lying across a snow-white horse. She looks toward the camera, her red (almost orange) hair spilling down onto the horse's mane. On the cover of "China," she stands behind a hive-shaped stone structure, once again looking toward the camera. It is unclear whether she is standing within the structure or whether the structure is merely a façade. Finally, there is the cover art for *Little Earthquakes*, showing Amos, dressed in jeans and a blue tank top, pressed inside of a square box. A small blue piano is also in the box, and both of her hands hold on to the outer edges of the box. On the back of *Little Earthquakes*, the same box appears, but this time it is empty.

The easiest photographs to read are the ones from *Little Earthquakes*. Too easy, one might add. A young woman is trapped inside a box, but through her struggles (represented by another photograph inside the *Little Earthquakes'* booklet), she escapes. Otherwise, the images on the other singles from this period seem as though they should mean more than they do. Certainly, a viewer might think, a garland of onions and a stone structure shaped like a beehive symbolize something significant. It would also be fairly easy to look up onions or necklace in a symbol dictionary and gather that the garland may represent a sensual or magical binding to the earth. But one could also—combining her lack of clothing, the onions, and the necklace—generate a number of other meanings. The white of the horse and Amos' coat may suggest the coolness of the season, while the stone-brick structure may represent the wall that builds up around the couple in "China." But closer scrutiny of these early photographs (images) is finally less than satisfying.

Unlike the early cover art on PJ Harvey albums, Amos' cover art seems to be a depiction of her (Amos as Amos). In this sense, the photographs on *Little Earthquakes*, "Crucify," "Winter," and "China" work much like traditional cover art for popular performers: they serve as an introduction and sell a particular image of the artist. But one might guess that these photographs—like Amos' realization of women's weak position within the social structure in "Crucify"—are only snapshots of a life or lives coming into focus. Amos is a young girl who struggles against social limitations on the cover of *Little Earthquakes*, she is the girl with beautiful red hair on "Winter," she is the wise woman who explores feminine symbolism on "China," and she is the eccentric earth mother figure on "Crucify." Amos, then, is simply trying on different identities, offering herself as a work in progress.

The difficulties with these images, even as works in progress, are multiple, with Amos seeming unsure of what she wishes to say and unsure of how she wishes to portray herself. This is complicated by a touch of art school pretension, with each image seeming to present only half-formed ideas. Instead of leaving the impression of thoughtfulness, they suggest eccentricities; instead of revealing Amos' presence, they suggest her uncertainty. Amos' efforts with her early songs, however, are much more confident. Like the photographs, her early songs focus on young girls and women struggling to build or un-cover identity—to uncover the true self—from the fragments of the past. Constructed from memories, life experience, and fiction, Amos' early songs are portraits of her personas as they peel back layer after layer.

"Winter"

> Once in midwinter when the snowflakes were falling from the sky like feathers, a queen sat sewing at a window, with an ebony frame.

> —The Brothers Grimm, "Snow White"[2]

In the first verse of "Winter," a young girl puts on her new boots and wipes her nose, preparing to go out into the snow. She has forgotten her mittens, however, and places a hand in her father's glove. But neither the gloves nor the boots prepare her for the deeper snowdrifts. Soon, she has tripped into the drifts, and as she falls—on each chorus—she hears her father's voice. He reminds her that he will not always be able to be there for her, even though he will always wish her near. He hopes that she will learn to love herself as much as he loves her, and then warns her that every-thing—that life—will change quickly. As winter changes to spring during the second verse, the girls around her begin competing for boys. As the years pass by, though, she remains alone, questioning herself in the mir-ror, wondering what has happened to her youth. Finally, in the last verse, she has grown old, realizing that while the fires of her youth remain, her dreams have been put aside.

Amos' gently lilting piano sets a melancholy, minor key mood, suggesting, even before "Winter" begins, a sense of loss. Each cascade of piano notes also echoes the vulnerability of Amos' aching vocal. Set against a backdrop of strings, the piano and voice create an air of fragility, underlining the vulner-ability of the girl as she reaches adolescence. As the song continues, a swell of strings and background voices highlight the emotional tension of the lyrics. All of these elements, piano, strings, and voices, create a poignant backdrop that movingly undergirds the story of one girl's personal tragedy.

The images of a frozen landscape and childhood evoke the magical world of fairy tales in "Winter." Throughout the song, seasonal imagery is emotion-ally sterile and cold, with snowmen, ice, and snowdrifts occasionally relieved by the warmth of memory, spring flowers, and burning fires. The winter imagery of a young girl preparing for a day outside is enhanced by images bor-rowed from fairy tales, underlining her wish to return to youthful innocence. In each chorus, her father tells her that all of the white horses are still in bed, but as she grows older, she questions a mirror, asking where the crystal palace has gone. Both the white horses and crystal (of the crystal palace) also evoke the white of the winter snow and ice, while the mirror suggests her struggle with her changing identity. Finally, earlier in the song, there is a reference to Sleeping Beauty, a sleeping beauty that trips her. While the image may seem to suggest a negative association with a fairy tale heroine, the reference may refer to no more than the fact that the girl is asleep to her potential.

The narrative of "Winter" seems to unfold in the present tense, as though all of one woman's life, first as a young girl, then as a young woman, and finally as an older woman, has been crammed into one song. But even in the first stanza, Amos' persona says that she feels warmth in her heart when she thinks of winter, leaving the impression that she is only reliving memories and supplementing them with an older person's reflections. The language— the snowdrifts, and the flowers (girls) that compete for the sun (boys)—also takes a number of metaphorical turns that more closely resemble an older person's reflection. Since the point of view does not unfold in the present or reflect the thoughts of an adolescent girl, it would be easy to guess that the story is being told by the woman in the last verse whose hair has turned gray, that she is remembering the guiding voice of her father and her inability to find her way by herself.

But there are few if any older women in Amos' early work. Instead, another possibility exists, that the latter part of "Winter" is no more than the girl/young woman's imagined end; that unless she can learn from her father's advice and unless she can form her own identity or find herself, she will lose her dreams. This possible narrative point of view also seems plausible because the older women's observations seem more generalized when compared to the detailed images of childhood from earlier in the lyric. From the point of view of Amos' persona, the challenges of adolescence—entering the world, forming an identity, and forging intimate relationships—are the central issues to the success or failure of the rest of her life (the older woman of the song seems to have no hope of reviving her dreams). Learning that Amos wrote the song about her own father might also increase the impression that "Winter" was written from the point of view of a young woman looking backward and forward at the same time.

The fairy tale atmosphere of "Winter" is stark and clear, but still hopeful. The girl and any girl, on the cusp of adolescence, must venture out into the world without the protection of her father. The awakening of desire further complicates this change. Marina Warner wrote in *From the Beast to the Blond* that "husbands or lovers will take a measure of the love that in innocence she might have once given to her father."[3] Instead of meeting the challenge, however, the young girl is paralyzed by it; she worries that as she grows older, her winter-toned dreams will be of the past, of childhood and lost innocence. If, at this juncture of her life, she experiences a failure of nerve because she could not learn to love herself as her father has loved her, her life will literally pass her by. While bleak, then, "Winter" nonetheless offers the possibility of something better for those willing to make a leap of faith beyond childhood.

"Girl"

I had good memories of who I was before I was five, and then I became everybody else's idea of who I was.

—Tori Amos[4]

On the first verse of "Girl," one girl watches another girl who is crawling in the shadows. The girl crawling in the shadows is clutching a photograph of the first girl, and the first girl believes the clutched photograph holds a message for her. On each chorus, the first girl also expresses her belief that the girl in the shadows has belonged to everyone else except herself, and hopes that, one day, she will belong to herself. The second verse unfolds against a backdrop of surrealism, featuring screaming flowers and water-filled violins; the first girl has cut her knees and feels as though she is falling down like a felled tree. On the song's bridge, a series of disconnected images—a river, flying pigs, drugstores, and smothered hearts—lead to the final verse. Finally, the first girl rides to work each morning, attempting to do as she has been told, while men/women in white coats enter the second girl's room.

In the beginning of "Girl," Amos' piano lines almost feel as though they are careening sideways against the heavy heartbeat of a bass drum. As with "Winter," the minor key sets the mood, though the mid-tempo pacing injects a greater urgency into the melody line. On the first verse, Amos' breathy vocal adds to the urgency; on the chorus, a terse string arrangement appends an undercurrent of tension. In the second verse, Amos achieves a ghostly aura by doubling her vocal, while an electric guitar thickens the off-centered, sonic ambience. The arrangement swells as the second chorus feeds into the bridge, with heavy bass, guitar, strings, and multiple overlapping voices. This musical outburst dissolves into an almost tranquil plateau as the bridge pauses before the third verse. Amos' voice vacillates between solo and doubling here, and on one line, is shadowed by a deep male voice. The terse arrangement—careening piano, a doubled voice, and minor key mood—generate an out-of-kilter atmosphere, a lack of balance that never rights itself in "Girl."

The images in "Girl" might be described as surreal, revolving around spiritual wounds and mental illness. The shadows of the opening lines are shadows in the mind of Amos' persona, places that are hard for her to see or recall clearly, while the photograph serves as a mirror. The image of a girl crawling may suggest that she is disturbed, but not necessarily mentally ill; the image of a girl with cuts on her knees is likewise disturbing, but not representative of mental illness. Both suggest emotional vulnerability and, with the fallen cherry tree, the possibility of a breakdown. Other images, screaming bluebells and water-filled violins, clearly suggest mental illness, while white-coated attendants suggest a mental institution. In the last verse, Amos brings these images together, with her persona twisting and holding tight as she goes to work each morning, just as, one might imagine, someone might move within the physical constraints of a straitjacket.

Attempting to sort out which lines of the lyric belong to which girl (and which lines possibly apply to both girls) is simplified by returning to the title. The title, "Girl," is singular, partially solving the song's riddle: despite the fragmented nature of the narrative, the song is about one girl watching herself. The girl in the shadows clutching a photograph, then, is clutching a photograph of herself: she simply no longer recognizes herself, thus the need to send a message to her own heart. The two roles, one girl working, another in a mental institution, are either imaginings of two possible life paths or the memory of an earlier trauma. All lines in the lyric of "Girl," then, belong to the same girl. The narrative of "Girl" is a puzzle of sorts, with one girl trying to reconcile fractured images of herself.

Underlying the trauma of "Girl" is the loss of identity. Amos' persona notes, in the second verse, that although she is no longer seventeen, she continues to suffer the emotional wounds of a teenage girl. The loss of identity, then, may be rooted once again in adolescence: as she looks at a photograph of herself, she is attempting to understand what happened to an earlier, perhaps more innocent or whole version of herself. The chorus offers a clue to understanding how she lost her identity: in attempting to fulfill other persons' expectation of her, the girl has allowed her own identity to become fragmented, thus making her belong to everyone else but herself. Within the lyric, however, she is unable to recognize these multiple portraits or fragmented images of herself. When she calls for her baby at the end of the third verse, she is in essence calling for herself.

As in "Winter," Amos presents a bleak prospect in "Girl." A girl reaching adulthood can obey the rules. In the song's last verse, this is emphasized by quoting from an authority figure who reminds her, as though she were a student in school, to sit down and be good. Amos further emphasizes this line by underpinning her vocal with a male voice. While she may be rewarded by the system—she will be considered a good girl; she will receive a paycheck—she twists and holds tight as she rides to work, prefacing her ride to work with the imaginative statement that there are burning castles in her heart. Work or any activity in which a young woman must follow the rules, then, offers a safe choice as she reaches adulthood. The choice, however, is also emotionally deadening: by following the rules, Amos' persona has lost track of her own dreams and now belongs to everyone else but herself.

There are a number of unresolved elements within the lyric, however. Does obeying the rules, doing what one is supposed to do, lead to mental illness or only emotional sterility? And what happens if a young woman chooses not to obey the rules? Does Amos' persona fear that if she chooses to ignore the rules she will either be labeled mad or perhaps literally become mad? Or would disobeying the rules offer her a chance to rebuild her own identity? "Girl" complicates the lyric of "Winter," suggesting that even if a woman leaves her isolation and ventures out into the world, the world has expectations for her to follow. While remaining pliant may be the easiest route, being pliant, even with the social rewards that come with it, is ultimately self-defeating. Refusing to play by the rules may be the braver course, then, but it also leaves one without a net (just as the young girl will not always have her father to protect her in "Winter"). In truth, then, either choice, to follow the rules or choose her own path, is fraught with danger. Within the lyric of "Girl," however, the contemporary woman has little alternative: the risky move, even if it leads to madness, is really the only choice.

"Precious Things"

As "Precious Things" begins, a seventh-grade girl is running after a boy named Billy, though the chorus makes it clear that she is older now and only remembering these events. He tells her that although he considers her ugly, he likes the way she plays. The "play" seems to suggest something sexual. Instead of being insulted, however, she thanks him for his backhanded compliment; she also continues to carry his picture and dresses up for him every day. She simultaneously expresses her disdain for beautiful, Christian boys like Billy: they may be able to give her orgasms, she says, but that does not make them Jesus. Next, she remembers attending a party, wearing a peach dress and not being noticed. She expresses contempt for all the pretty girls: while each one is seemingly special, they all secretly hold evil in their hearts.

In the present, however, she wishes to let these memories go, to let them bleed and wash away.

More directly than in "Crucify," Amos' imagery centers on sexual desire, vulnerability, and Christianity. Perhaps the most powerful image is the recurring one of blood. This potent symbol is not easily contained or limited to any one meaning. In one sense, blood alludes to the sexual maturity of Amos' persona; in another, it seems to refer to the same self-sacrifice as the crucifixion of "Crucify." The idea of self-sacrifice also seems to suggest that these violent memories will only be relieved by violence, that they will not be soothed by Christian forgiveness or Zen meditation. There is also the juxtaposition of the peach dress that the young girl wears to a party and the fascist panties inside the hearts of nice girls; one, an image of adolescent innocence, the other, of mean girls, sexually aware beyond their years.

Like "Crucify," "Precious Things" is a musical force of nature. On one piano, Amos builds taut lines that tightly hold the emotional tension as the angry mood builds toward an overflowing chorus. Besides the piano line, an unidentified sound on the right track mimics a person short of breath, adding to the overall anxiety of the lyric. Even before the lyric begins, it is easy to gain an impression of someone running, of someone who is afraid. While the piano lines continue to spin a web of tension on the chorus, the sonic pallet thickens as booming percussion and a deep male vocal enter the mix (and the male voice resembles the male voice that appeared on "Girl"). The male voice undergirds Amos' vocal like a dark shadow on the title line. As the chorus reaches its end, the musical fury subsides momentarily and Amos emits a cry somewhere between pained anguish and liberated release.

This temporary calm breaks midway through the free-floating bridge, however, releasing a torrid burst of anger. The arrangement, with multiple voices, piano, and percussion, swells to its highest point here, preparing for the climax as the song jumps from the bridge back to the chorus.

More obviously than "Winter," "Precious Things" is clearly a memory song, taken from the point of view of an older girl/woman looking back at her growing pains in early adolescence. The narration seems to be divided between the present and the past, with, generally, her memories occupying each verse and her desire to put these memories behind her occupying each chorus. But as is common in Amos' early work, the division between past and present is seldom clear-cut. A great deal of her persona's anger, in fact, spills into the memories, seemingly expressing feelings that she did not have—or that remained below the surface—at the time of these incidents. While the pronouns and identity of the narrator may be less confusing than with "Girl" or "Winter," she nonetheless, like those personas, remains divided within or against herself.

Partly, "Precious Things" is an attempt to expunge painful memories, but even Amos' persona fails to understand the hold these memories continue to have over her. While a great deal of anger is focused on the beautiful Christian boys and the pretty girls, it is also focused on the naiveté of her earlier self: part of her may wish to come to terms with these memories, but part of her simply wishes to eliminate her perception of her weaker, earlier self. No matter how angry she is at the Christian boys, she did, at one time, desire them; no matter how much she despises the pretty girls, she did, at one time, wish to be one of them. This leaves her with an unstated puzzle: how can she reconcile these two versions of herself, one, a person who desired to be with and be one of the beautiful people, and the other, a person who despised the beautiful people and all that they stood for?

"Precious Things," then, is filled with paradoxes like many other songs on *Little Earthquakes*. At first, the song offers an obvious choice: women must learn to let go of painful memories and sexual trauma or these memories will overpower the present. Like the choice to move into the broader world in "Winter" and the choice to not follow the rules in "Girl," letting go of painful memories seems the obvious or only possibility. But once again, part of the problem with this obvious choice is that letting go involves reconciling with her earlier self. This is complicated not only by her persona's negative perception of her weakness, but also because she seems to partially blame herself (as in "Crucify") for what has happened in the past, and may even blame herself for its continued hold on her. If she had not desired the beautiful Christian boys, if she had not desired to be one of the pretty girls, then none of this would have happened.

It is also possible that her recriminations in "Precious Things" extend beyond her adolescent self: she may still wish to be seen as beautiful and she may still desire beautiful boys. As the final repetition of "precious" brings the song to a close, the residue of pain and anger remain like an open wound. Whether self-sacrifice—allowing the blood to wash these memories clean—will permanently or just temporarily remove these mental scars and allow Amos' persona to go forward, however, remains far from clear in "Precious Things."

"Silent All These Years"

Like "Precious Things," "Silent All These Years" can loosely be described as a narrative. The narrative, however, must be teased out of elliptical phrasing, and stray details must be placed aside. Even then, the narrative of "Silent All

These Years," a seemingly casual sexual relationship between a woman and a man, is only one of the song's subjects.

In the first verse, Amos' persona asks an unidentified person, perhaps her male friend/boyfriend in the song, if she can trade places or exchange identities with him temporarily. She then tells him that her dog will not bite him if he remains still, and that the Antichrist is in her kitchen, yelling at her. She notes repeatedly in the song that she wishes, but finds herself unable, to speak. In the second verse, she comments on the fact that her boyfriend has found a new girl who he considers intelligent because she thinks deep thoughts, and then she offers her own version of a deep thought: he better pray that her period arrives soon. In the last verse, she tells him that the sky is falling, which precedes his mother's arrival. The arrival of his mother also seems to set off a crisis for the boyfriend, and she tells him that he will have to stand where she has stood. She offers her hand to help him through his difficulty.

While the male/female relationship may seem to hold the center in "Silent All These Years," the central imagery revolves around silence and finding one's voice. Indeed, while the relationship also echoes the theme of silence, it seems to work more as a front or lead-in to Amos' real concern. On each chorus her persona wonders if she is a mermaid, and whether the listener returns to Han Christian Andersen's tale or Disney's version of "The Little Mermaid," the undercurrent is the same: the Mermaid, like Amos' persona, loses her voice. The jeans she wears on her human legs underline the loss of her voice: the jeans belong to her boyfriend and they have an unidentified girl's name on them. On the second verse, she screams like the bluebells in "Girl," but her scream is lost within a paper cup. All of these references also help make an essential distinction that her silence is not voluntary: she wishes to speak and is attempting to speak, but her words will not come. She wishes for someone to understand her, and the listener is left with the impression that when she does speak, it will be revelatory.[5]

Musically, "Silent All These Years" is closer in mood to "Winter" (melancholy) than "Crucify" or "Girl" (terse); the pacing, however, is less lackadaisical than "Winter." The arrangement of piano, strings, and voice(s) is simple and is developed quite subtly across the song's four-minute, twelve-second length. "Silent All These Years" begins with a nervous, hesitant piano line, and Amos uses the same line as a connection between the first and second verses. After the opening of the first verse, the arrangement builds slowly, first with Amos' vocal, then with strings, reaching its peak on each chorus. As Amos returns to the final phase of the chorus and repeats the title, the strings and her vocals are dropped, and the nervous piano line returns. The instrumental arrangement grows to its height on the bridge, the most up-tempo section of the song, supporting Amos' emotionally tinged outburst.

Compared to Amos' persona in "Girl" or "Winter," the narrator of "Silent All These Years" is easy to identify, though understanding who she is speaking or referring to is perplexing. In the first verse, Amos' persona asks another person if he will exchange places with her: is this the same "you" who will never quit speaking in the second verse? Or is there a connection between the Antichrist in her kitchen who is yelling at her in the first verse and the "you" in the second verse who never quits speaking? The reference to a second girl on each chorus, a girl whose name has been printed on the jeans she is wearing, is just as confusing. Is she simply an old girlfriend, or is she perhaps the new, intelligent girlfriend who the boyfriend claims to have found? The lack of voice, one might suggest, has garbled the thoughts of Amos' persona, creating a cast of interchangeable characters and underscoring her unrealized identity. Her own voice, it would seem, is trying unsuccessfully to rise above the din of the voices around her. The narrative point of view may be that of a young woman, then, but her identity remains unknown, even to herself.

The silence underneath "Silent All These Years" is never explicitly stated, but seems to refer in general to female silence and more specifically to female sexual trauma. Within the song, women are also silenced because men feel free to talk when they please, thus limiting a woman's opportunity to speak. Amos also suggested the song's connection to sexual trauma when "Silent All These Years" was reissued in 1997 to raise money for Rape, Abuse, & Incest National Network.

As in "Winter," "Crucify," "Precious Things," and "Girl," a choice is presented in "Silent All These Years": whether to push oneself toward speech or to remain silent. And once again, the choice seems obvious: speaking is certainly better than keeping the trauma repressed. But it is easy to imagine that Amos' persona has remained silent, became silent to begin with, because no one cared enough to listen or learn the cause of her trauma. Indeed, from the social stigma, it is easy to imagine that she feels shame for the traumatic event, even if perpetuated by someone else. To speak may be the best course, the only real course, but it also risks the possibility of further social marginalization.

"Silent All These Years" is, ironically, a song filled with words on the subject of being unable to speak. There are other ironies. While her confession of silence is made to herself within the lyric, her confession is nonetheless—as a released recording on a major record label—quite public. Also, while Amos' persona freely explores her silence, she never returns to the origins of her silence: whatever trauma she has experienced, she never confesses it. In this sense, "Silent All These Years" might be seen as exploratory, with Amos' persona only partially aware of the reasons for her own silence. As with other paradoxes in Amos' early work, there is no convenient way to resolve these contradictions: her confessions are intensely private, but presented in a public forum; her explorations are painfully candid, but cloaked in obscurity; and she seems to express a desire to move forward, but remains trapped in the past. An attempt to resolve these paradoxes would fuel her next work.

Gospels of Defiance

I've never thought of myself as a confessional writer because I associate confession with religion and needing to be absolved and forgiven.

—Tori Amos[6]

"God" and "Cornflake Girl," respectively, were the first two singles issued from *Under the Pink* (1994). The tinted black-and-white photograph of "God" shows a bust portrait of Amos, and while there is a great deal of information in the photograph, much of it is barely perceptible beneath a palette of white and light grays. The context of the cover of *Under the Pink* is much less clear, with Amos, in the lower half of the frame, wearing white and standing on an undefined, fragmented white surface, perhaps ice or pieces of tissue paper. The backdrop is grayish blue. And finally there is the cover photograph of the single "Cornflake Girl," with Amos standing inside a dark wooden box and wearing a black dress, covered by netting that resembles a fishing net. While her face is fully lighted, she stands within a shadow, a shadow that also surrounds the box she is in. In all three cases, Amos makes direct eye contact with the camera.

As with the images of the *Little Earthquake*–era recordings, Amos still seems to be appearing as Amos, but with a difference. Any awkwardness that may have appeared on earlier covers, as with her slightly questioning gaze on "Crucify," is gone. Likewise, a clear symbolic connection now exists between Amos and larger ideas that she wishes to represent. Whereas the earlier photographs feature Amos in a variety of nonconnected roles with no underlying theme, the cover art for "God," "Cornflake Girl," and *Under the Pink* features Amos in three variations on the same role, with each brought into focus with a central theme. Each image, whether dark and mysterious or light and ethereal, features a relaxed but self-assured figure, a universal image: Amos, with these three photographs, presents multiple images of a feminine deity.

Amos, by placing herself on the cover of a single titled "God," underlines this connection. On the back cover of the booklet of *Under the Pink*, Amos stands atop a giant world of fluff, watching over it. On the cover of "Corn-flake Girl," she stands like Time or the Fates in shadow, balancing the other portraits by recognizing the darker side of existence (pain, disease, death). While the representative roles of each image may spill over into one another to a certain degree, a viewer might loosely imagine these three images—wisdom ("God"), judgment ("Cornflake Girl"), and watchfulness (*Under the Pink*)—as a new feminine trinity.

In offering a female version of the deity, Amos leaves the impression that she now understands how she wishes to portray herself and how she wishes to portray the feminine ideal to which she will aspire. She may also realize that by presenting herself as the deity, she will provoke a reaction. But while each of these images openly challenges the church, male authority, and traditional female portrayal, they do so with easy confidence. Artistically speaking, Amos is in sync with her muse, offering images that connect forcefully with her new songs. These images also seem to open a new chapter in her confessional style, seemingly resolving or breaking free of previous themes that focused on vulnerability. Confession, as Amos realized on *Little Earthquakes*, could be harnessed to uncover a person's identity, but confession could also be harnessed to forge new, undreamed of identities; confession in song could be used as a public forum to reach other women who had experienced personal trauma, but confession in song could also be used as a tool to explore new horizons for women. Having confessed and explored her emotional and spiritual past on *Little Earthquakes*, Amos was now ready to carve out a new path.

"God"

> I've written a song called God . . . about patriarchal religion, and how it's just *fucked the whole thing up. Basically I say to Him, "You know, you need a babe and I've got nothing to do Tuesday and Thursday this week!"*

—Tori Amos[7]

In "God," Amos' persona directly addresses her remarks to God or the traditional idea of God, and her address is accusatory. She states directly that he does not always follow through, and asks if he needs a woman to look after him. She does admit that he makes pretty flowers, but this positive attribute does not make up for a multitude of sins and omissions, including the literal or metaphorical burning of witches. Mostly, she sketches the male deity as indifferent and lazy, driving his new four-wheel, keeping a number nine iron in the back seat, and leaving whenever the wind blows. There are also several cryptic references, the first reading like a partial inversion of the Lord's Prayer, accusing God of failing to give strength to women, and the latter asking if he would let an undefined "her" know if he decided to cause the sky to fall.

Part of the symbolism is present-day, with golf clubs and four-wheel drive vehicles painting God as the contemporary carefree man. This is juxtaposed against more archaic references to witches burning and the reference to the Lord's Prayer. The inverted Lord's Prayer holds the center of the song, though the spoken vocal by Amos is so low in the sound mix that one may need a lyric sheet to understand what she is saying. She basically says that the Lord does not give strength to women or to anyone who will destroy kings. Finally, the threat of a falling sky may point to nothing more complex than a children's story; Chicken Little believes, after being hit on the head with an acorn, that the sky is falling. It is also important within Amos' worldview that Chicken Little is female.

Musically, "God," along with "Waitress" (discussed later in this chapter), is one of Amos' most aggressive arrangements, with screeches and electric guitar adding a noisy element into the musical mixture. Some radio programmers disliked the aggressive guitar of the single, and a non-guitar version of the single was issued. Even as "God" starts, the screeches, percussion, and heavy bass are loud in the mix, creating an immediate aural impression. Amos adds emphasis to the "noisiness" by allowing all instruments to drop out when she reaches the hook referring to God's departure each time the wind blows. Here, her voice, previously supported by an echo-drenched heavenly choir, sings in a vacuum. Amos' breathy, sensual vocal also generates an immediate physical presence while underlining the irreverence of the lyric. There is also the curious "who whos" that open and close the song, an ironic reference to the woo woos scattered throughout the Rolling Stones' "Sympathy for the Devil." Combined, the noise factor and brooding minor key, like the lyric, is much more in your face than gentler pieces like "Icicle" (discussed later), delivering the lyric like a slap.

The narration of "God" is unusual in relation to Amos' early work, though the confusion of cryptic pronouns continues. While the listener assumes a female narrator is accusing God of his sins against women, neither the specifics of her life or her age seem to matter. She is simply any woman because one woman, according to her Amos' persona, has suffered just as much from God as the next. While she seems to ask God a number of questions, these questions are rhetorical: she has already made up her mind about how she feels about him. A more interesting query, perhaps, is to ask who exactly the narrator is addressing. Obviously, the title of the song and the lyrics call this person/entity God. But is she addressing the general idea of a Godhead, or the specific idea of a Christian God within Western society? While it would be easy to note Amos' Christian background as evidence for the latter position, the lyric never singles out Christianity; only God is mentioned, not his Son. Amos' persona, any woman, then, is addressing the broader idea of a God within a patriarchal culture.

One thing that is easy to lose here and that is easy to lose on many of Amos' early songs is her off-centered, black humor. If "Crucify" offers a blasphemous image of contemporary women suffering in the manner of Christ for sins not committed, then "God" is likewise blasphemous but with a difference. In a sense, "Crucify" is focused on how women suffer, and while it might offer a sacrilegious comparison between women and Christ, it infers the connection and there seems to be little dignity in it. "God" directly insults the deity, asking if he needs a woman to look after him, and suggesting that he is both lazy and indifferent to the plight of women. Amos' dark humor, however, make these insults even more bold with her careless and carefree persona offering a direct challenge that includes insults. She throws out the word "toasty" to describe witches burning, and then offers that God travels with a golf club in his car: he would rather play golf than worry about the fate of women.

"God" has a fearless quality. Amos' persona defies traditional religion and traditional ideas of God, identifying both traditions as male centered and, in regard to women, uncaring. Her anger is righteous, and, as is often true of her lyrics, she gives direct voice to thoughts that are generally not spoken out loud. In this way, the lyric to "God" is like an inverted prayer, accusatory and angry as opposed to thankful and entreating. As an inverted and very public prayer, "God," unlike "Crucify," seems less confessional than confrontational: Amos' persona is less interested in revealing her deepest feelings than challenging injustice.

But the idea of "God," as with the single's cover photograph, is not the rejection of religion or God, per se, but the rejection of how these traditions have allowed men to either harm women or treat them indifferently. If "Crucify" underlines the problem of how women suffer in contemporary society, suggesting that women partially share the burden of their own suffering, "God" places the blame directly on patriarchal power; if "Crucify" offers the choice between self-love and self-sacrifice, "God" offers that women should defy all arbitrary power. In "God," the self-absorbed complexities of ambiguity and choice represented by the self-regulated narrators of "Winter," "Girl," and "Crucify" have been replaced with a fixed vision of rebelliousness. With "God," Amos has openly declared that the traditional rules laid down by men for women are unfair and that she will no longer obey them. By implication, "God" is not a call to sisterhood but a call to arms.

"Waitress"

"Waitress" is nearly as straightforward as "God," with one waitress—Amos' persona—announcing in the opening line that she wishes to kill another waitress. Furthermore, she expresses her belief that if she kills her quickly, it will be an act of kindness. Her initially stated reason rests on the simple fact that the second waitress has worked at the restaurant a year longer than she. Later, she adds that she believes that the boys think she—the other waitress—is kind, suggesting that the narrator believes otherwise. Amos' persona is critical of her own impulses, though, expressing that she cannot believe the violence within her. Later, she also expresses her wish that she could kill this feeling toward violence. While she wishes to rid herself of these violent impulses, she nonetheless retains her basic dislike of the second waitress; this waitress, she believes, is not who she pretends to be.

The imagery in "Waitress" is fairly simple, with words like *bitch* and *kill* set against *peace* and *kindness*. Amos, however, also combines these words in ways that alter their context, offering *killing* as *kindness* and following *peace*, which is nearly spit out vocally, with *bitch*. Perhaps the most evocative line is in the last stanza, which states that there are too many stars and not enough sky. Here, the waitresses and perhaps all women are the stars, while the sky is the limited field they must play upon; this limited field includes competition with one another, and competition with one another for men. One other image is presented, a club sandwich, when the narrator wonders where the waitress' power lies; unlike the reference to stars, however, the image seems intentionally absurd.

Musically, "Waitress" starts broodingly in a minor key with piano accompaniment, but builds into a mesh of thrashing percussion and an angry vocal that peaks on each chorus. As with "God," one might describe "Waitress" as alternative rock, save for the quieter piano passages. Unlike "God," however, "Waitress" begins ominously, with Amos' emotive vocalizing set against a bare backdrop of percussion and sweeping reverberation that pans between the right and left speakers. As she utters the first words at a sluggish ballad pacing, a menacing undertow accompanies her piano. Amos pauses briefly before the chorus and returns to wordless vocalizing, creating a small, quiet space before unleashing the noise fest of the chorus and her angry vocal. Electric guitar and thrashing percussion accompany the vocal, and temporarily, the piano seems to disappear from the mix. Interestingly, Amos brings "Waitress" to close without repeating the chorus, allowing it to fade out with the third verse. While this seems to place an emphasis on her persona's fading anger, the residue of the dynamic chorus remains.

The narration in "Waitress" is simpler than much of the narration in Amos' earlier songs on *Little Earthquakes*. A waitress is simply expressing her negative feelings toward another waitress, and her belief that she should feel differently about her than she does. Perhaps the oddest thing about the narration is the rarity of the point of view: within popular music, few songs seem to have been written from the point of view of a waitress. It is also interesting that despite her strong feelings toward the other waitress, she offers mostly weak or trivial reasons for her feelings: the other waitress has worked at the restaurant longer, and, in the last verse, there is the insinuation that the other waitress is not as kind as she appears. At the same time, abstract reflections reveal Amos' persona as thoughtful, leaving the impression that she understands her own pettiness. As such, she is as divided as earlier Amos' personas, struggling to reconcile an inner conflict more than her stated conflict with the other waitress.

As in "God," "Waitress" succeeds on two accounts: (1) because of its dark humor, and (2) because of its directness. Amos once again shows that she has an ability to get to the heart of a particular subject—the competition between women—and confess or speak what is seldom said out loud. Amos' persona hates the waitress and says that she hates the waitress; she understands that her hatred clashes with her belief system and wishes that she felt differently; nonetheless, she hates the waitress and cannot find anything good to say about her. Here, Amos admits that female competition is a problem, but one that will not be easily solved because of the limited field that women have been allowed to play upon. Even waitresses, after all, are judged on body image and personality, and must compete with one another for customers and tips.

The explicit anger expressed by Amos' persona is made more palpable by the lyric's dark humor. By combining words like *peace* and *bitch*, and by offering the idea that killing someone quickly would be an act of kindness, her humor helps balance the overall harshness of the lyric and its delivery. The direct delivery also infuses the lyric with humor, shocking the listener by calling the waitress a bitch and saying, without qualification, that she wishes to kill her. Even Amos' delivery of the line stating that she believes in peace is aggressive: the listener may take her at her word, though she never leaves the impression that she believes in peace. Overall, the black humor supports the darkness of the theme, but also keeps the lyric from seeming too melodramatic. By including humor, Amos winks at the listener: she, too, understands that admitting a desire to kill someone will seem over the top, no mater how real the feeling.

If Amos' lyric treats the subject of female competition in a straightforward manner, she nonetheless leaves an undercurrent of female anger that spills over from the song. By delivering many of the lyric's lines with such conviction, her negative expressions—wishing to kill the waitress and calling her a bitch—may leave more of a residue than the remainder of the words. In a sense, Amos has allowed her persona to confess her sin of hating the waitress while never losing her anger; confession, in other words, has not exorcised her demons, but may actually be feeding them. "Waitress," which may seem to have been designed to expunge the emotional tide of female competition, nonetheless celebrates it.

Still, within this fairly short lyric, the waitress/narrator succinctly presents her moral philosophy: she knows how she should feel, even if she does not feel that way. And while this does not resolve the dilemma presented by "Waitress," it does place the problem in the open, challenging women to recognize their own demons in regard to female competition.

"Icicle"

In "Icicle," Amos' persona seemingly narrates the story of a young girl masturbating in her hiding place as her family sings songs of praise downstairs. The loose structure of the lyric, as will be shown, allows for more than one reading of the events within the elliptical storyline. As the song opens, the young girl speaks to an icicle hanging outside her window, saying that she has a hiding place as spring approaches. In the second stanza, she mentions Easter dresses, and her father instructs those present to bow their heads as it says in the good book or Bible. The girl, however, believes that the good book is missing pages. She lies down in her hiding place, resting her head, and decides that instead of taking of the body of Christ, she prefers to take from her own body. While others are singing prayers downstairs, she is masturbating upstairs. She refers to another person who is wearing her pajamas, though whether the person is in her hiding place with her or downstairs with her family is unclear. The song ends with the expression of several vague regrets, though how they relate to the remainder of the song is unclear.

The symbolism of "Icicle" is similar to that of "God," rich in Christian imagery. The approach of spring will melt the icicle of the title, and it will also bring the young girl's sexual awakening, similar to the arrival of spring in "Winter." At the beginning of the second verse, she references a monster that an undefined "they" greet while wearing Easter dresses, though the reference is unclear. Is it religion? Christ? God? Uncles and aunts? She also offers her belief that the good book is missing pages. While the idea of missing pages may suggest any number of books left out of the Bible, such as the Apocrypha, the missing pages seem to refer more generally to the negative tone of the Bible toward sexuality and specifically female sexuality. This also works in conjunction with the imagery of Holy Communion, with Amos' persona replacing the Eucharist with autoeroticism, taking from her own body. A listener might also note the irony of the young girl's hiding place: while others pray openly downstairs, she cloisters herself away for her own kind of prayer.

Musically, "Icicle" is a virtuoso performance, with Amos accompanying herself quietly with multiple pianos (and/or keyboards). Unlike either "God" or "Waitress," then, "Icicle" surges from quietly peaceful to expressively intense. Instrumentally, two minutes of piano work precede the lyrics, with Amos slowly building the intimate mood. While there seems to be a threat of exposure in "Icicle," the piano work and vocal never suggest fragility or vulnerability as does the music in "Winter." Instead, as a familiar church instrument, the piano mimics both the build of a charismatic prayer and the young girl's sexual experience. The loudest portion of the song, as has been common in many of Amos' other songs, arrives on the bridge when her persona expresses undefined regrets. Even with this intensity, the interplay between Amos and her piano remains an intimate and private one.

On the surface, the narration of "Icicle" seems fairly straightforward, that of an adolescent girl relaying her experience, perhaps on an Easter Sunday. The nonspecific regrets expressed in the bridge near the end of the song, however, seem to be made by an older woman looking back. This redirects the listener's attention to other expressions within the song that seem to have been colored by time. While one might picture an imaginative young girl speaking to an icicle or internally describing fear as a monster, she might be less likely to articulate the idea that the Bible is missing pages or refer to her autoerotic experience as "getting off." It is common in Amos' early work to use an older narrator who is looking back at earlier events, but it is also a technique that complicates the lyric of "Icicle" considerably. In fact, the presence of an adult narrator may even scramble what may, at first, seem obvious in the song. In this scenario, it is possible that Amos' persona, and not the young girl, is addressing the icicle and masturbating. Her sexual experience, then, is mixed in with memories of her youth, allowing the narrative to overlap itself in various places between the past and the present.

This allows for at least two readings of "Icicle." Taken as the experience of a young girl's sexual awakening, "Icicle" is quite different than that of an earlier song like "Precious Things": Amos openly celebrates youthful rebellion for choosing an autoerotic experience over a traditionally religious one. While her persona expresses concern that she may get caught, she expresses no shame over her act. "Icicle" is an affirmation of emerging female sexuality, only balanced against the nonspecific regrets at the end of the song. The regret expressed later in the song, however, may indicate that while the young girl's attitude toward her body is a healthy and holy one, maintaining that attitude amid family, church, and other social pressures is difficult. What initially feels natural may later be experienced as religious guilt and shame. Still, "Icicle" leaves the listener with the image of a young girl frozen in time, untroubled by the coming of spring, and, unlike many of Amos' earlier narrators, temporarily free from guilt and shame.

Interpreting "Icicle" from the point of view of the older narrator, however, is perhaps more intriguing. In this scenario, the regret that Amos' persona experiences becomes clearer: she regrets her religious instruction as a child and its influence upon her. By mingling her memories with an autoerotic experience, she is basically defying her earlier teaching. Also, from a Christian viewpoint, "Icicle" may be more sacrilegious than "God," equating sexual ecstasy with religious ecstasy. Amos' imagery is clear: when a woman takes from her own body, she is performing an act as sacred as the Eucharist. In this sense, "Icicle" pushes the defiance Amos expressed on "God" even further, replacing traditional religious symbols and ceremonies with a spirituality centered on one's own body. It is the body and its natural desire, not the good book or traditional ceremonies like the Eucharist, that is sacred. To embrace one's sensuality, then, is a religious act, one that might be celebrated in Amos' missing pages. In this sense, the lyrics of "Icicle" become the missing pages of the good book.

An Unfinished Portrait

On "Flying Dutchman," an early B side from 1992, Amos' persona addresses her words to a young girl, saying that she understands the pressures and questions that assail her from the adult world. The adults wonder what you will be when you grow up, or whether you will amount to anything. She tells the young girl that there is an alternative, that she can visit the Flying Dutchman, a fantastical rocket ship ride that will allow her to travel from the sky toward the Milky Way; perhaps the magical rocket ship can take her anywhere. The song, more directly than most of Amos' lyrics, promotes the free-floating dreams and values of childhood over the constricting dreams and values of adulthood. The adult world clearly wishes to limit a young girl's choices early on, to lay her dreams aside as childhood playthings, and refocus her imagination on the responsibilities of adulthood. While exhilarating, this vision of unfettered childhood freedom finally seems, like the Flying Dutch-man of the song, little more than a desire to return to a less complicated preadolescent world. In this way, a desire to return to preadolescence is less a road map to a girl's future than an escapist fantasy.

By the time Amos recorded *Under the Pink*, however, she knew that escape into childhood was a beautiful but impossible dream. A woman might return to childhood temporarily, perhaps to rediscover fragments of a lost self, but she could not remain there or build a life out the past. In "Honey," a B side initially slated for inclusion on *Under the Pink*, Amos' persona must reconcile a relationship that she has held on to, even though it has become unfulfill-ing. The lyric reveals itself slowly, built around the sexually evocative line in the chorus that he has become too used to her honey. At first, it appears that her lover has grown tired of her and that the relationship—from his point of view—had become too familiar; instead, he has already left her for someone new, but has continued his tryst with Amos' persona nonetheless. Unlike the sad narrators of "Leather," "Pieces of Me," "China," and "Baker, Baker," however, Amos' persona finally brings the relationship to an end, sending him on his way like a cowboy riding into the sunset. The temptation to live in the past, whether that past is a childhood fairy tale or a relationship that has ceased to be fulfilling, is finally replaced with the bittersweet present.

The transformation also dramatically shifts the confessional format that Amos has relied on to imagine her visions. In a song like "Me and a Gun" from *Little Earthquakes*, Amos seemed willing to rely on traditional singer-songwriter methods to reveal and confess the emotional scars of her own life. If "Me and a Gun" seemed different than a Joni Mitchell song like "Blue" (1971) , this was only because the subject matter, rape, seemed more contemporary and more brutally expressed than any Mitchell song. Sung a cappella, "Me and a Gun" explicitly recounts a rape, with Amos' persona of-fering a public confession that will allow her to share this trauma with other women who have had the same experience. In a sense, then, Amos' work on *Little Earthquakes* ends here, potentially leaving her personas, like multiple personas in the work of traditional singer-songwriters, as victims. Although these personas have bravely uncovered their pasts, it seems unclear whether they will now move beyond the past or remain defined by it.

In later work like "God" and "Icicle," however, Amos has traded confes-sion for assertion, passive memory for agency. She has exchanged the psy-chology of untangling one's past with a righteous affirmation to live in the present, whatever that may entail. Even when affirming the present, though,

Amos either refuses or is frequently unable to pull the fragments of her vision into a whole. The listener may never know why her persona would rather hang with the raisin girls in "Cornflake Girl," or, in another *Under the Pink* song, what it means that her and her friends are in the wrong band ("The Wrong Band"). In Amos' lyrical world, logic and clarity are frequent casualties to the deeper truths of waking dreams and buried memories. Ultimately, her vision, dredged from the emotional depths of her own life, can only be revealed piecemeal; like breadcrumbs in a fairy tale or missing pages from the good book, her piecemeal vision offers the listener a rich lyrical and musical portrait of contemporary women writ large. More than that, it is a vision that offers women the chance to embrace the present and move into the unknown.

Notes

1. Sharon Lamb, *The Secret Lives of Girls: What Good Girls Really Do—Sex Play, Aggression, and Their Guilt* (New York: Free Press, 2001), 41.

2. Jacob Grimm and Wilhelm Grimm, "Snow White." *Grimms' Tales for Young and Old*, trans. Ralph Manheim (New York: Doubleday, 1977), 184).

3. Marina Warner, *From the Beast to the Blond: On Fairy Tales and Their Tellers* (New York: Farrar, Straus and Giroux, 1994), 390.

4. Liz Evans, *Women, Sex and Rock 'n' Roll: In Their Words* (San Francisco, CA: Pandora, 1994), 7.

5. Jean Chevalier and Alain Gheerbrant, *The Penguin Dictionary of Symbols* (New York: Penguin, 1996).

6. Carla A. DeSantis, "Tori Amos: The Crispy Cornflake Girl," *Rockrgrl*, November/December 1998, 15.

7. Evans, *Women, Sex and Rock 'n' Roll*, 7–8.

CHAPTER SEVEN

Fumbling towards Ecstasy:
Sarah McLachlan

I love music and art that show a person's duality, the beauty and the ugliness each one of us has within ourselves. To be able to love both of those aspects is a real challenge. If you succeed, you find harmony.

—Sarah McLachlan[1]

As Sarah McLachlan's "Possession" (1993) opens, the sound of an organ slowly builds into a dense sonic tapestry. The buildup lays an expectant backdrop, and as McLachlan's voice enters, the song remains suspended in ambient space. Her voice creates a slight uneasiness as she speaks/sings the first lines, rushing the delivery of each line ahead of the music. Her lead voice is accompanied by multitracked vocals that appear on the left and right channels, voices that echo symbolically—the voices that McLachlan refers to as being trapped in time—and literally as an audio echo. McLachlan's persona, speaking of isolation, night, solitude, and unsatisfied yearning, is like a voice crying in the wilderness, warming to unexpressed, unlived passion. Secluded in his own private world, he prepares to reach out to the object of his desire.

Even before "Possession" properly begins, the mingling of the warm vocals, rushed delivery, and instrumental swirl, pull the listener into its musical world, inviting her to surrender to the flow of the aural soundscape. After nearly a minute of suspended stillness, "Possession" is set in motion by percussion and a persistent bass. The voice of McLachlan's persona, rising from the thickened aural tapestry, speaks of an intense passion toward an unidentified other. The persona's passion will merge with the desired object, kissing her so forcefully as to take her breath away. In a sense, the possession of the listener by the music prepares her for possession by McLachlan's persona: within the creative space of the song, the listener is overtaken and possessed by her persona.

As is common with McLachlan's lyrics, the words of "Possession" are more impressionistic than narrative, sketching a state of mind, a mood, and disconnected emotions. It is difficult to literally interpret the meaning of "Possession," and this impressionistic approach repeats itself throughout McLachlan's work: who is the narrator and to whom is the narrator speaking? A listener can argue that this approach allows each listener to interpret the lyric personally, but one can just as easily argue that McLachlan's approach is overly ambiguous. The lyric of "Possession" is also short. At four minutes and thirty-seven seconds, "Possession" is fairly long by pop-music standards, perhaps more so because of the suspended beginning. The lyric, however, is brief, consisting of an opening verse, two regular verses, and a repeated chorus.

In the first verse, McLachlan's persona speaks of an unkind world where betrayal is the norm and truth is enslaved. The rarity of honesty he perceives in the object of his desire increases his possessiveness; he believes she is speaking to him and that they understand one another. He speaks of her words, and although he defines them as cryptic riddles and rhymes, he also says that they keep him alive; his feelings are so strong, in fact, that he wishes to breathe the same air that she breathes. In the second verse, McLachlan's character surrenders to his own desire and refers to his surrender as entering the night. He fears his overwhelming desire but is nonetheless willing to sacrifice everything, including his pride, to it. Once he has given into his own desire, allowed himself to be possessed by it, he believes that nothing stands between him and the object of his desire. Having repressed his desire, having chosen solitude for so long, he will no longer be denied.

Because the lyric never reveals how the object of his desire feels, the listener is left to interpret these emotions subjectively. Is it a possession of darkness, suggesting the unwilling surrender of another person? Or is it a possession of enveloping love, the conjoining of two souls? Does the depth of the bass add an undercurrent or counterpart that works against or worries the ethereal ambience? Or does the depth of the bass work in tandem with the seductive quality of the overall arrangement? It would be easy, it seems, to support either view of "Possession," one revealing love as the merging of two souls, a gentle surrender, the other a dark obsession where one person wishes to possess the other.

In the first scenario, a listener could view "Possession" as an attractive pop song with a typical—for a song within pop music—focus on love and desire. In this reading, "Possession" is a feel-good song accompanied by feel-good music that draws the listener into the warm swirl of desire. As McLachlan sings of possession, she is presenting the lyric from an intimate first person point of view, revealing her persona's sensuous longing for connection. The intensity of certain lyrics—kissing a person so hard as to take her breath away—expresses no more than the intensity of her persona's passion. Love, in essence, is like possession, a longed-for intermingling of two souls.

The second reading of "Possession," however, is much more troubling. Here, possession becomes an unhealthy, obsessive desire that has no relation to the feelings of the other person. Instead, McLachlan's persona has imagined a connection and assumes that the other person feels the same, that this object of his desire is personally speaking to him or signaling him in code. Within this interpretation, the uneasiness of the opening, with McLachlan's voice slightly out of time, and the persistent bass line, working like an overstimulated heart muscle, matches the character's emotional imbalance. Here, the first person delivery echoes his isolation while his attempt to reach out and connect is sabotaged by his inability or unwillingness to communicate with the object of his desire. The intensity of the lyrics, his desire to take her breath away, is a desperate attempt to awaken the passion in the other person that lies—he believes—just beneath the surface, a passion of which the object of his desire may be unaware. To love, then, is to give in to one's own passion, and to spiritually and physically possess the object of one's desire.

For fans with an in-depth knowledge of McLachlan, the interpretation of "Possession" is further complicated and prejudiced because of its basis in reality. While in the broadest sense the lyric may be about the possessive nature of love or the desire to possess or merge with another person, it was also easy to read the lyric from the point of view of an obsessed fan who longs to possess a popular singer like McLachlan. In this reading, the riddles and rhymes become the singer's lyrics, with the idea that the singer is speaking directly to a fan through her songs. This interpretation was further supported when one fan, Uwe Vandrei, sued McLachlan, stating that she had used passages from his fan letters to write "Possession." Before the case came to trial, however, Vandrei committed suicide.

Does knowledge of the backdrop of "Possession" make it more difficult for the listener to interpret the lyric and music? Does this general knowledge, that the lyric is being delivered by an obsessed fan, add depth or a dark hue to the lyric? Or was the depth and swirling undercurrent of "Possession" already apparent in the lyric and music?

Even with this information, however, it is easy to argue that the relaxed flow of "Possession's" soundscape renders much of this discussion beside the point. While set in a minor key and underpinned by heavy bass, the melody line and rich arrangement nonetheless remove the teeth from the lyric and backstory; the tone of McLachlan's multitracked vocal and the wash of the organ, guitars, and percussion create a soothing emotional setting, a comforting ambient space. Somewhere between New Age and mainstream pop, the ethereal sea of voices and aural reverberation ebb and flow like a gentle ocean tide. In a cultural feminist sense, the expressions in "Possession" are also essentially feminine. If the emotion of the female voice expresses yearning, it is no more than a universal desire that we all feel for connection, a desire with which most listeners can sympathize. The emotional mood of the music, then, smoothes all lyrical wrinkles, inviting the listener to surrender to the warmth of the singer's voice and beauty of the arrangement.

This interpretation of "Possession" is supported by what might be described broadly as McLachlan's cultural feminist approach to her music, an approach that injects her music with traditional feminine qualities. Under some strains of cultural feminism, a listener might consider the ebb and flow of the music as matching the natural rhythms and cycles unique to women. "Possession," then, describes the need to love and the need for love, the desire and fear of possession from a feminine point of view, and the movement between these polarities mimics the easy-flowing current of the music. Cultural feminism also comes into play when one considers McLachlan's image. The cover art of *Fumbling towards Ecstasy* (1993) features an idealized portrait of the singer, perhaps recalling images of St. Catherine, somewhere between spiritual and sensual ecstasy. In the photograph, McLachlan is presented as recognizably feminine within a cultural tradition of femininity.

McLachlan's cultural feminism complicates this duality between words and music in "Possession" and on the remainder of *Fumbling towards Ecstasy*. If one argues that "Possession" has a feminist message, argues that the songs on *Fumbling towards Ecstasy* have feminist messages, then these messages are in constant threat of being devalued by the music and the soft feminism of the lyrics.

Is McLachlan's music, then, merely pretty, a sophisticated but still typical example of popular music? Or does her vision run deeper, expressing a disquieting darkness beneath a calm surface? Does McLachlan, with her music, explore new modes of expression, modes that circumvent traditional male rock? Or does the production surface of her music simply draw from a melodic and harmonious pop tradition in order to sugarcoat her darker lyrics? Does McLachlan's work represent the elevation of mood over meaning?

Or does the medium of her music provide her a singular voice for artistic expression? Only by looking at both sides of McLachlan's music, only by equally weighing multiple interpretations of *Fumbling towards Ecstasy*, can the listener hope to resolve or properly evaluate these ambiguities.

Reading *Fumbling towards Ecstasy*

Mood over Meaning (Reading 1)

The title itself—*Fumbling towards Ecstasy*—is a poetic phrase, though more entangled than it might appear at first glance. Combining *fumbling* and *ecstasy* may seem playful, suggesting perhaps a sexual experience, though the word *fumbling* suggests awkwardness and lack of awareness. This is quite different than tumbling, and the middle word, *towards*, even suggests that while a person may be moving toward ecstasy, she has not yet attained ecstasy. Obtaining ecstasy, then, almost seems like an accident, something that just happens along the way. It is a happy accident, though, perhaps an accident that human biology and intelligence drives us toward. The words of the title, then, seem less concerned with specifics than a broader metaphor on life itself: as we live our lives each day and interact with others, we are clumsily moving toward ecstasy.

The photograph on the cover of *Fumbling towards Ecstasy* extends this metaphor on life. The photograph features a romantic portrait of McLachlan, captured in the throes of physical ecstasy. In one sense, the cover offers an example of what we might expect from a popular recording artist in the mainstream. Unlike the photographs of Harvey, which are frequently threatening or unnerving, or of Amos, which are frequently odd or mystically puzzling, McLachlan's image is presented as an image of desire for the viewer's pleasure. While it would be easy to point to many more provocative photographs of women as objectified artists in the broader field of popular music, the image of McLachlan nonetheless pushes the envelope within the singer-songwriter genre. Maria Raha wrote in *Cinderella's Big Score: Women of the Punk and Indie Underground*, "Album covers like Fiona Apple's *Tidal* and Sarah McLachlan's *Fumbling Towards Ecstasy* offered softly lit portraits in the tradition of Hollywood circa 1940s, lending the singers an air of ethereality."[2] The image of one moving forward in the frame, fumbling toward ecstasy, is playful, but thanks to the deeper shadows and splashes of blue-green surrounding McLachlan's lucent skin, also moody. The image, then, represents both the ecstasy of love, especially of physical love, but also the pitfalls of love gone wrong. McLachlan, after all, is pictured alone.

McLachlan notes in one of her early documentary films, *Sarah McLachlan: Fumbling towards Ecstasy Live* (1994), that when she started writing songs, she emphasized mood over meaning. She also expressed her belief that while she moves beyond this style of writing on *Fumbling towards Ecstasy*, mood remains an integral part of her vision. In the same film, she notes how she continues to relate many of her songs to specific colors: "Lots of blue—it's blue sort of melancholy and kind of a little hint of sadness . . . and cold, isolation. . . . It's romantic stuff. . . . I'm a sucker for romantic stuff. . . . Blue is a romantic color."[3] The expression of mood, then, remains integral to each song's meaning on *Fumbling towards Ecstasy*.

McLachlan's musical approach on *Fumbling towards Ecstasy* can also be seen as an extension of her own musical preferences. In a number of interviews, she has mentioned a narrow range of CDs as singular influences on her work, noting that these recordings have replenished her artistically, and that she felt no need to reach outside of them. Three of those choices, Tom Waits' *Closing Time* (1973), Talk Talk's *Spirit of Eden* (1988), and Brian Eno's *Thursday Afternoon* (1985), provide insight into the musical world McLachlan would build on *Fumbling towards Ecstasy*.

Waits may seem like the odd person out in this group, though fans of his 1970s work may remember *Closing Time* as a fairly straightforward affair. Most familiar is "Ol' '55," a winsome ballad that McLachlan would record and include as a bonus track on *The Freedom Sessions* (1995). Waits' trademark gravelly vocals are not nearly as pronounced as they would be on later material, leaving fewer rough edges to mask his unabashedly romantic appeal in songs like "I Hope That I Don't Fall in Love with You." This makes *Closing Time* fairly typical for its time period, a time period crowded with singer-songwriters, and easy to view as falling within the tradition of singer-songwriters like Joni Mitchell. In this sense, Waits served as the urban counterpart to John Prine, offering a series of clear-cut songs featuring wry observations about love and life filtered through a romantic gaze.

Eno's *Thursday Afternoon* is an entirely different kettle of fish, sixty-one minutes of ambient music with no vocals. While critics usually avoid referring to Eno's ambient music as New Age, his achieved results create a similar artifact. What is central in its relationship to McLachlan's music, however, is Eno's ability to use music to generate and extend mood. Traditional song structure of verse, chorus, and a buildup toward climax, then, is less important than creating ebb and flow, recurrent patterns, and sonic balance. Eno's extended mood montage also features a heavy emphasis on harmony, seemingly removing any dramatic conflict or sharp edges within the music. By removing these elements, he seems to have circumvented traditional Western musical motifs, motifs that have been described by some critics as masculine. Within Eno's soundscapes, then, there are no climaxes or choruses to be highlighted. Instead, the listener is left with an integrated whole that might be loosely described as Eastern or, by cultural feminists, as feminine.

McLachlan's third influence, Talk Talk, started off as a popular new wave band, but by the time *Spirit of Eden* had been issued in 1988, they had developed a more complex and less commercial sound. One thing that the listener will notice on *Spirit of Eden* is that there are only six songs, and while it might be easy to mistake it for an EP, the tracks, at a little over forty minutes, do equal album length. The individual songs, then, are quite long by traditional standards. The opening track, "The Rainbow," is over nine minutes, and three minutes of music elapse before the vocals begin. The length of songs, then, is not predicated on a barrage of words as with Bob Dylan, but on the need to integrate sound and words into an intertwining musical quilt. There even seems to be a connection, in style, arrangements, and pacing, between the six songs on *Spirit of Eden*. This makes the overall album seem more like a series of connected musical suites in which repeated themes and ideas interlock and echo one another in a similar fashion to *Thursday Afternoon*. Unlike Eno, however, Talk Talk continues to emphasize climatic moments, bursts of sound and passionately delivered lyrics, generating a more elastic emotional palette.

Loosely understood, these sources provided McLachlan a bedrock for building her own artistic methodology. She would start with basic songs within the singer-songwriter tradition, like Waits, and it is perhaps surprising how traditional her songs sound in basic and/or demo form. An unlisted, second version of "Possession," for instance, appears at the end of *Fumbling towards Ecstasy*, and it features McLachlan as a soloist, accompanying herself on piano. The simplicity of her approach echoes the earlier, piano-based songs of Joni Mitchell from *Ladies of the Canyon* (1970). McLachlan's lyrical style, however, was less concrete than Mitchell's, giving her lyrics a free-floating quality of impressionism.

The lyrics are also are intimate and open, personal and easily integrated into the listener's point of view. Attempting to limit the meaning of a specific lyric to McLachlan's autobiography or narrative logic, or an attempt to critique a lyric based on literal interpretation, is a failure to understand her open-ended approach. The lyrics on *Fumbling towards Ecstasy* are not meant to be taken literally but impressionistically. In this sense, they sketch a mood, emotion, or situation and allow the listener to fill in the details. The mood may point the listener toward a particular interpretation or feeling, but the mood does not define the subject, per se. As a result, each lyric retains a certain looseness, perhaps even an air of mystery. McLachlan noted in the documentary, *Sarah McLachlan: A Life in Music*, "[One of] the beautiful things about songwriting and my desire to leave things vague to a certain degree, because I want people to draw their own stories, or their own—whatever the song does to them, however it moves them—that's what's important to that person."[4]

With the initial building block of a basic song, McLachlan moves to the next stage. The fact that alternative, basic versions of McLachlan's material are easily available helps clarify the transformation that takes place when she enters the second part of the creation process. Here, she creates—with the aid of her producer—ambient soundscapes to accompany her songs, adding musical accompaniment that enhance and mirror the mood of the words and melody. In this fashion, McLachlan's songs become larger collages of mood and sound, a rich blend of ambient pop and New Age.

While tracing McLachlan's influences through her favorite albums might make the process of her artistic maturation look like a natural one, she worked through this process one album at the time. Even listening to her previous album, *Solace* (1991), it is clear that she had not discovered this happy medium. *Fumbling towards Ecstasy*, then, is the accumulation of McLachlan's artistic method, one that remains nearly intact on her follow-up album, *Surfacing*, three years later in 1997. The success of her work during this period, in fact, may even be attributed to her comfort level: the match between voice, music, and vision seems a perfect mesh between 1993 and 1997.

McLachlan's relationship with producer Pierre Marchand has also played a large role in the realization of her artistic process. With Marchland's studio expertise, McLachlan's songs are built from multiple elements—vocals, keyboards-synthesizers, guitars, and percussion—to create a carefully layered track that, with the various parts working in unison, leave the impression of sheer simplicity. Even when parts of the arrangement counter or complicate the melody in some way, an overall balance is reached between each strand until the arrangement forms an intricate web of sound and reverberation. In this way, *Fumbling towards Ecstasy* creates a rich harmonic surface that leaves little to distract the listener from the flow of the music and voice.

This layering is illustrated on a version of "Plenty" that appears on *The Freedom Sessions* (1995). This EP includes a number of alternate versions of songs from *Fumbling towards Ecstasy* along with a live version of Waits' "Ol' 55." In this version of "Plenty," McLachlan and producer Marchand have built the track from multiple overdubs of vocals (McLachlan's), keyboards, and drum programming. The track is very much like a stripped-down version of the official album track from *Fumbling towards Ecstasy*, and McLachlan notes that many of these vocals were used in the final version of the track. She also wrote in the liner notes of *The Freedom Sessions*, "This version started in the studio early on during the making of *Fumbling towards Ecstasy* with a vocal experiment of over-dubbing different sounds to make a collage that would lie under the lead vocal."[5] Together, the multiple vocal parts create a rich tapestry that serves as a unified background or underpinning.

The final version of "Plenty" is even more complex, with electric guitar and percussion added. One might argue that certain elements, a stray guitar phrase or McLachlan's emphasis on particular words, create a countervoice that pulls the listener out of the flow of the song. For instance, at the end of the first chorus there is a short, dramatic instrumental passage featuring electric guitar crescendos and industrial percussion, sounds that might be said to support the violence of the emotion expressed in the lyric. A listener might also consider the emotional emphasis McLachlan's vocal places on the second verse disruptive, especially in the latter half of the verse that follows this instrumental passage. These emotional upsurges, however, are less variations or interruptions than—as with Talk Talk's *Spirit of Eden*—extensions of her emotional palette. If a guitar or voice is emphasized, then, it rises up from the arrangement, coloring the passage of music, but never overly detracting from the overall soundscape.

McLachlan finally enriches and underpins the musical world of *Fumbling towards Ecstasy* with her connection to nature and the natural, enfolding her philosophical bent quietly into the fabric of her work. In interviews centered on the release of *Fumbling towards Ecstasy*, she frequently spoke of her isolation in the Canadian wilderness for seven months while writing for the album. Here, she reconnected with herself and the countryside around her, discovering her own rhythms and natural self. The process of deprogramming, however, would take time.

> When I was making *Fumbling*, I went a little crazy because I was living in this cottage by myself in the woods for seven months and it was winter, about minus 35 degrees Celsius every day. It was just hellishly cold, and I regressed to animal form. I went a little nuts. I had just come off of the road again from a year of touring and had been with people 24 hours a day. To go from that to complete nothingness, to complete solitude was just such a shock.[6]

In essence, the philosophy that underlines McLachlan's work during this period, and the philosophy underlining her feminism, was one of harmony with one's self and harmony with the world around you. For McLachlan to return to nature, then, was to return to her natural rhythms and true self;

for McLachlan to create new songs, then, was to follow a process that would expel elements that worked against this harmony:

> In feeling so connected to nature I tapped into something great. It made me realize how incredibly tiny I was in comparison to the universe, but at the same time I felt really connected to it and really important in it, and it gave me a real freedom. I didn't edit myself. I just let things flow. I have never felt so strong or so in touch with everything as at that point.[7]

As the notes of the piano sound out quietly on the reprise of "Possession," McLachlan radiates the calm acceptance of one who has expelled her demons and surrendered to both the dark and light of love.

The Dark Stuff (Reading 2)
> *If the lyrics are going to be dark, I have to temper it with some nice-sounding music or it will be too much. . . . People don't want to be hit over the head.*
>
> —Sarah McLachlan[8]

McLachlan borrowed her title for *Fumbling towards Ecstasy* from a well-known Wilfred Owen poem, "Dulce et Decorum Est." The image in the poem—one of fumbling as a dark kind of ecstasy—is a haunting one, with World War I soldiers fumbling for gas masks during an attack. In the poem, one soldier fails in his fumbling, and is soon drowned in a "green sea" of nerve gas. The narrator describes his failure, struggle, and fate in detail, noting that if anyone could follow the wagon—as the narrator had—where they had tossed the soldier, they would never again say how honorable it was to die for one's country.

This will perhaps seem like an odd reference point to underpin a pop album with a heavy focus on relationships. But "fumbling" works as a far-reaching metaphor, one that finds poetry in life's darker moments, a blind dance as we clumsily search for happiness on our way toward death. In this blindness, men and women play a dangerous game with one another, searching for an elusive thing called "ecstasy," but frequently crippling themselves and each other in the process. Recalling reading Owen, McLachlan told an interviewer, "[He] wrote about being in the field in the war and all the horrors that went on. But somehow, without glamorizing or romanticizing it, he made it incredibly beautiful. In the same breath, he'd be talking about something horrendously grotesque."[9] Love is perhaps the purest form of ecstasy, but love can take many forms: possessive love, physical love, love until death, and love as betrayal. The pitfalls may seem to outweigh the benefits, the search for ecstasy—even for a moment—may seem no more than an impossible dream. But to live without love or to close one's self off from love is to live without the possibility of ecstasy or of "fumbling towards" ecstasy. The metaphor of a man reaching for a gas mask may seem an extreme metaphor for the search for love, but it serves to focus attention on the dark mood and potential despair beneath McLachlan's vision: love has many dark corners, and ecstasy may never be obtained.

The photograph on the cover of *Fumbling towards Ecstasy* continues this metaphor, capturing McLachlan's image in the midst of her own fumbling. In the photograph, she seems to be moving forward, caught in the ecstasy of the moment and unaware where it is taking her. But her ecstasy, represented by her expectant face—parted lips, half-closed eyes—is also surrounded by heavy shadows. In essence, McLachlan presents herself as an idealized figure, embracing desire, spirituality, and ecstasy as inseparable, unveiling herself as a symbolic spiritual figure for a new era. Like Tori Amos on the cover of the single "God," McLachlan presents herself as an image of the Goddess, reveling in her sensuous nature, but also expanding her femininity by combining it with spirituality and—as cover art—presenting it publicly. It is an accepting image that embraces the dark and light, the physical and spiritual, an image that embraces all sides of femininity. Finally, it is the image of someone fumbling for her own gas mask, lost in a sea of green, bravely, perhaps carelessly, moving towards ecstasy.

When thinking of the darkness that underpins *Fumbling towards Ecstasy*, it is also interesting to note McLachlan's multiple references in interviews to personal experiences that might be felt within the texture of the songs, even though these influences may not necessarily be spelled out within individual lyrics. One reference, for instance, was to a trip that McLachlan made to Thailand and Cambodia to work on a documentary about AIDS. During the nine days of filming, she would witness both the current destitution of AIDs and the historical memory of Pol Pot's killing fields, destitution that far surpassed anything she had experienced at this point in her own life. In *Muse* magazine, McLachlan said that she knew she would be unable to prepare herself mentally for what she would experience on the trip. Even though she realized that it would be shocking, the actual experience was even more overwhelming than she had imagined. Within the darkness, however, McLachlan would find the possibility of balance. In one particular instance, she visited an outdoor museum in the Killing Fields where eight thousand skulls had been retrieved from a nearby site. At the same time, she recalled, it was a beautiful day, and beside the museum, schoolchildren were singing. She described the experience as both heartbreaking and transcendent.[10]

A second reference was to a documentary that McLachlan had watched on AIDS, *A Promise Kept*, which would have a direct bearing on one of *Fumbling towards Ecstasy*'s songs, though once again, not in an obvious way. The song, "Hold On," does focus on death, but AIDS is never mentioned. On *VH1 Storytellers—Sarah McLachlan*, she recalled her inspiration:

> I was watching a documentary called *A Promise Kept*. It was made in Canada, it was about this woman who discovered her fiancé was HIV-positive. And basically, the story followed her and her husband. They got married. He got progressively sicker and she took care of him right up until the end. She was telling the story with just such beautiful clarity and honesty. It struck home in a way that I couldn't really describe except by writing this song. And I really feel like it's something that came out of me through her.[11]

Finally, McLachlan referenced how disturbing a number of fan letters had become. In her real life as a singer who had found a modicum of fame in the early 1990s, she discovered the love of her fans also had a darker side:

> I had a few obsessed fans who were writing me a lot of letters based on this romantic, sexual fantasy world that I wasn't in, but they believed me to be there with them. Writing "Possession" appeased me—it was just sort of a sicko fantasy in my brain that wouldn't go any further.[12]

Filtered through the dark recesses of McLachlan's own mind, *Fumbling towards Ecstasy* is a dark journey of betrayal, sacrifice, and possession that eventually leads to redemption, revealing love as a chimera that one must embrace in spite of the dangers. These dark undercurrents, however, are not openly apparent, because within the world of *Fumbling towards Ecstasy*, two levels of experience greet the listener: one, an ethereal surface of shimmering beauty; the other, a dark lyrical swirl. One calms and comforts the listener, whispering that everything will be all right, while the other reveals a seductive undertow, pulling the listener into the deeper current. The two are intricately connected, the first preparing the listener for the latter and the latter adding deeper hues to the sonic beauty. While this may seem like a surprise attack, first lulling the listener and then delivering unpleasant news, it might be more accurately described as a measure of sweetness to balance a bitter pill.

This binary, however, is less than perfect: there are a number of places on *Fumbling towards Ecstasy* where the music is born out of chaos, suggesting that order—in music as in life—may be temporarily held together, but only within an artificial structure like a song or album. In everyday life, fumbling may be the norm.

"Possession"

The music of "Possession" begins in slow motion, a dream-like opening that is a repeated musical pattern on several of *Fumbling towards Ecstasy*'s songs. The musical landscape forms only slowly, as though it were being born out of chaos. After nearly a minute, McLachlan's vocal begins haltingly, with her persona's words struggling to rise from the musical tapestry. Why, a listener might ask, is so much time required to set a mood or begin a song? In part, the elapsed time serves to set the darkened mood, but it also serves to imitate a voice deeply buried within an emotional tapestry: McLachlan's persona's effort to speak is one that requires a great deal of effort. This intensity is born out of great frustration, perhaps driven by an inability to connect emotionally and physically with other people. The person with whom the narrator has become obsessed must carry the burden of all of his fantasies and frustrations, must meet an impossible standard of his expectations. The voice of McLachlan's persona, out of time, hesitant, and alone, rushes ahead in a struggle to synchronize with the music.

"Possession" represents love as suffocating, as the desire to possess or be possessed by another. In a straightforward sense, the word *possess* expresses McLachlan's persona's desire to possess another person, perhaps not unlike her (McLachlan). Possession also seems to be a point of demarcation: the persona has stepped over the garden variety "obsession" or "fixation" into the realm of stalkers and the capacity to cause harm. In an interview preceding the release of *Fumbling towards Ecstasy*, McLachlan offered a clue to the narrator she wished to capture: "For 'Possession,' I put myself into the rapist/murderer's point of view. I wrote it from his perspective."[13] The song, then, was more than criticism of fans and more than criticism of possessive love; it was also an exercise in imagination, an attempt to understand these dark desires within herself.

This may also remind us that the word *possession* can be interpreted within a religious context. Within this context, the narrator is possessed by the dark force of his desire. The path that he dreads to take as he moves toward the song's conclusion is one that he no longer feels capable of controlling. He moves by compulsion, by an elemental force fed by his naked and concentrated desire; his very movement toward the object of his desire is not unlike a "fumbling towards ecstasy." But it is a badly confused fumbling, partly because it is so disconnected from the object of his desire; he believes he knows her; he believes, without knowing, that she wishes for the same thing as him. His path, then, is a course set for collision, an unwanted imposition that promises to end in violence. Literally, his unchecked and unwished for kisses promise to take her breath away.

The intensity of "Possession" seems to be momentarily relieved at other places on *Fumbling towards Ecstasy*, but the respite is often a chimera. Once again, the listener finds herself seduced by the rich textures of the sound, only to be caught once again in a riptide.

The lilting surface and easy pacing of "Wait" belies the murky nuances that make up the song's lyrics. The opening stanza mentions a blackened sky, empty dreams, and vultures that stand in wait—hardly good signs. An anonymous "we" has dreamed of renewal, only to see its hope fail. Now, McLachlan's persona remains with her lover, surveying the failure and accessing their future together. The lyric, then, weaves two separate and very loose narratives, one referring back to the disillusionment of youthful dreams, the other referring to the narrator's inability to return the love she's been given. The chorus also focuses on youthful dreams and the desire of each generation to start fresh with its own ideas and idealism. McLachlan's own interpretation of her lyric focuses on this part of the narrative, noting the disappointment the young experience when dreams fail. Each new generation believes it can accomplish what the previous one did not, only to find that they are no different. After learning this, a residue of disappointment remains, leaving one's dreams empty, and leaving one temporarily unable to respond to life and love.

As one might guess, this night-drenched mood, filled with empty dreams and a darkened sky, is a bad omen for the lovers. McLachlan's disillusioned persona finds herself—in the face of disappointment—wishing for sympathy in the form of a lover, believing that throwing herself into a relationship will ease her distress. Because of her disheartened state, however, she finds herself incapable of receiving what he offers, or perhaps finds herself afraid that a new disappointment will be more than she can handle. In the final verse, her motive becomes clearer. Here, she tells her lover that even if she leaves him, her departure in no way reflects her feelings about him; at the present, she is simply unable to return what he offers. The word *wait*, then, is symbolic of both the wait for a new generation who will once again believe in dreams and the time needed before McLachlan's persona will be ready to experience the give and take of love again.

The dark flow, moving from unbalanced love in "Possession" to premature love in "Wait," continues with "Plenty," a lyric focusing on love as betrayal. The lyric is much more complex than the average "love gone wrong song," more an impressionistic sketch than a filled out narrative. The listener knows nothing of McLachlan's persona or her lover, only that the depth of her feeling causes the shock of the betrayal to register more piercingly. A listener might call her sentiment toward love old-fashioned, when she expresses that once she believed that she would be completed in love, and describes her life as an empty space that was filled by her lover. So deep was her faith and commitment, she refused to listen to others when they questioned the faithfulness of her lover. This refusal to listen may even lead the listener to the uncomfortable revelation that her lover had never been faithful.

There is also an odd reference near the end of the second verse that almost seems like an opening of a new theme, though it remains undeveloped within "Plenty." When McLachlan's persona learns that her lover has been unfaithful, her world comes to a standstill. Within that moment, however, she learns something new about herself: she discovers within that moment that she feels free in a way that she has never felt. It is as though she has discovered, in the midst of her world crashing, another possible way of living.

This theme is fleshed out later on *Fumbling towards Ecstasy* in "Elsewhere." Here, McLachlan offers a flow between two states that may remind a listener of Pete Seeger's "Turn! Turn! Turn!" There is a continual movement between companionship and solitude, and the vacillation between the two states, the song suggests, is the natural order of relationships. Daughters cling to mothers, then move toward independence; lovers obliterate the individual self, forming a union of desire, then move once again toward self-reflection, quiet, and solitude. Even within intimate relationships, a listener might conjecture, there is always a balance between sharing and privacy, between common desires and individual growth.

The middle of *Fumbling towards Ecstasy* expands on the disappointments of love, from physical and emotional abuse ("Good Enough"), to the vulnerability of unselfish love ("Mary"), to smothering love ("Circle"), and to love as a game of deception ("Ice"). Each of these songs, seemingly, offers yet another reason to avoid love. These songs, and this expansion on the theme of disappointment in love, are further supported by the texture and mood of the music. With relaxed ballad pacing, McLachlan's voice, and warm harmony, "Good Enough," "Mary," and "Elsewhere" flow easily into one another. The occasional tempo change, as with "Circle," enriches and worries the emotional grain of *Fumbling towards Ecstasy*, lest the musical soundscape become overly familiar to the listener. Even when the pacing remains relaxed, as it does later in the album with "Fear," McLachlan complicates the sonic tapestry by adding a hesitant opening and a mesh of voices and sound.

The impressionistic narrative of "Good Enough," building its structures from two mise-en-scènes, includes one of McLachlan's darkest lyrics. In the second verse, an adult asks a child if she would like candy and adds that the child's mother has already given her permission. The child, however, tells her that she cannot come outside. McLachlan's persona then fills in the backstory, noting that the girl's shoulder has been cracked in an act of violence, and that she has been left frightened. There is a similar dark mood in "Ice," though the game of deception is closer to emotional abuse. McLachlan's persona seems to have been deceived and seduced by a man who—from the start—meant her harm, and she damns his behavior. The delicate arrangement of "Ice" mimics the thinness of the ice mentioned in the first line of the lyric as well as the fragility of McLachlan's persona. It is unclear, however, whether she is aware of his game from the beginning, and if so, willing to accept what he offers, even if it is offered dishonestly. Either way, she assures the listener that he can never win his game: he has done no more, she believes, than deceive a fool.

"Hold On" focuses on the death of a loved one, and in this case, was inspired following the viewing of a documentary about AIDs, *A Promise Kept*. *A Promise Kept*, however, is never mentioned in the lyric of "Hold On." Instead, the listener focuses on McLachlan's persona, who expresses both her willingness to do anything for her lover or friend and her prayer to God to take care of him when he dies. Her friend/lover is ill, but the illness is undefined; each day that remains is held precious. While the bumpy, emotional ride of *Fumbling towards Ecstasy* is hardly over, it does peak on "Hold On." While possession and betrayal are painful, the ultimate disappointment in love is death itself, robbing you of your loved one.

Intriguingly, however, "Hold On" diverges from other songs on the album by focusing on a disappointment that cannot be blamed on anyone. Still, the disappointment is profound. Even on the rare occasion when your blind search for love leads to ecstasy, you have no guarantee how long it will last and no guarantee that it will not be brought to a sudden end by death. Death, then, is the ultimate irony of this fumbling, adding one more element of chance to the nature of love. It also adds another level of fear. If we are afraid to love because we worry that lovers will betray or smother us, then we are also afraid to love because our lover might—because of death—leave us without warning. As we have no guarantees in life, we have no guarantees in love.

The following song, "Ice Cream," offers perhaps the most abrupt shift on *Fumbling towards Ecstasy*, a seeming love song in the midst of love gone wrong songs. While "Ice Cream" is clearly upbeat, especially following the first nine songs, it is less straightforward and holds more darkness than is immediately evident. The tracking itself, allowing "Ice Cream" to follow "Hold On," is seemingly perverse. Why follow a song about love and death with one about sensual love? One about the pain of watching your friend/lover die with one that compares love to ice cream? In a sense, though, the transition is logical within the world of *Fumbling towards Ecstasy.* If "Hold On" focuses on the physicality of death, then "Ice Cream" focuses on the physicality of love, comparing it to the sensation of eating ice cream and chocolate. The songs are at opposite ends of the same continuum. "Ice Cream," then, is a psychic journey that remembers the sweetness of sensual love, a journey that remembers the electricity of a new lover's touch. In one interview, McLachlan even joked about the sexual nature of the lyric:

> Well, when you bring food and love into the same sentence, sex is definitely going to come into play. . . . When you think of love and chocolate, personally, I think of . . . Well, I don't want to get into it! Lots of things come to mind. Ice cream, same thing. Licking ice cream out of someone's navel is wonderful. Especially if you're in love with them. Whipped cream and mangoes actually is the best.[14]

If "Hold On" represents the emotional depths of *Fumbling towards Ecstasy,* then "Ice Cream" represents a turning point. The remainder of the album moves toward letting go of pain and hurt, of moving beyond fear to quietly accept and make peace with the deeply ingrained need to love and be loved. If "Ice Cream" represents a turning point, both "Fear" and "Fumbling towards Ecstasy" map out the next step in the healing process. Even as you leave behind the fear that others may hurt you, you may still express doubt before reentering the fumbling: what if you have nothing to give to others? But this question—what do we have to give and what will others see in us?—is clouded in mystery like love itself. Worrying about what we have to offer, then, may be no more than one more evasive maneuver that prevents us from letting go of the past. As the album dovetails into "Fumbling towards Ecstasy," McLachlan's persona accepts or gives in to her need for love and her need to express and feel all of her natural feelings—rage, sadness, and love—that well up inside of her.

Intriguingly, a second version of "Possession" is tacked on to the end of "Fumbling towards Ecstasy," and the track is not listed on the album credits. While using the same song to open and close *Fumbling towards Ecstasy* may seem a little too clear-cut thematically, the second version of the song presents much more than a convenient coda or bonus cut. Within the album's expansive narrative, "Possession" provides the first glimpse of disappointment in love, while the second version reveals McLachlan's final thoughts and her reconciliation with the possibility of love. In both "Fear" and "Fumbling towards Ecstasy," McLachlan's personas have let go of the past and are moving forward, despite pain, despite betrayal, and despite uncertainty. At first glance, then, "Possession" may seem to be a poor choice to build on this theme of reconciling oneself to the need for love and the need for connection as part of the human condition. The lyric, after all, is exactly the same. The difference, however, is embedded in McLachlan's vocal performance and the arrangement. Performing solo, she turns the original meaning of "Possession" inside out, offering a quiet resolution to the turmoil that has preceded it.

Intriguingly, the opening of this second version of "Possession" is—at its beginning—more chaotic than the original. Even before the noise, there is a long, forty-plus second pause with no sound at all. For the listener unfamiliar with the album, it would appear that *Fumbling towards Ecstasy* was over. This silence makes way for the chaotic noise of instruments at the beginning of the track, an anarchic sound that may remind the listener of a rock band warming and tuning up before a performance. This gives way to the simplicity of the opening notes of "Possession" on piano, followed by McLachlan's voice. Unlike every song on *Fumbling towards Ecstasy*, nothing is double-tracked here, leaving the listener with a warm sound that might be referred to as natural or authentic. It is as though McLachlan is taking a moment at the end of the album to reveal herself, to say what she has personally learned during the journey of making *Fumbling towards Ecstasy*. The possession by love, possession by a lover, and possession of a lover need neither be suffocating nor overpowering, neither something to fear nor resist. Having exorcised the demons, she is ready to let love be whatever love will be.

Reconciling *Fumbling towards Ecstasy*

There are times when her music does reek too much of new-age candles, herbal teas and pre-Raphaelite maidens in leafy glades.

—Robin Eggar[15]

Women have a unique understanding of other women that men, for the most part, just don't have.

—Sarah McLachlan[16]

While the end result of any artistic statement like *Fumbling towards Ecstasy* may seem natural, artists make a number of choices—which songs they wish to record, which arrangements they wish to use, how they wish to record the songs, and so on—during the process. When McLachlan released a number of earlier versions of these songs on the *Freedom Sessions* in 1995, she provided a glimpse into her working process and also a reminder of the choices she had made: the songs on *Fumbling towards Ecstasy*, in fact, could have been recorded and presented in a number of different ways. In trying to reconcile divergent readings of *Fumbling towards Ecstasy*, a listener might ask: were McLachlan's choices in approach and arrangements the best way to record the material she chose to record? Or were there other possibilities that would have clarified the album's darker undercurrent? To make this more specific, would a different presentation of McLachlan's music on *Fumbling towards Ecstasy* have resolved the album's ambiguity between sonic beauty and lyrical darkness?

One of the best examples of a different possible direction for *Fumbling towards Ecstasy* is McLachlan's recording of "Ice" on *The Freedom Sessions*. As an experiment, she played electric guitar on the track. And while electric guitar is hardly unusual across the expanse of *Fumbling towards Ecstasy*, it generally worked smoothly within the dynamic of each arrangement. McLachlan abandons this principle on this earlier version of "Ice," adding biting, stray electric guitar notes to a spare mix of percussion and plodding bass line. McLachlan viewed this version as a failed experiment:

> This was one of my first attempts to control an electric guitar plugged into an amp turned to 10. I'm not sure what the plan was but it certainly added some tension, if not distraction, to the original soft acoustic feel. Often mistakes are the best way to learn how not to do it.[17]

Is this version of "Ice" a failed experiment? It surely wouldn't have fit well with the other material on *Fumbling towards Ecstasy*, and a listener could also argue whether McLachlan's smoother vocal style is a poor fit for an edgy approach. But biting guitar and plodding bass do build an equally effective arrangement that generates a creepy, haunting mood that matches the deception of the lyric. The intention of the lyric is clarified and, because of the dissonance, the theme is communicated even without the words. Here, there is little chance for the listener to misunderstand "Ice."

At other places on *The Freedom Sessions* McLachlan flirts with the blues. This may seem like an odd choice, because there is little about her work on *Fumbling towards Ecstasy* that even suggests the blues. Even McLachlan's vocal style might be referred to as faux soul, because most of the blues influences have been erased. As with her edgy version of "Ice," however, there seems to be—by borrowing from the blues—an attempt to achieve a more authentic feel, not unlike the second version of "Possession." This is further bolstered by using a stripped-down arrangements. Under the influence of the blues, a different version of "Elsewhere" has been radically altered, and McLachlan, at least during the verses, even adopts a looser vocal style and slurs her syllables. Instead of piano, acoustic slide guitar dominates the instrumental arrangement. Recorded live, "Elsewhere" has the feeling of a loose jam that develops spontaneously. If McLachlan's approach seems less effective here than on the disjunctive "Ice," it nonetheless captures her searching for a fresh way to deliver her lyrics.

A listener might note that neither of these efforts works as well as the finished versions, but it is difficult, in each case, to know what stage of the recording process these songs had reached. Neither "Ice" nor "Elsewhere" sound finished on *The Freedom Sessions*. With more polish, both may have provided a totally different blueprint for *Fumbling towards Ecstasy*, and both would have provided a blueprint that differed radically from McLachlan's easy-flowing pop.

There is one other side of McLachlan's musical personality mentioned earlier in this chapter that can be found on demos, singles, and live tracks, one that seemingly rejects all artifice in recording. Whether listening to the second, stripped-down version of "Possession" at the end of *Fumbling towards Ecstasy*, or hearing the demo of "Mary," McLachlan, at her base, draws heavily from the traditional singer-songwriter tradition. She lists both Joan Baez and Cat Stevens as early influences, and she recorded a version of Joni Mitchell's "Blue." Both the unplugged approach and the grittier blues approach seem to be attempts to maintain an intimacy and direct connection to an audience that may seem lost in the artifice of pop production values. The influence of pop production inserts an ambiguity into the singer-songwriter genre that is difficult to resolve. A singer-songwriter promises an audience an intimate connection, but the wrong kind of music—perhaps overly produced, perhaps overly complicated—may work against this aim, creating a situation where the music works against itself.

The final results of McLachlan's musical vision on *Fumbling towards Ecstasy* do transcend the traditional singer-songwriter approach, enriching the more traditional approach but never losing intimacy. She stops short, however, of creating a style that could be described as truly innovative, or of creating a style that can deliver the darker side of her vision clearly and forcefully. Within the atmosphere of the studio, McLachlan and Marchand's approach complicates the singer-songwriter tradition by combining it with a rich musical tapestry that may remind the listener of the work of innovators such as Brian Eno and Talk Talk or even Sinéad O'Connor. But McLachlan and Marchand steer these songs toward a mainstream, pop tradition, combining an ethereal sound with ambiguous lyrics. By moving in the direction of mainstream pop, McLachlan and Marchand limit both the depth and emotional range of *Fumbling towards Ecstasy*, and by doing so, limit the impact of the album.

McLachlan's musical vision does present a darker inner texture, but her overall approach, from her impressionistic lyrics to her New Age pop structures, is unable to deliver that darker vision convincingly. Her vision also suffers from its commitment to a singular mood, a "blue sort of melancholy and kind of a little hint of sadness," a mood that holds awkward ground somewhere between melancholy and sensuality.[18] As a result, her musical approach is too singular for an expansive artistic statement. While it would be unfair to categorize her work as a calculated combination of pop tunesmith and traditional singer-songwriter, it is likewise difficult to totally sell her work as a radical departure from either category.

This leads us to look back at the content of *Fumbling towards Ecstasy* itself and attempt to comprehend how far McLachlan has wandered from the singer-songwriter tradition as defined by Mitchell, Baez, and others. While it may seem less than obvious, love remains triumphant on *Fumbling towards Ecstasy*, whether a listener reads McLachlan's work as light or dark. In either reading, love is the chosen path by the time the listener arrives at "Fumbling towards Ecstasy." But even in earlier songs on the album, love is always present, and McLachlan's heroines are always filled to the brim with the capacity to love. Love may be betrayed in "Plenty," but McLachlan's persona expresses that she would—had she not been betrayed—have remained committed for life. To give unselfishly of oneself, as in "Mary," may open a woman to exploitation, but to give love unselfishly is a gift in itself. The potential to love is a given in these songs, regardless of how that love is treated, and seemingly, in McLachlan's musical world, the capacity to love is a woman's gift.

By presenting multiple takes on what love is and is not across the expanse of *Fumbling towards Ecstasy*, McLachlan has offered a much more complex point of view than the average pop album that concerns itself with relationships. Still, the content of McLachlan's songs is much closer to cultural feminism, a more softly focused feminism not unlike her portrait on the cover of *Fumbling towards Ecstasy*. In "Mary," a woman gives to others selflessly, hoping that they will not take too much from her; in "Plenty," a woman has placed all of her belief in the power of love to fulfill her emptiness; and in the reprise of "Possession," a woman learns to calmly accept love as possession. The album's Zen-like acceptance of love in its many guises is less a compromise with the human heart than passive acquiescence with the natural order. The first step toward happiness in love is to find harmony in oneself and harmony within nature and life's natural cycles. The male/female dynamic is part of that natural order in McLachlan's musical world that her characters come to accept and learn to live within. Even if a listener interprets *Fumbling towards Ecstasy* as dark, then, the material still romanticizes traditional femininity.

It is easy to argue, though hard to prove, that McLachlan's softer approach to feminism made her music more acceptable to the mainstream. In this sense, the softness of her musical palette matched the softness of her message. Women listeners were invited to feel Sarah's pain, and, singing along, feel their own pain. Since the structure of male/female relationships was accepted as the natural order, there was no need to explore traditional gender ideas in any depth. Like an updating of the traditional singer-songwriter boilerplate, *Fumbling towards Ecstasy* worked as a contemporary *Blue*, with McLachlan offering an acceptable and safe model for the new woman singer-songwriter in rock.

Notes

1. Marc Woodworth, *Solo Women Singer-Songwriters: In Their Own Words* (New York: Delta, 1998), 2, 3.

2. Maria Raha, *Cinderella's Big Score: Women of the Punk and Indie Underground* (Emeryville, CA: Seal Press, 2005), 224.

3. Sarah McLachlan, *Fumbling towards Ecstasy: Live* [DVD] (Vancouver, Canada: Nettwerk, 2005); originally *Sarah McLachlan—Fumbling towards Ecstasy Live* (New York: Arista, 1994).

4. Sarah McLachlan, *A Life in Music* [DVD] (Toronto, Canada: Casablanca Media, 2005).

5. Sarah McLachlan, "Liner Notes," *The Freedom Sessions* (Arista, 1995).

6. Megan Olden, "The Art of Contradiction," *Mondo*, Winter 1996/Spring 1997.

7. Olden, "The Art of Contradiction."

8. Robin Egger, "Sarah McLachlan: Her Own Woman," *Sunday Times*, January 11, 2004.

9. Bill DeMain, *In Their Own Words: Songwriters Talk about the Creative Process* (Westport, CT: Praeger, 2004), 173.

10. "A Journey That Led to the Extremes of Human Kindness and Cruelty," *Muse*, Winter 1994.

11. Sarah McLachlan, *VH1 Storytellers—Sarah McLachlan* [DVD] (Chatsworth, CA: Image Entertainment, 2004).

12. Olden, "The Art of Contradiction."

13. John Mackie, "McLachlan Gives Heart to Darkness," *Vancouver Sun*, October 28, 1993; quoted in Judith Fitzgerald, *Building a Mystery: The Story of Sarah McLachlan & Lilith Fair* (Kingston, Canada: Quarry Press, 1997), 106.

14. Mackie, "McLachlan Gives Heart to Darkness," quoted in Fitzgerald, *Building a Mystery*, 96.

15. Eggar, "Sarah McLachlan."

16. McLachlan, *A Life in Music.*

17. McLachlan, "Liner Notes."

18. McLachlan, *Fumbling towards Ecstasy: Live.*

CHAPTER EIGHT

Tuesday Night Music Club: Sheryl Crow

I pictured myself as a loner off living like a Jack Kerouac character or, worse, someone out of a Charles Bukowski book, one of those down-and-outers who works at a gas station and has no one, no family.

—Sheryl Crow[1]

The success of our relationship was, I felt, due to my efforts to be alert to his moods and desires without imposing my own. I was allowed to share his observations, which I enjoyed, and he liked company—as long as it was sympathetic.

—Carolyn Cassady, on her relationship with Neal Cassady[2]

"All I Wanna Do" began its life as a poem titled "Fun" by Wyn Cooper, published in *The Country of Here Below* in 1987. Trimming the poem and then adding a chorus and music, Sheryl Crow and her colleagues transformed the poem into a song vaguely reminiscent of "Stuck in the Middle" (1973) by Steelers Wheel. Lyrically, the chorus may also recall Cyndi Lauper's "Girls Just Want to Have Fun" (1985). "All I Wanna Do" would kick-start Crow's career in the summer of 1994, almost a year after the release of *Tuesday Night Music Club* (August 1993), eventually reaching number 2 on the Billboard Hot 100; the song received two Grammys, one for Record of the Year and another for Best Female Pop Performance. The success of "All I Wanna Do" and sales of *Tuesday Night Music Club* (number 3 on Billboard 200) would also land Crow squarely in the mainstream of the 1990s popular music scene.

But "All I Wanna Do" is a rather odd summer song, with the promise of the chorus hiding the tarnished lives of the song's characters. As their lives are sketched out during the verses, no one in the song gives the impression of having any fun. Instead, they are sitting in a bar drinking beer at noon on Tuesday, watching the car wash across the street where workers, dressed in skirts and suits, come during lunch to wash their cars. The bar crowd seems to have nowhere to go and nothing to do.

Crow's persona offers little information about herself, but instead focuses on the man sitting next to her at the bar, William. As Crow's persona points out, the name *William* seems somewhat formal, and she imagines that his name is really Bill, Billy, Mac, or Buddy. Her physical description of Billy is brief and unforgiving: he is ugly. The formality of his name also seems appropriate for someone who expresses a rather simple, though odd, desire: to have fun before he dies. It is odd because it would be easy to assume that most everyone knows how to have fun; but Bill doesn't even know where to begin, and Crow's persona underlines this by wondering whether he has ever had any fun. He expresses his frustration by peeling off the labels of Budweiser bottles and by lighting matches, which he lets burn down to his fingers. When he finally blows out the matches, he curses. Is he a regular, and thus like everyone else in the bar, or is he an interloper on the scene? Do his frustrations emanate from the rat race, or is he just another loser, perhaps out of work or unlucky in love? Since "All I Wanna Do" is a slice of life, these questions are never answered.

There are several unusual things about the content of "All I Wanna Do" when considered within the realm of popular song. First, there is an element of class with the working men and women, wearing suits and skirts at the car wash, juxtaposed against the denizens of the bar. Secondly, there are also hints that the poem/lyric, with references to car washes and Datsuns, is stuck in the past, perhaps in the 1970s. Also, there is an irony buried in the song's overall structure. When the song is over, it is the chorus that seems to echo most loudly, even though no one in the song—at the car wash or at the bar—seems to be having any fun.

The most transformative quality of the song, however, and the one that allows Crow to assert herself as the author, is the vocal. While Crow's persona never identifies herself as female, her feminine voice makes it easy for the listener to make this inference, especially without evidence to the contrary in the lyric. And while we know even less about Crow's persona than the frustrated William, we do know that she, like William, is sitting in a bar drinking and watching the world go by instead of working or keeping house or raising children.

These bare facts—Crow's voice and the gender of her persona—may seem minor, but they aren't. Even without noting her persona's gender, the lyric of "All I Wanna Do" is a comment on the straight world where workers—at phone and record companies—spend their spare time at lunch expending yet more effort washing their cars. While the world of the barroom may be derelict, and peeling labels from the bottles of Budweiser may appear quietly desperate, it still seems superior to joining the rat race. The fact that Crow's persona is a woman adds another layer to the lyric/poem. She drinks beer, just like everyone else in the bar, and admits to enjoying a beer buzz in the morning; likewise she, like everyone else in the bar, is suspicious of the romantic couple who enters the bar. Crow's persona has made herself at home in a world of derelicts as frequently celebrated by male writers like Ernest Hemingway, Henry Miller, Jack Kerouac, and Charles Bukowski. Within the world of "All I Wanna Do," it's accepted that she can enjoy and pursue the same dissipated lifestyle as everyone else in the bar.

It would be easy to point to a number of Crow's songs that express a conventional view of male/female relationships. And listening closely to songs like "Strong Enough" and "I Shall Believe" might lead a listener to believe that very little—in regard to the dynamic of male-female relationships—had been altered from traditional pop fare in her work, and that Crow's songs are conventional. Her personas are vulnerable to their emotions and to their need for love, and this need for love remains the Achilles' heel of many of Crow's characters. But this conventional male-female split only represents the more conservative side of Crow's musical vision.

More interesting is the way songs like "All I Wanna Do" borrow from classic rock philosophy, digging deep into the founding doctrines of hipsters, Beats, and American mystics. It's easy to forget that while R&B, folk, country, and the blues may form the base of rock's musical heritage, the Beats' rebellion against post–World War II middle class values in America provided a philosophical base. It was a philosophy that rejected the clichés of the American Dream—a home in the suburbs, a middle management job, and two and a half kids—for a life of adventure played out on the highways and back roads of the nation. The *Rolling Stone* emphasized this connection with *The Rolling Stone Book of the Beats: The Beat Generation and American Culture* in 1994. It was a tradition vaguely rooted in expatriates like Henry Miller in the 1930s; a tradition that matured with the works and lives of the holy trinity of Beat, Jack Kerouac, Allen Ginsberg, and Neal Cassady in the 1940s and 1950s; and a tradition that spread—through these authors and rock itself—to the American counterculture in the 1960s. It was tradition that had, to a certain degree, lapsed since then, but could still be found in writers like Charles Bukowski and rock revivalists. "All I Wanna Do," borrowing from both 1970s rock music and Beat philosophy, reminding listeners of the connection.

Most interesting, however, is the additional twist Crow added to her reminder of classic rock philosophy in "All I Wanna Do." Crow's persona is a woman. As a woman, she is claiming this territory, the same territory once claimed by Miller, Kerouac, Ginsberg, Cassady, and Bukowski; once claimed by Jerry Lee Lewis, Elvis, Little Richard, Mick Jagger, and Kurt Cobain, as her own. In the lyric, no lines are drawn between herself and the other characters. By claiming the Beat tradition as her own, Crow's female characters are at home in bars, as members of rock bands, and especially as searchers on the open road. By claiming it as her own, she has also turned her back on the traditional roles of wife, mother, and homemaker. By expanding Beat territory to include Crow's persona in "All I Wanna Do," she opens the territory for all women.

This background of rock philosophy helps make another point in "All I Wanna Do" more obvious. While a listener might assume that the people in the bar, drinking in the middle of the day, are society's rejects, this very fact—within the realm of Beats and rock—is to their credit. Their refusal, even if there is no joy in it, is a victory against the straitjacket of the straight life. A refusal to work and join the rat race; a refusal to marry, pay a mortgage, and raise a family; and a refusal, finally, to accept the social restraints of gender. The people at the bar refuse to join the people who rush from their jobs to the car wash during lunch hour. Within this framework, William/Billy seems like a casualty of the straight life, a well-trained company man who doesn't know how to sit Zen-like in a bar (he nervously peels the Budweiser labels) and who doesn't know how to appreciate a good beer buzz in the morning. The bar where Crow's persona and her colleagues waste away the day, then, is more than a place to hang out and drink. It's a place where people like Billy, and presumably everyone in the bar, can come for salvation from the straight life.

Even though much of the lyric of "All I Wanna Do" was borrowed from Cooper's poem, its focus on down-and-outs, blue collar work, surreal atmospheres, and a cynical attitude toward love fits in well with much of Crow's overall philosophy. There is always the temptation to settle down, to find a man to love and a place to call home, but good things seldom seem to last and there's always a new road to travel. Indeed, even trying to make something last may spoil it. Crow draws portraits of a number of women who enjoy living just like the Beats, and like the Beats, find settling down ultimately stifling. The woman in "All I Wanna Do," then, reminds the listener of the hitchhiker in

"Everyday Is a Winding Road" or the woman who refuses to put down roots in "Run, Baby, Run." Whether women who live as Beats find the answers they are looking for is immaterial. It is the freedom to look for the answers that matters, whether that means the freedom to travel the open road or the freedom to sit on a barstool and drink beer in the middle of a Tuesday.

Every Day Is a Winding Road

At the heart of Crow's work on her first two albums, *Tuesday Night Music Club* and *Sheryl Crow*, lay a vision of American life drawn from beatniks, hipsters, and the '60s counterculture. It was a sketch that ran counter to mainstream consumer society in the United States during the 1990s, and one that seemed, since it drew from Kerouac, Hunter Thompson, and the love of the open road, somewhat old-fashioned. As in the setting for "All I Wanna Do," Crow often presented a life philosophy that harked back to an earlier era, partly reflecting her age (thirty-three when her second album was issued in 1996), but also her commitment to these earlier writers and ideas. Crow's vision of the open road seemed to promise an escape from the emptiness of the American Dream, a vision that had even deeper meaning for contemporary women: domestic life may have provided men with a brief respite from daily experiences in the world, but for women, home continued to be a sterile prison. While men ventured out into the world and were offered creative outlets, women, even if they joined the workforce, were responsible for the care of husbands and children, bound by the thankless tasks of cooking, cleaning, and washing clothes for others.

Crow's albums were coincidentally released during a time when women associated with the Beat Generation were receiving wider recognition. In 1983, Joyce Johnson issued *Minor Characters*, a memoir that detailed her own life within the Beat community during the 1950s, along with her relationship with Kerouac. In 1990, both Hettie Jones, who had married LeRoi Jones, and Carolyn Cassady, who had married Neal Cassady, issued memoirs: *How I Became Hettie Jones* and *Off the Road*. By the mid-1990s, two broader collections were issued, *Women of the Beat Generation* (1996) and *A Different Beat* (1997). While many of these women had lived adventurous lives compared to most American women during the 1950s, and while a number had been published authors in their own right, many of the titles—*Off the Road* and *Minor Characters*—reveal that even within the Beat community, many traditional attitudes remained entrenched regarding women.

Still, these women revealed an important pre–second wave feminist chapter, and, as they were rediscovered during the 1990s, offered women a lesson in counterculture politics. Many of these women had lived dual lives, remaining in traditional roles while either wishing or attempting to move beyond them by following in the footsteps of the men around them. These women offered financial and emotional support and served as homemakers to men who espoused freedom from work, family, and home; at the same time, these women expanded the social and psychological space—whether that meant living on the Lower East Side in New York City, smoking marijuana, or hitting the road themselves—that women could inhabit within American society (or at least at the edges of American society). This same split between home and the open road would serve as a fault line for many of Crow's characters. Her musical vision reveals and revels in this split, offering a new role for women as agents working against middle American stasis, but still tempted by love, even if imperfect, and a place to call home, even if only temporarily.

Crow's rebellion against the straight life is clear in a song like "A Change Would Do You Good" from *Sheryl Crow*. The lyric unleashes a series of stream-of-consciousness phrases that defy narrative logic—a strategy, in itself, that supports the flux of the title: when life becomes too predictable or safe, or when you are backed into a corner, any change is preferable to continuing with the same old, same old. Elements that we might associate with the stability of middle America—the house and answering machine—must be traded in to return to school or catch a train, anything that requires movement, a fresh angle, or novelty, even for the sake of novelty. While we may wish to change for multiple reasons—a bad job, unsatisfying relationship, or midlife crisis—Crow seems to cast a wider net: change, even for the sake of change, is better than standing still.

Crow's philosophical debt, however, has been filtered through and balanced by her more modern sensibility. While she may have borrowed a large chunk of her philosophical approach from an earlier time, she nonetheless felt free to update and balance it with life-in-the-1990s realism and, on occasion, a dash of Gen X cynicism. It was as though she believed in Woodstock, but also remembered the Rolling Stones' concert at Altamont; that she had seen D. A. Pennebaker's *Monterey Pop* (1968), but also Dennis Hopper's *Easy Rider* (1969); and that she realized that while LSD may give you visions, it can also give you flashbacks. Even so, much of what made Sheryl Crow, Sheryl Crow, seemed to connect her directly to another time and place.

Crow's seemingly old-fashioned connection to the bohemians and the Beats also helps explain her heavy reliance on classic rock forms. With its love of freedom and rejection of straight America (the middle class, a home, marriage, a job, etc.), rock inherited the bohemian and Beat philosophies. A listener is likely to discover traces of a number of classic rock performers, including Rod Stewart, Steve Miller, the Eagles, Eric Clapton, or Bob Seger, in *Tuesday Night Music Club* and *Sheryl Crow*. Partly, her reliance on past rock styles is a personal choice: since she enjoyed this kind of music, it perhaps seems natural that parts of it would filter into her music. But her reliance on rock music from the 1960s and 1970s also has a philosophical link, connecting her with a time period when rock seemed to present a shared social vision derived from the counterculture lifestyle.

That Crow's philosophy and sound fit easily into mainstream radio during the 1990s may have been a happy accident, but the sound itself reinforced her commitment to and reflection of these older ideas. If Crow sometimes seemed out of sync with other women singer-songwriters in the 1990s and out of sync with popular radio even while it included her, it was because she, in many ways, gave the impression of showing up late for the 1970s. Having been too young to join the ranks—as a performer—of bands like the Who, the Rolling Stones, and Led Zeppelin during the 1970s, she would now claim this primarily male territory as her—and other women's—own.

"Run, Baby, Run"

Most of us never got the chance to literally go on the road.

—Joyce Johnson[3]

"Run, Baby, Run" is the first track on *Tuesday Night Music Club*, and serves as an introduction to both Crow and the darker side of life on the road. In the lyric, Crow's persona was born in the torrent of the 1960s and flanked by two extremes—a free-love hippie mother and a father involved in the protest movement. After her mother disappears, her father makes plans for his daughter's future. But instead of following his plan, she learns a deeper lesson from watching him: that she should keep moving, leaving before anyone has a chance—like her mother—to say goodbye. She is restless, even sitting in a taxicab: she searches—by turning the radio dial—for the comfort of familiar songs. Moving may not be the answer, but it at least protects her from being let down by other people.

The lyric provides little information about the everyday life of Crow's persona, except that this motif—the need to keep moving—dominates everything she does. While she is obviously an adult now, the song never defines her age or occupation. If she had been a man, society's worst criticism might have focused on her inability to commit or settle down or grow up; if she had been a man, however, society might have also seen her in a more positive light, as a wanderer, a romantic, or perhaps a contemporary Beat. As a woman who wanders, however, she seems to hold a less stable position within society, and while Crow's portrait is sympathetic, it nonetheless leaves the listener to ask uneasily: how will society describe a woman who will not settle? Is it possible to describe her in the same way as a man, as a free spirit? Or is it more likely that she will be described as a lost soul who needs love, a husband, and a family?

Perhaps what the listener finally wishes to know is whether this continual movement has made Crow's persona unhappy. The minor key and ballad pacing add a melancholy undercurrent to "Run, Baby, Run," suggesting that her need to keep moving is somehow problematic. The mood makes it easy to suggest that she is running away from relationships, roots, and a place called home. The haunting melody line also suggests a sense of undefined loss. Crow's persona is unwilling to look more closely at her own behavior; unwilling to consider another way; unwilling to question her deeper self.

Strangely, though, the lyric does not sketch her as unhappy, and while Crow's musical and lyrical portrait might be described as sad, it is also tinged with romanticism. Even the backward glance to the 1960s is tinted with nostalgia as it outlines two broad camps in the counterculture movement: the hippies and the protesters. In the second verse, Crow's persona peers out of her rain-streaked taxicab window to look at workers who are described as fighting, which seems to imply that they are protesting, not literally fighting. Her gaze is described as hopeful. Crow's persona also seems content. Later in the verse, she is described as smiling to herself because she understands what she needs to do in order to get by in the world. Here, once again, she seems to be replaying her father's life, and while it is still easy—despite the romantic tinge—to interpret the song as being critical of her need to run, the lyric never suggests that she is missing out on something (family, home, etc.) by running.

The lyric of "Run, Baby, Run" has an unusual point of view, relayed by an unidentified narrator, not the song's main character. This narrative method—covering one of Crow's personas as though she were a character in a short story—is not uncommon in Crow's work. She noted of her own style, "Writing about characters rather than in the first person isn't a popular way to write songs now."[4] Like a short story, too, she, along with her cowriters, pays attention to small details like the rain on the taxi window. She has a tendency to stay close to her characters, as though she were describing the world through her characters' eyes. While the listener is given enough information to understand the background of the story, Crow's fictional approach on "Run, Baby, Run" is still more of a slice of life than a story. Because of the distant narration, it seems doubtful the listener would assume that the character was Crow or was based on her. Instead, it feels more like a portrait of someone from Crow's generation, perhaps an old friend or a family member.

In the end, Crow's feelings seem torn between the romance of the road, the legacy of the 1960s, and the emptiness of her persona's life. These feelings, however, are only artfully communicated by the pacing, minor key, and lyrical suggestions. For "Run, Baby, Run," then, the lure of the road may be the lure of an empty promise, but the other options—to love and perhaps be left behind—seem even worse. Crow, here, keeps her artistic cards close to her chest, perhaps uncertain whether her character is making the right choice. Other Crow songs, however, would clarify her split vision.

"Everyday Is a Winding Road"

"Everyday Is a Winding Road" may come as close to anything in Crow's early work to codifying what resembles a life motto. In "Everyday Is a Winding Road," Crow's persona has hitched a ride at the beginning of the song with a vending machine repair man. She has embarked on an adventure, reasons for which the song will slowly, though only partially, reveal. Naturally, the vending machine repairman spends a great deal of time on the road, and Crow's persona mentions the rather odd fact that he was high on intellectualism. She, on the other hand, seems content to watch the road open up before her. The chorus repeats her metaphor/motto of life as a winding road that leads—a little at a time—toward something that makes everything okay. Life, for women just like men, is an ongoing journey toward an unknown goal. While a listener might assume that past experiences might count for something on this journey, Crow's persona dismisses them like the highway in the rearview mirror. It is the Zen-like approach to life that promises revelation.

In the second verse, Crow's narrator provides more background on the driver who has a daughter (Easter) who was born on Tuesday night. This information seems like a humorous aside to Crow's first album, *Tuesday Night Music Club*. Learning more about the vending machine repairman, however, only leaves her to reflect on her own life. Why does she feel alone and believe that she does not understand herself? In the third verse, which only qualifies as a short verse, she expands on her personal predicament, describing herself as living in an anarchic state and subsisting on cigarettes and coffee. Her alienation is so complete that she even questions the reality of all of her experiences. Still, the repeated chorus, the easy, open flow of the crunchy electric guitar, remains upbeat and hopeful. She seems to believe, despite everything, that she is getting closer to where she wishes to be; she shows no signs of abandoning the open road to start a family like the vending repairman, or of having any desire to ever do so.

In essence, this leaves the listener with a split portrait of Crow's persona. Is she a reliable narrator? Or is she deluded like the narrator of another Crow song, "Maybe Angels"? Is the road a place for her to find *the* answer or a place for her to escape from her own problems? A listener may note that Crow's persona, for all of her exuberance, often seems at a loss within the narrative of "Everyday Is a Winding Road." At one point, she says that she is getting closer to where she wishes to be; at another, she says that she has been living in a state of anarchy. She seems to suggest that despite her desire for adventure, she is less than completely happy and less than completely balanced in her life. It would be easy to wonder if she is running from her own past or perhaps attempting to escape from current responsibilities.

One simple suggestion in regard to this ambiguity is that even while she may be, at least partially, deluded or temporarily lost, the listener should nonetheless accept her and what she says at face value. In other words, her life is in chaos, but she has turned to the open road as the place where she can resolve this imbalance. The music and her attitude of the song matches this mood, remaining upbeat and thus indicating that her current path is the right one. The fact that she is not exactly where she wishes to be—mentally, physically, or spiritually—does not indicate failure or ambivalence, but only a recognition that all people—men as well as women—must search for equilibrium from time to time.

Her road trip, then, is an act of faith into the great unknown where she will find the right answer; it is also an effort to escape from the patterns and ways of thinking that have produced her current anarchic state. As it was for Kerouac, Ginsberg, and Cassady, going on the road, while distinctly American (the open road, manifest destiny), is, when the journey itself replaces the destination, a rebellious act against mainstream culture. To commit to the road is to abandon family, work, and home; it is to abandon the predictability of everyday events—rising in the morning, dressing for work, leaving the suburbs for one's place of work, and arriving home each evening for family dinner—for chance happenings. The road, then, becomes a church to the churchless, a place for discovery and rediscovery, a place where one hitches rides, a place where one meets vending machine repairmen, and a place where one can hear the wheels of one's own mind turn.

Crow's portrait, like the lyric of "All I Wanna Do," adds one more level by the very fact that a woman is singing it. One cannot imagine, from the way in which women are portrayed in popular media, anything more dangerous than a woman hitching rides from unknown men. Crow, however, suggests the open road—both literally and metaphorically—as the most exciting way to experience life. Women, then, should be afforded the same experience—even though it may be dangerous—as beatniks, hipsters, and bohemians. And while danger may be a real possibility (though Crow never focuses on this possibility), the very idea of the road revolves around chance, and it stands in stark opposition to the safety of home (the vending machine repairman seems to have the best of both worlds).

"Maybe Angels"

Crow's underlying philosophy here—the road as both a metaphor for life and a place to find life's answers—may seem less clear on a song like "Maybe Angels," also from *Sheryl Crow*. Part of the problem in "Maybe Angels," however, centers on the unreliability of Crow's persona/narrator. This returns to potential problems with Crow's fictional style of writing lyrics when experienced within popular music tradition. Literary majors are taught to look for unreliable narrators; audiences for popular music, however, are more accustomed to associating the narrator with the singer and have to learn this on their own. These associations—that the narrator and singer are one and the same—seem to become even more true with singer-songwriters in rock. Crow's purpose in "Maybe Angels," then, may not be self-evident.

Crow's persona in "Maybe Angels" is an American eccentric, looking for answers at the margins of mainstream spirituality. Her bags are packed, but she knows that the freeway that runs behind her house will not take her where she wishes to go. She seems to have already been offered answers by a group of fundamental Christians, but she states that they have no idea how to save her. Instead, she seems willing to put her faith in nondenominational spiritualism, specifically, in angels, and plans to travel to Roswell, New Mexico, to wait for their return. Crow creates a lyric so absurd that one finally understands her portrait as satirical.

While satirical, however, "Maybe Angels" nonetheless draws a not unkind portrait of one American type, the searcher/dreamer in pursuit of the elusive, just-around-the-corner truth. Like the characters that populate the surrealistic "A Change Would Do You Good," Crow's persona feels as though she doesn't belong anywhere. Everyday life is dull compared to the tabloids that she reads, and she even has a sister who claims to personally know or be in touch with several famous dead persons, including Jesus and Kurt Cobain. While the beliefs of Crow's persona are tainted by her expressed fear of real life, she welcomes the chance to meet angels or aliens. While it is doubtful that a listener would take the narrator seriously, Crow nonetheless celebrates the very qualities she satirizes in this gentle portrait. The road to Roswell may be a fool's journey, but that doesn't mean that her persona cannot learn something along the way. The narrator of "Maybe Angels" may be deluded, but she shares a peculiarly American delusion that has its charms.

If Crow sometimes expresses ambiguity over the happiness of her narrators and personas, she never questions the value of roaming or searching for elusive answers. Freedom of movement does not guarantee happiness; one may still have to work toward it or at least keep on keeping on. But she does argue through these songs that women, whether they are happy, sad, or somewhere in between, should have the same right to explore, roam, and search as men.

Home

If Crow is suggesting that the search for meaning begins on the open road, then why don't all of her characters forsake the straight life for the highway? What do women have to gain by playing the roles of daughter, wife, and mother? What is the temptation that prevents every woman from taking off the apron, opening the kitchen door, and heading out toward the open road? Simply put, affairs of the heart.

Crow's women, like the women in Sarah McLachlan's work, feel the emotional need for relationships with men. Also as in McLachlan's work, these emotional needs are problematic because they often lead women into less than satisfactory situations and relationships. Songs like "I Shall Believe" and "Strong Enough" still seem to hold a slim hope for love, but Crow nonetheless frequently expresses a deep cynicism within her lyrics that seems to question whether heterosexual relationships can ever be satisfactory. She sketches a world, then, where women continue to be drawn into relationships that, eventually, cause more pain than pleasure. Even had women wanted to escape to the open road, these entanglements, combined with working for a living and the requirements of everyday life, prevented women from taking flight.

When expressing the emotional need for love in her songs, Crow often sounds very traditional, as though her characters would like nothing better than to find a good man and settle down. Songs like "Strong Enough" and "I Shall Believe" remind one of the kind of tough-but-vulnerable staples that helped Janis Joplin and later Heart fit so well within the classic rock paradigm during the late 1960s and 1970s. In one sense, these women were "one of the boys," tough and uninterested in feminists' desires for an equal playing field: they could hold their own.[5] In a second sense, however, they embodied traditional femininity and longed for a real man who would love and take care of them.

With this combination, "Strong Enough" from *Tuesday Night Music Club* fits easily into the classic rock canon. Since few of the song's details are filled in, Crow's persona seems like a traditionally irrational woman, asking for someone who is strong enough to love her in spite of her difficult self. As the lyric opens, she is angry, and she has no intention of helping her lover understand what is wrong. She does ask him, in the chorus, to lie to her; and she also promises that she will accept whatever he says, as long as he will stay with her. She tells him that he cannot change the way that she feels, and seems to place the burden of the current, unnamed crisis on her own shoulders. Crow's persona is laying her emotional cards on the table, challenging her lover to support her with his strength. She is even willing to accept less than his best, as long as he will only remain with her.

A similar vulnerability or desperation is expressed in *Tuesday Night Music Club*'s last track, "I Shall Believe." Again, Crow's persona is willing to accept whatever her lover tells her. The difference, however, is that she does raise a slight objection, reminding him that not everything will necessarily turn out the way he wishes for it to turn out. Still, she places herself in a vulnerable position, asking him not to give up on her, asking him to tell her that everything will be all right.

"Sad, Sad World," issued on an EP for "Everyday Is a Winding Road," explores a similar vein. Here, however, the relationship seems to be already over with no hope of being revived. The lyric, addressed to her lover at a distance (she seems to be addressing him mentally), appears to be an attempt to sort out the emotional aftermath. Crow's persona is much like the ones in "Strong Enough" and "I Shall Believe," willing to accept the blame for the failed relationship. Even though she knows he hates her, the refrain repeats that it is a sad world without him; she also notes that she is a bad girl for letting him down. Although she directs some recriminations at him, that he would like her better if she was unhappy and that his friends talk too much, these seem small asides to the main drama of the relationship. The word *lie* is also used again, but this time with her promising that she has never lied to him. Once again, Crow's persona is vulnerable, and in this scenario, is hoping to find a satisfactory end to a relationship when none seems possible. Even though none of the relationships in these songs seem particularly healthy, Crow's personas seem more than willing to continue with or make the best of them.

One recurring matter is how little Crow's personas expect in each of these songs. In "Sad, Sad World," "Strong Enough," and "I Shall Believe," Crow's characters play traditionally passive feminine roles, women who, more than anything, wish for love. They are willing to accept this arrangement, even if it is built on lies. Nothing substantial is expected from the men, and all of these women seem more or less desperate. Again, a listener might recall a number of women who worked within classic rock during the late 1960s and 1970s. They are women in the traditional sense, with a heart that longs for a real man on which she can lean. Simon Reynolds and Joy Press noted of

Janis Joplin, that she "revels in neediness and pathos. She doesn't seem to be in control of her passion, but controlled by it."[6] Reynolds and Press also spoke more generally about other problems that emerge when artists rely too heavily on the idea of traditional femininity:

> Another approach attempts to infuse rock with "feminine" qualities; rather than imitate men, it tries to imagine a female strength that's different but equivalent. . . . This affirmation of "feminine" qualities consolidates female identity against the attacks of both straight society and rebel counterculture. But, even as it valorizes the "feminine," it runs the risk of confirming patriarchal notions of what femininity is (emotional, vulnerable, caring, maternal, etc.).[7]

Unlike McLachlan, though, Crow circumvents this pitfall by bringing a more critical view toward these unsatisfactory relationships in other songs. It is interesting, for instance, to juxtapose Crow's vision of life on the road in "Everyday Is a Winding Road" with another song from *Sheryl Crow* describing life in middle America, "Home." "Home" is told from the point of view of a woman who remains committed to her marriage even though she has grown tired of it, and it is one of Crow's most moving songs. As she wakes up one morning, she realizes the full weight of her commitment to one person; she is afraid of reaching the point in life where she no longer feels anything out of the ordinary, specifically romance. Married to her husband at seventeen, she can no longer remember the initial spark that inspired the relationship; still, she realizes that she made a promise and believes that it must be kept. She escapes from the present, though, filling her hours reading romance novels and dreaming of romantic getaways evocative of those books: she dreams of traveling to the Riviera, dancing beneath the night sky, and then watching the sun come up with a stranger by her side. Despite her determination to remain committed to her marriage, however, Crow's persona realizes that her unhappiness is undermining her relationship with her husband: she no longer feels the same and to continue living as though she does is to live a lie.

In a sense, "Home" leaves the impression that Crow—who had never married and, at the time of *Sheryl Crow*'s release, was thirty-three (the narrator of "Home" is thirty-two)—is imagining how her life might have been different if she would have married at seventeen. Although the chord progression is stunning, offering a lovely soundscape, it is tinged by the melancholy of the lyric. The life Crow's persona sketches is one of despair, and one that—in the absence of happy songs about marriage—seems to personify her view on both relationships and permanence. The problem may actually have less to do with the husband and wife in the song than the fact that they attempted, through marriage and a place called home, to make something permanent that was not meant to be permanent. One half-humorously presented view on the Beats and relationships stated that the Beat would never ask someone out on a date because that would eventually lead to a relationship, which would eventually lead to marriage, family, and a home; all of this would eventually lead to divorce, which would leave the person alone, exactly where he had started before the date.

Just as depressing is the portrait Crow sketches in "No One Said It Would Be Easy" from *Tuesday Night Music Club.* In the lyric, a couple seems to be living on the edge of emotional and economic bankruptcy. The arrangement and the pacing are similar to "Run, Baby, Run," though perhaps more lackadaisical, a pacing that matches the lethargy of the unfolding drama. In the first verse, Crow's female persona reveals that the couple is in more trouble than she had imagined: his father, driving a Mercedes-Benz, stops by unexpectedly and slips his son rent money. Her boyfriend/husband, however, is unconcerned about their problems, and indifferent to her efforts to maintain a normal life: he offhandedly empties his dinner plate outside of the kitchen door and then suggests that they eat out. The second and final verse reveals more domestic discord; even when he looks at her and smiles, she wonders who he is really thinking about. The chorus twists a familiar cliché about no one saying that life would be easy by adding an inverted cliché: no one said that life would be so hard. Despite the desperation in this portrayal, Crow's persona believes that the couple will remain together, partly because she cannot image life being any different.

It seems impossible to find hidden love or a romantic tinge to the couple's situation within Crow's lyrics, leaving the listener to wonder why the couple—without love, without friendship, and without happiness—stays together. For Crow, the unstated answer seems as depressing as the situation itself: out of habit. This couple may have once cared for one another in Crow's worldview, but everyday living—a place called home in which one works to pay rent, cooks and eats regular meals, washes laundry and keeps house, and sleeps in the same bed—wears one down, eventually replacing love with resentment. Home, whether a place or a permanent relationship, eventually becomes more of a prison than an enveloping place of warmth and growth.

It is interesting to note that all of these songs—"Home," "I Shall Believe," "Sad, Sad, World," "Strong Enough," and "No One Said It Would Be Easy"—are ballads with many of the traditional trappings of ballads. Each song allowed Crow to wear her heart on her sleeve, presenting her personas as emotionally vulnerable women who long for a good man to complete them. The pacing and arrangement of each of these songs remind one of other classic rock ballads—"Wonderful Tonight" (Eric Clapton), "Dog and Butterfly" (Heart), "Angie" (Rolling Stones), "Can't You See" (Marshall Tucker Band), "Love Hurts" (Nazareth's version), and "Free Bird" (Lynyrd Skynyrd). The point here isn't that Crow's songs are overly familiar, but that she's working within a specific tradition—the rock ballad—that allows more room for emotional expression than the average rock song, and that frequently focuses on some aspect of love.

What Crow brings to the tradition is a woman's point of view, following in the footsteps of and expanding the themes of writers like Ann and Nancy Wilson from Heart. All of these songs focus on relationships and on domestic life; while two of her songs seem to express some kind of hope for the future ("I Shall Believe" and "Strong Enough"), none of the relationships in these songs seem particularly happy or worthwhile. Crow's relationship songs, then, seem to bring a harsh realism to the rock ballad. While Crow's personas value the freedom of the road, they also leave the impression that they wish that men and relationships could be different, that they could fulfill their promise. There are no mixed feelings in a "Sad, Sad World" as there are in "Free Bird" or "Heard It in a Love Song," no mixture of tearful goodbyes comingled with the exuberance of freedom. Only sadness that emotional longings and beautiful ideas—love, a place called home—ring hollow in real life.

"If It Makes You Happy"

As a group, then, Crow's personas and characters are pulled in two directions: one wishing to believe in love while realizing its pitfalls, the other drawing from the Beats and the possibilities of the open road. This split can be most easily seen in "If It Makes You Happy," from *Sheryl Crow*. The emotional center of the lyric, carried in the chorus, rests on the sketchily outlined premise of romantic troubles. But the verses are nonsensical, reminding a listener of the more surrealistic passages of Tom Wolfe's *The Electric Kool-Aid Acid Test*. Here, Crow's persona pursues her bliss, but her bliss is always tarnished by looking at what might have been in the rearview mirror. The choice of directions, despite the heartbreak, is nonetheless clear: following, searching for, or finding one's own path is always the right way.

In the lyric, Crow's persona seems to be relating her life to a lover or ex-lover, first from a distance, and later, by his side. At the beginning of the song as she details her experience from the road, she almost seems to be writing a letter or making a phone call. Because the language is surrealistic, what she delivers sounds as though it were filtered through a stoned person's mind. She mentions playing a show, which helps the listener place her as a performer, not unlike Crow. She also says that she has done all of these things (performed, traveled), because she promised him that she would; the listener gathers that she seems to have promised him that she would follow her dream, and that perhaps she became a well-known rock singer in the process. Instead of being happy that she has kept her promise, however, he seems to be depressed. Upon returning to his side, she has to wait on him because he seems too down-and-out to leave his bed. In her absence, he seems to have sunk deep into himself and neglected the daily chores of living.

This, at least, is an interpretation of what the lyric of "If It Makes You Happy" might infer. In truth, however, the narrative of the song is more suggested than revealed, and the dreamlike language works to obscure more than it discloses. In the first verse, the lyric of "If It Makes You Happy" resembles a fantastic laundry list of loosely connected experiences. Instead of performing for an audience, Crow's persona says that she put on a poncho and played for mosquitoes—a very odd description of a performance. She then explains a search through what she describes as thrift stores that are jungles where three items—Marilyn Monroe's shampoo, Geronimo's rifle, and Benny Goodman's corset and pen—were found. At the end of the first verse, she admits that she has made all of this—her description—up, leaving the listener even more puzzled.

In the second verse, the lyric is more clearly focused on the relationship between Crow's persona and her lover or ex-lover. She notes that he is down or depressed, and seems to dismiss his state: everyone, she says, has been there—in that state—before. She waits on him, bringing him comic books to read in bed and making him French toast, after she has scraped the mold off of his bread first. She then offhandedly admits that she still gets stoned, and infers that she is not the type of girl one takes home to meet the family. The first verse is repeated once more, though a new tag is added: even though they both continue to get along, nothing seems to be all right. Neither character, it seems, can say what they mean, and both are left—at the end of the song—in a stalemate.

A listener might complain that the song basically falls within the traditional boundaries of songs about "love troubles," with Crow's persona attempting to console an unhappy man. He is unable to say what he really wants, and she is left to guess his true emotional needs. In the second verse, she plays the traditional feminine role, waiting on her depressed friend/lover. Instead of focusing on Crow's persona and the goals that she has reached or is in the process of fulfilling, the emotional weight of the song rests with the friend/lover's discontent. She comes to his bedside, not vice versa.

The problem with this interpretation is that the song's surrealism—both in language and in the lyric's storyline—undercuts any foundation of traditionalism. When Crow's persona arrives at the bedside of her friend/lover, her attempt to care for him parodies the traditional role that a woman performs in the home. Instead of restocking his kitchen cabinets and refrigerator, she makes a partial attempt at homemaking by relying on whatever he already has at hand. This is why she has to scrape the mold off of his bread before she can fix French toast. Indeed, even bringing him comic books in bed leaves the impression that she is waiting on a sick child, not an adult male. To cap off her lack of traditional homemaking skills, she reminds him that she is not the kind of girl a guy brings home to meet the family. She is still the same girl who has no intention of giving up her original promise that she made to him, a promise that seems to guarantee her absence.

What does a listener make of the arcane references in the first verse? On one level, they remain impenetrable, meaning that any attempt to interpret them is, at best, an educated guess. The poncho seems to be both a symbol of the West with Mexican accents and, perhaps, a fashion accessory. Crow's persona, in an attempt to "make it," is performing in a poncho before record-biz types—mosquitoes—who suck one's blood to make money. There is also the odd reference made by Crow's persona that she drank until she was thirsty again. This, like much of this lyric, seems to mean the opposite of what is said, and it is difficult to connect this line to earlier ones. A listener might guess, however, that this continued thirst—despite the fact that she continues to drink—refers to a quote made by Jesus in the Gospels related to thirst. Jesus speaks of living water, a spiritual experience that leaves one satiated forever:

> Jesus answered and said unto her, "Whosoever drinketh of this water shall thirst again:
> But whosoever drinketh of the water that I shall give him shall never thirst; but the water that I shall give him shall be in him a well of water springing up into everlasting life."[8]

That Crow's persona cannot gratify her thirst may indicate that the process—the attempt to make it in the music business by appealing to the money men who run the show—is spiritually unsatisfying.

But what can one make of thrift stores that are like jungles where Crow's persona and those who traveled with her found a rifle, shampoo, and corset belonging, respectively, to Geronimo, Marilyn Monroe, and Benny Goodman? Generally speaking, these individuals serve as broad symbols, tying into the West again (Geronimo), Hollywood (Monroe), and American jazz (Goodman). The Goodman reference also contrasts with the reference to John Coltrane in the second verse: one was the king of swing, the other a postbop experimenter. But again a listener might ask, why rifle, shampoo, and corset and pen? Explaining the meaning specifically may be less important (and this is true of Crow's other surreal lyrics) than a more generalized meaning. Life on the road, on the stage, and in jungle-like thrift stores is the opposite of domestic life as pictured in the second verse; and these symbols, a hodgepodge of Americana, also represent a wilder and more adventurous America. Crow's persona may not be completely happy on the road or with the business end of the music industry, and she may feel pity for her friend/lover at home, but the road at least offers her a chance for adventure. Her surreal language here and in other songs also help sketch a portrait of different currents within the American experience, currents—like the Beats—that deviate from mainstream.

On the Road

On both *Tuesday Night Music Club* and *Sheryl Crow*, Crow has offered a strong argument that women should remain open to change and weary of romance; more specifically, she has argued that women should have the same freedom to ramble and search for answers as men have always had. And if Crow's call for emancipation with a Beat consciousness seemed to arrive late for women, it followed a certain historical and social logic. As daughters to second wave feminists, blessed with the pill and legal abortions, women in the 1990s were no longer tied to home and hearth by biology. Joyce Johnson noted of women who lived in the era of the Beats, "For unmarried young women, sex was more than adventure, more than a broadening of experience; it was a high-risk act with sometimes fatal consequences, given the inadequacy of birth control."[9, 10] With broader social independence, women were no longer restricted to the role of daughter, wife, and mother. They were now free to create their own roles.

It might be easy for a listener to think that it is absurd for a woman to take her chances hitching rides with strangers, and that Crow's vision of life on the road is merely a catchy metaphor. The problem with this interpretation, though, is that there is a potential to remove the danger from Crow's Beat portrait, a potential of reducing her lyrics to feel-good sentiment. While she leaves her vision open for multiple interpretations, reducing it to metaphor alone overlooks one key element in her work: her vision of the life on the road as described in "A Change Would Do You Good," "Everyday Is a Winding Road," and "Maybe Angels" must be similar to life on the road as experienced by traveling musicians like Crow. And the life of a musician is clearly a life separated from the traditional roles that many women have historically played in middle America.

Life on the road, living in hotels, traveling in buses, eating in cafés, and killing time before the show in another American town or city is as far removed from the idea of home and family as one could hope to get. The hipster or beatnik, like the musician, has centered her lifestyle on movement, impermanence, and chance. Whereas Americans love cars and the idea of the open road—traveling, vacationing, and the Sunday drive—the musician creates a lifestyle that takes the love of travel and the open road to an extreme.

The lifestyle advocated in "Everyday Is a Winding Road," then, is the opposite of the one most Americans live, and furthermore, the opposite of even the most progressive roles reserved for women. For most American women, the house is home, the place where one physically lives as well as the place one receives spiritual nourishment. The home is the command center and safe house from which adults and children gird themselves to meet the consumer culture of work, school, church, and shopping malls; the home is also the place where adults and children retreat from consumer culture for nourishment, entertainment, and rest. Even when the family leaves their haven for a vacation, it is less a temporary respite from consumer culture than a chance to participate in American consumer culture at a new locality. At Dollywood, Disneyworld, or the Rock and Roll Hall of Fame, a family simply sets up a second residence and fills it with a scaled-down version of goods from one's first home. Even where these excursions include authentic experiences or an element of chance, these experiences are short-lived. Soon, families return to the command center of the house/home.

Crow's vision acknowledges that women like herself may wish for a place to call home, may desire stable relationships, and may even long for true love. But over and over again, the idea of home and lasting relationships prove hollow: neither men nor women seem particularly reliable in Crow's fictional world. Through restlessness and human nature, poor communication and raw emotions, Crow's code offers that people grow bored and restless, and that attempting to make true love last or the idea of home permanent usually backfires. The very act of attempting to make these things permanent is perhaps the beginning of the end. Home, from the perspective of one who is always on the road, is a romantic notion seen from a distance; a long-term relationship, from the point of view of someone actively seeking out life's adventures, is likewise romantically unreal.

The lifestyle advocated in "Everyday Is a Winding Road" and lived by musicians like Crow reverses these values. If there is a place called home, it is only a temporary rest stop where one recharges her batteries before returning to the road. And even were a traveling musician to have a family and home, these institutions would perform a much smaller, and much less central, function in one's life. Home may even be a place that a musician longs for while on the road—a place that promises order, stability, and regular, nongreasy meals. But the stability and promise of order offer no more than the promise of more stability and order: life, at home, will never allow the possibilities and chance of the open road.

Notes

1. Marc Woodworth, *Solo Women Singer-Songwriters: In Their Own Words* (New York: Delta, 1998), 275.

2. Carolyn Cassady, *Off the Road: My Years with Cassady, Kerouac, and Ginsberg* (New York: William Morrow, 1990), 208.

3. Joyce Johnson, "Beat Queens: Women in Flux," in *The Rolling Stone Book of the Beats: The Beat Generation and American Culture*, ed. Holly George-Warren (New York: Rolling Stone, 1999), 48.

4. Woodworth, *Solo Women Singer-Songwriters*, 281.

5. Simon Reynolds and Joy Press, *The Sex Revolts: Gender, Rebellion, and Rock 'n' Roll* (Cambridge, MA: Harvard University Press, 1995).

6. Reynolds and Press, *The Sex Revolts*, 274.

7. Reynolds and Press, *The Sex Revolts*, 233.

8. John 4:13, 14, *Bible Gateway*, www.biblegateway.com/passage/?search =John%204:13-14&version=9.

9. Johnson, "Beat Queens," 48.

10. Johnson describes her own traumatic abortion in her autobiography *Minor Characters* (Boston, MA: Houghton Mifflin, 1983).

Epilogue: Afterglow

In the summer of 1998, the single "Thank U" seemed to introduce a new, more reflective—and mellower—Alanis Morissette with the unexpected first line that referred to antibiotics: why not, the lyric suggested, quit taking them? This odd first line was set to a relaxed, meandering piano line that shifts spaciously and continuously from right to left speaker as the song opens. The vocal likewise begins quietly, almost as though Morissette is talking to herself, reminding herself of the things that are important. The lyric poses a number of open-ended, philosophical questions: Why not quit eating when one is full? Why not quit chasing illusions and fame? Why, she seems to suggest, are we never satisfied—why do we always need more? Musically and lyrically, "Thank U" seemed very far away—in space and time—from the angry "You Oughta Know."

It had been three and a half years since *Jagged Little Pill*, seemingly a long time between albums for a popular singer. But in many ways, Morissette had remained in the public eye. The singles from *Jagged Little Pill*—"You Oughta Know," "Head Over Feet," "You Learn," "Ironic," "Hand in My Pocket," and "All I Really Want"—would make strong showings on the charts in 1995–1996. "You Learn" and "Head Over Feet" would return to Billboard's Top 40 Adult Recurrents chart in 1997. Both *Jagged Little Pill* and "You Oughta Know" won Grammys in 1996, and "Ironic" was nominated for two Grammys in 1997. Warner Brothers also issued the video, *Jagged Little Pill: Live*, which won a Grammy for Best Music Video, Long Form, in 1998. In a sense, the sheer popularity of *Jagged Little Pill* seemed to demand a fairly long break between albums as the public continued to absorb it and as Morissette and her label continued to promote it. Early in 1998, Morissette issued her first new material since the songs of *Jagged Little Pill*, recording "Uninvited" for the *City of Angels* soundtrack. The song rose to number 1 on Billboard's Mainstream Top 40 and number 3 on the Adult Top 40.

Morissette also seemed forever present because of the women singer-songwriters in rock movement itself. She had been narrowly defined by the media as an angry young woman, and popularity made her the de facto leader of a broad movement within rock music. As the movement around her expanded, many new performers—Tracy Bonham and Meredith Brooks, for instance—were described as the "new Morissette." At the height of the women singer-songwriters' movement between the release of "You Oughta Know" in the summer of 1995 and the release of "Uninvited" in the spring of 1998, Morissette seemed to be everywhere.

In truth, however, Morissette had dropped out for an extended period of time, living in Los Angeles and traveling to India, attempting to find—by her own account—equilibrium in the wake of fame. The shock of "Thank U," then, was much different than the shock of "You Oughta Know." In "You Oughta Know," listeners had been surprised at the public voice of a woman who they didn't really know expressing unabashed anger, and they had been surprised at her expression of raw sexuality. "Thank U" had surprised listeners who had grown to know Morissette by listening to the singles and watching the videos from *Jagged Little Pill*. Three years of personal growth, change, and experience had been poured into "Thank U," an abrupt shift from 1997's "Ironic," leaving the impression that her transformation had been much more sudden than it had been in real time. The anger that had seemed so potent had dissipated, and "Thank U" offered a Zen-like acceptance of the good, bad, and ugly in life, and a willingness to forget the past. Life was ugly and beautiful, the chorus of "Thank U" suggested, and we should embrace both. Morissette said of the song,

That was the first song that was written for the record. I'd gotten back from India, and I'd seriously let go of everything, and so many things I'd realized while I was over there, and with having had a year and a bit off, I had spent some serious time just stopping and reflecting and purging. And I guess at the end of the day, I was very grateful.[3]

In a press release, she further explained the song:

[It was the] first song written with glen for the record . . . after having stopped for what felt like the first time in my life and experiencing a deep stillness, i was left with an overwhelming sense of gratitude, inspiration and compassion . . . it felt natural for this to be the first song release as it encapsulates the heart-space from which all the songs on this record sprung.[4]

"Thank U" also suggested that the women singer-songwriters' movement had room to grow by expanding on old themes (anger) and exploring new ones (peace within one's self). While the theme of anger, and the idea that women singer-songwriters were all angry, had always been too narrow of a cliché, "Thank U" nonetheless was the polar opposite of the first single from *Jagged Little Pill*, "You Oughta Know." Even more to the point, the second verse of "Thank U" seems to reference the first song, when Morissette's persona asks a series of questions: What if she quits blaming her former lover/friend for everything that is wrong with her life? What if she actually forgave him and let all of those feelings go? While Morissette admitted in one interview that it was important to purge negative feelings as she had on *Jagged Little Pill*, at some point—she believed—she needed to move on. "[I've examined] my role in it, just taking a lot more responsibility for things and not feeling like such the victim."[5]

For all the serenity of "Thank U," however, the song remains rather awkward. The opening line referencing antibiotics seems oddly topical, while the drifting, loose structure of the song seems—at over four minutes—long. "Thank U" is not a bad song, and it does give the impression of growth and newfound maturity. But it also carries all the unease of Morissette's mental and spiritual growing pains, a partially formed expression about a newly formed philosophy of life. This awkwardness also translates into a more self-conscious writing style that indulges in familiar clichés within the singer-songwriter genre. It would be easy, for instance, to view her self-conscious lyric as navel gazing, and her music, having shifted from in-your-face rock to a gentler adult contemporary pop-rock, as having lost its bite.

If "Thank U" gave the impression of a new, more mature Morissette, the rest of *Supposed Former Infatuation Junkie* was as sprawling and unfocused as the album's title. There is an unrelenting quality to tracks like the opener, "Front Row," where a barrage of words and a thick, repetitive rhythm deliver an oblique sketch of a relationship. The overlapping voices/vocals by Morissette on the choruses are clumsy and muddled. As with "Thank U," "Front Row," at slightly over four minutes, feels way too long. In fact, part of the problem with *Supposed Former Infatuation Junkie* is that the album, at over seventy-one minutes and stretching out over seventeen songs, is just as unwieldy as these songs.

The album also seemed to serve as a spiritual battleground for a philosophical clash between the past and the present. On songs like "Can't Not" and "Are You Still Mad," Morissette seemed to still be drawing from a surfeit of anger, making "Thank U" seem no more than a temporary conversion. Musically, she seemed equally divided, adding what might loosely be described as Eastern flavors to indie rock, creating an anxious sonic approach as muddy and meandering as *Jagged Little Pill* was clear and straightforward. *Supposed Former Infatuation Junkie* seemed to capture a genuine effort to uncover personal truth, but it felt like a work in progress, and much of it seemed less accessible musically and lyrically.

It would be easy to fall back on previous criticisms of the singer-songwriter genre when listening to *Supposed Former Infatuation Junkie*. The title itself seems to conjure up the self-absorbed singer-songwriter who offers personal confessions combined with philosophic reflection on her life. Morissette wrote of the title in a press release,

> in the past when i felt infatuated with someone i wanted to pass through that phase if not skip over it entirely because i felt out of control and overwhelmed . . . relationships equated confusion and pain to me . . . upon realizing why relationships exist and understanding myself more, i can now enjoy the heart-palpitating phase of infatuation once again.[6]

Indeed, the press release itself—offering explanations for the title, the songs, and the pressure of recording—seems to be overkill. After all, she had just recorded an album that provided a "snapshot of that time in my life," but a snapshot that has to be explained further with press releases and interviews. "Are You Still Mad," for instance, seemed to revisit "You Oughta Know," and Morissette wrote of the song,

> on jagged little pill i viscerally reacted to certain people/situations that resulted in a cathartic release . . . on this song i allow myself the emotional reaction (which i think is important) while also taking responsibility for my role in the

relationships which resulted in a sense of closure that had not been realized by my simply reacting or solely pointing the finger.[7]

Again, for a traditional critic of the singer-songwriter, this statement sounds a little like the kind of psychology a reader might find in a self-help book. Simply put, it would be easy to interpret *Supposed Former Infatuation Junkie* as a self-absorbed singer-songwriter album that was oblivious to the social and political world—including women's issues—outside of it.

But this critique would also miss the underlying spiritual quest on *Supposed Former Infatuation Junkie*, and a broader understanding of what was happening to the women singer-songwriters in rock movement in 1998. Morissette spoke frequently about her spiritual search during her interviews at the time of the release of the album. And as she noted about "Are You Still Mad," she was interested in taking responsibility for her own actions. The struggle within *Supposed Former Infatuation Junkie*, then, was more than a struggle to write and record a new album in the *Jagged Little Pill* mode. It was a struggle for personal enlightenment and maturity. Morissette told Sarah Chauncey of *Canadian Musician*,

> As a young teenage person, I was very self-absorbed in a way that I think you almost have to be at that age. . . . I feel this transition between caring so much about healing myself and fixing myself, to doing that at the same time as looking outward and seeing things on a grander scale, as opposed to this little, tiny microcosm that I was.[8]

Part of the idea of *Supposed Former Infatuation Junkie*, then, was to expand the pie:

> I do think that it's natural to indulge the part of us that is victimized. I don't think it's good to skip over that part. But there does reach a time in your life, whatever age you are, where you have to realize that we have a role to play in controlling our reality, too. It's not just something that's randomly given to us. Our reality is very much dictated by what we believe.[9]

This spiritual search was reflective of a basic shift in the women singer-songwriters in rock movement during 1998. It had been six years since Harvey's and Amos' first releases, and five years for Phair and Crow. Love and McLachlan had been recording even longer. That meant that the women who had put the singer-songwriters' movement on the map were growing older and that within their music, their focus was changing. It seemed to make sense, for instance, for an emerging performer to interpret childhood trauma and failed adolescent relationships in song; but once they'd purged this material, it was time to move on to adult themes. Love and Phair had become mothers; Love, Amos, Phair, and McLachlan had married. In 1998, Harvey turned twenty-nine; Phair, thirty-one; Love, thirty-four; Amos, thirty-five; McLachlan, thirty; and Crow, thirty-six. If anything, the concerns of Morissette, who turned a mere twenty-four in 1998, were more pronounced than those of her singer-songwriter peers. Far from uniform, however, the personal growth and changes that these performers were experiencing would push the women singer-songwriters' movement in many directions in 1998, finally depriving it of the very qualities that had held the movement together for the past six years.

Surfacing

The artistic and personal shifts present in Morissette's *Supposed Former Infatuation Junkie* were reflected in 1998 releases by Amos, Harvey, Crow, Phair, and Love (Hole). Each of these singer-songwriters seemed to be, broadly speaking, tackling more mature themes, from the aftermath of a miscarriage, to making a relationship work on a daily basis, to understanding the ravages of fame. The indignities of childhood (Phair, Amos) had been explored and laid to rest, the challenges of young adulthood (Harvey, Love) met, and the open road (Crow) was now mostly in the rearview mirror. Many of these singer-songwriters had expressed interest in love, even though relationships, more often than not, seemed to have more negatives than positives. How did a woman in the 1990s resolve these issues as she reached her late twenties and mid-thirties? Did she give up on companionship because it seldom seemed worth the effort? Or did the desire for companionship and perhaps a family require compromises? All of these issues would be complicated by the fact that these women, on a personal level, were musicians, often traveling and living, from mainstream society's point of view, unconventional lifestyles.

These themes seemed promising, however, offering fans a chance to watch and relate to Amos, Harvey, Crow, Phair, and Love as both—the fan and the performer—grew older. But the awkwardness of growing older and tackling new themes was frequently accompanied by equally awkward aesthetics. Whether it was an attempt to try new things in the studio, shift the stylistic focus of a performer's approach, or just a general lack of imagination, these albums—even when quality wasn't an issue—lacked the sure-footedness and impact of earlier efforts. Earlier work—Amos and Harvey on their first two albums, Phair on *Exile in Guyville*, Crow on *Sheryl Crow*, and Love on *Live through This*—had seemed to be imbued with aesthetic purpose, a sense of knowing what sonic effect they wanted to achieve and how they wanted to achieve it. Now, the new work seemed uncertain, self-absorbed, and scattered. As a result, many of these albums—even when well received—seemed more appropriate to listeners who were already fans than good places to start learning about the women singer-songwriters' movement.

Amos' *From the Choir Girl Hotel* seemed like a step forward after the disorganized *Boys for Pele* in 1995. Whereas *Boys for Pele* was over-long and included many ideas that seemed unfinished, *From the Choir Girl Hotel* was tighter and each song received a fuller treatment. While the subject matter was diverse, Amos spoke in interviews about a personal trauma that underlined the album: "I got pregnant at the end of the last tour, it wasn't planned, but I was very ready at that point in my life to be a mother. Then, when I miscarried, the music just started to come."[10] As she had in the past, however, Amos continued to write opaque lyrics, making it difficult for the listener to find the thread of her miscarriage running through *From the Choirgirl Hotel*.

Musically and lyrically, *From the Choirgirl Hotel* was much different than either *Little Earthquakes* or *Under the Pink*. Amos seemed to have borrowed from Crow's writing style, looking at the characters in her songs from a distance, as though she had removed herself from much of the project emotionally. Musically, she relied more on mainstream rock and less on piano, radically shifting from the blueprint of the earlier albums. The lyrical and musical shift also seemed to alter what had made Amos' vision so distinct in 1992–1994 and, finally, make the current album less pointed and less fun. Gone was the cutting black humor, sacrilege, and angular musical edges; listeners could still find Amos' idiosyncrasies in the mix, but they seemed to be delivered by a mature voice that had stripped the material of its urgency. *From the Choir Girl Hotel* may have been a good album, but it did not seem like a good Tori Amos album.

Harvey's *Is This Desire?* was one of the better releases by women singer-songwriters in 1998, but nonetheless seemed to be drifting away from the philosophy that had undergirded her early work and the movement itself for the past five years. Harvey told Stephen Dalton in an interview for *NME*,

> The labels that were attached to me during the first couple of albums seem to have stuck very solidly. . . . The first two albums were very angry and direct sexually because that's how I was then, eight years younger. But I feel that I've moved a long way with my songwriting now.[11]

Her new themes, however, were more scattered and less easily attached to her personally. While Harvey has called *Is This Desire?* very personal, she frequently seems more like a fiction writer (like Crow and Amos) than a singer-songwriter on the album, viewing her characters and telling their stories from a distance. Whereas Harvey's lyrics had always been dense, she seems to have gone even further on *Is This Desire?*, relying on a private code only known to herself. In the *NME* article, Stephen Dalton referred to her approach as "novelistic role-playing."[12]

Sonically, the arrangements feel as inward as the lyrics, leaving *Is This Desire?* encased in a claustrophobic atmosphere, frozen in some unidentified time and place. The arrangements, however, do communicate the moods of her characters, from the joyful "The Sky Lit Up," to the darkly entranced "The Garden," to the aching title cut. *Is This Desire?* opened a new interval in Harvey's vision, but it was moving away from the themes that had made her music fit in well with the other women singer-songwriters from the mid-1990s.

Phair, five years after *Exile in Guyville*, was married and had a child; the title—*Whitechocolatespaceegg*—was taken from the appearance of her new son's head. In a page-long interview with *Option*, in fact, Phair focused on the challenges of life with her new baby more than her forthcoming album: "I thought there should be a whole new me and a whole new outlook. . . . But it's so much more about poop and changing diapers and sleep deprivation."[13] The interview made it obvious that Phair, like Amos and Harvey, was also ready to approach more adult themes. *Whitechocolatespaceegg*, more so than the albums recorded by Morissette, Amos, and Harvey, helped identify the fault lines that were pulling the women singer-songwriters' movement apart. Key words in a number of titles—"Only Son," "Uncle Alvarez," "Polyester Bride," and "Love Is Nothing"—gave away the drift of the album: love, marriage, and family would weigh more than issues of identity, gender, and sexuality. "Love Is Nothing" focused on the difficulties of two people making love work on a daily basis, while "Only Son" revealed the inner feelings of a son who believes that he has failed his family. These were adult songs custom-made for other adults.

Whitechocolatespaceegg had much to recommend it, though it lacked the unity, sharp edges, and impact of *Exile in Guyville*. While the songs were tuneful and the arrangements consisted of a stripped-down pop-rock, Phair's music had also mellowed with her new themes. It might have been easy for a riot grrrls or the indie community to criticize Phair's mellower vision of life and love in the suburbs, but it still seemed healthier than revisiting "Fuck and Run" at thirty-one. If her vision seemed less intense in many ways, it nonetheless satisfied the singer-songwriter tenet of offering honest reflection from wherever place one happened to be in life.

The difference between *Whitechocolatespaceegg* and new albums by Morissette, Amos, and Harvey was an important one: all seemed to be soul-searching and exploring themes associated with young adulthood. Only Phair, however, seemed to make herself and these new themes clear. In this way, it might be easy to imagine a listener coming of age with *Exile in Guyville* and now coming to some kind of new understanding of herself as a young adult while listening to *Whitechocolatespaceegg*. Harvey, Amos, and Morissette, on the other hand, had momentarily distanced themselves from fans by relying on personal code, symbols, and singer-songwriter clichés. Phair's vision remained fragmented, with songs like "Johnny Feelgood" seeming to reach back to *Exile in Guyville*. But *Whitechocolatespaceegg* did offer a model of growth that remained accessible to a broader audience, while Amos and Harvey's work seemed more likely to appeal to hardcore fans.

Even when focusing on quality alone, the best of these albums—Harvey's and Phair's—were quite different from one another, revealing how the movement—even at a high artistic level—was fraying. Harvey's vision, insular and fragmented; Phair's more open and domestic. Both albums represented artistic growth, backed by personal growth, and neither could be easily categorized as "angry young women" or the "Lilith Fair crowd." They were rich, multilayered works, perhaps not perfect, but solid. Even though these albums may have been difficult to categorize, the women singer-songwriters in rock movement may have still held together if all of the work released in 1998 had been this thoughtful. Instead of being pigeonholed by critics as angry (riot grrrls, Harvey, Amos, and Love) or soft (McLachlan and Lilith Fair), however, critics may have been forced to recognize a more multifaceted, multilayered movement. The quality, however, was far from uniform, and the scenario of a thematically expanded movement failed to materialize.

Other efforts in 1998 were more pedestrian. Both Crow's *The Globe Sessions* and Hole's *Celebrity Skin* seemed to live up to both performers' worst criticisms: Crow was stuck in the past, deriving her sonic blueprint from 1970s mainstream classic rock, while Love, having changed Hole's overall approach for the third time since 1991, proved her lack of sincerity. Of the two, *The Globe Sessions* worked best, offering a solid updating of the classic rock—Eric Clapton, the Steve Miller Band, and Rod Stewart—sound. It lacked the innovations of *Sheryl Crow*, however, and lyrically, she had mostly left the open road behind to explore failed love. *Celebrity Skin* seemed almost the opposite of *Live through This*, trading pop-punk and emotional rawness for straight pop surfaces. Love's rough-hewn vocals, however, seemed to cut against the grain of straight pop, while the song structures themselves were blasé. In both cases, Love and Crow seemed to be reaching for the same maturity in their new work as Harvey, Phair, Amos, and Morissette, delving into the ravages of fame (Love) and the personal disappointments of love (Crow). But without the musical force, personal connection, and lyrical sharpness of former work, *The Globe Sessions* and *Celebrity Skin* were robbed of urgency and relevance.

The year—1998—could have been a banner year for women singer-songwriters in rock. With all of these albums released in 1998 by artists who had helped found the movement, it might have been a chance to solidify the gains of women singer-songwriters in rock over the last five years, a chance to expand on what had been so energetically and artistically built. By exploring new themes as these singer-songwriters reached adulthood, Morissette, Harvey, Love, Phair, Crow, and Amos may have had the chance to explode the myth of the angry young woman and reveal the richness of the movement's work that had always lain beneath the surface of media clichés. Instead, the movement seemed to devolve and fray, losing its connection to many elements—the personal link between the listener and the singer, a personal exploration of women's issues, and a willingness to struggle against the ongoing backlash against women—that had defined and unified women singer-songwriters in rock since 1992. It was ironic, then, that just as Lilith Fair was announcing the continued triumph of women singer-songwriters in rock by entering its second year in 1998, the philosophical and political underpinning of the movement was coming undone.

It would be easy to point out that these albums, by themselves, did not represent every woman singer-songwriter in rock music in 1998. There were few releases, however, by other major women singer-songwriters in 1998. Sarah McLachlan had issued *Surfacing* in 1997, and it continued to do well commercially in 1998, but she would not release another album of new material until 2003 with *Afterglow*. Both Paula Cole and Meredith Brooks had reached large audiences with *This Fire* (1996) and *Blurring the Edges* (1997), respectively, though neither would release follow-up albums until 1999. Others who had issued promising albums, like Tracy Bonham, Poe, and Patti Rothberg, would not issue new material until 2000.

Even though there continued to be a strong market for women singer-songwriters and a strong presence of women singer-songwriters in alternative music, these delays offered a second blow to the women singer-songwriters in rock movement. Between 1993 and 1996, successive albums by new and established artists built the momentum of the movement, both commercially and artistically. By 1997–1998, however, the established performers were faltering and the new works by singer-songwriters like Brooks and Natalie Imbruglia seemed to tip the balance toward the worst clichés of the movement.

The momentum for the new women's singer-songwriter had grown from a fledgling possibility in 1992 to a full-fledged movement in 1995–1996. By 1997, Lilith Fair celebrated and even cemented that success, announcing in a visible public forum that the movement was an established fact and inviting other women to partake in the revolution they had been instrumental in initiating and sustaining. To many critics, the women in rock phenomenon was at the point of establishing itself permanently; one day soon, no one would even need to mention it as a phenomenon.

But by 1998 the movement had begun to unravel and lose momentum just as quickly as it had gained it in the early to mid-1990s. Whether a listener or critic focused on the albums by Morissette, Hole, Harvey, Crow, Phair, and Amos, or whether they focused on the development of less substantial women singer-songwriters in 1997–1998, it was easy to gather that the movement was in disarray or worse, that there was no longer a movement at all. Perhaps Lilith Fair and the radio presence of McLachlan and Imbruglia gave the appearance that little had changed since the explosion of *Jagged Little Pill* in 1995, but without new, high-quality material to sustain it, the movement faltered badly in 1998. It was a stumble that the women's singer-songwriters in rock movement would not recover from.

Renewing the Backlash

As the '90s came to a close, the decade's swing to the left, especially among young people, both in music and in politics, could only mean a dreaded swoop back in the other direction.[14]

The fraying of the movement was also representative of happenings on the political front at the end of the 1990s. An open cultural door, partially brought about by a new Democratic administration in Washington DC and the emergence of third wave feminism, seemed to abruptly shut as the decade drew to an end. Indeed, whether a bystander looked at the sometime conservative policies of the Clinton administration (welfare reform, trade policy) or the victories by Republican candidates in Congress (Contract with America), it was easy to wonder how wide the cultural door had been open to begin with. However wide, the heady cultural environment of the early 1990s that seemed to support the women singer-songwriters' movement was on the decline by 1998–1999. Part of this was wrapped up in the fate of the Clinton administration itself, as revelations of the president's relationship with Monica Lewinsky in January of 1998 would eventually lead to his impeachment by the House of Representatives at the end of the year. The political furor and debate over Clinton's sexual behavior, however, seemed more fragmented than the ones that had developed around Anita Hill (sexual harassment) or William Kennedy Smith (rape) in the early 1990s. There were no new books to rally around, like *The Beauty Myth* (1991) or the *Backlash* (1991), and no broadly popular movies with feminist themes like *Thelma and Louise* (1991) or *Fried Green Tomatoes* (1991).

On the musical front itself, a similar conservative swing took place at the decade's close. The years 1998–1999 would see the emergence of both rapper Eminem with his breakthrough *The Slim Shady LP* and teen idol Britney Spears with . . . *Baby One More Time*. Indeed, both performers seemed like a step back in time to the mid- to late 1980s, one evoking the violent misogyny of Guns N' Roses' *Appetite for Destruction* (1987) and *G N' R Lies* (1988), and the second evoking teen idols like Tiffany and Debbie Gibson, who had both issued their first albums in 1987.

Like the original cover art for *Appetite for Destruction*, the cover of *The Slim Shady LP* seemed to court controversy, displaying a parked car on a pier. A man and a child stand at the dock's railing against the backdrop of a full moon and the ocean; nearby, an open trunk of a car reveals the legs of a body. All of these details are in perfect synch with "'97 Bonnie and Clyde," a story narrated by a father to his daughter as they drive to dispose of the mother's body. Even Spears, while never offering music as malevolent as that offered by Eminem, nonetheless joined him with her own prefeminist ideas on women. On her first single (". . . Baby One More Time") from . . . *Baby One More Time*, she asked her boyfriend—metaphorically—to hit her one more time in the chorus. Spears also appeared in a controversial photo spread in *Rolling Stone*, one that included photographs of her wearing only shorts and a bra, and standing in front of a cabinet of baby dolls and stuffed animals. Both Eminem's misogyny and Spears' teen (she was seventeen at the time of the *Rolling Stone* photo spread) sexuality were widely criticized, but both acts were extremely popular.

The single event that seemed to represent the end of an era and offer yet another blow to women's progress during the 1990s, however, was Woodstock '99. Advertised as a celebration of the thirtieth anniversary of the original festival where peace and love had reigned, it would be remembered for looting, the destruction of property, and, most vividly, for violence against women that included several rapes. Rock critic Ann Powers wrote,

"It seems that Woodstock '99 did bring back one custom from the classic days of rock: treating women like sexual toys, often against their will."[15] The new values of Woodstock Nation '99 were the polar opposite of those of Lilith Fair. And while many people would point fingers—at bands like Limp Bizkit, at the promoters and the lack of security, and even at the behavior of the women who attended—what stands out about the event was the overall atmosphere of aggression toward women. A *Billboard* writer noted, "In the end . . . an overriding tone of misogyny—and the four sexual assaults reported to authorities by press time in connection with Woodstock '99—is what leaves the ugliest aftertaste of the event."[16]

Four rapes were officially reported, though many who attended noted other incidences of aggression and harassment toward women. Sheryl Crow, who performed at the festival, commented on her own experience: "[The number of rapes] seems like a low number. There were topless girls on guys' shoulders who were constantly being groped. These kids were out of control."[17] In one incident, a twenty-six-year-old male prison guard was accused (and eventually convicted) of sodomizing a fifteen-year-old girl outside the grounds after the festival had ended. Some of the behavior revolved around the mosh pit in front of the stage, also the site of another rape. Jill T. Stempel wrote in *Rockrgrl*, "In one case, a 24-year-old girl from Pittsburgh was stripped, assaulted and eventually gang-raped by fellow audience members after she crowd surfed to the front of the mosh pit during Limp Bizkit's testosterone-fueled set."[18] Adding to this violence, some of these incidences occurred in public places with security guards nearby, and no one seemed to interfere.

A number of commentators also blamed both the music and musicians for generating and adding to the level of violence against women. Jeff Stark wrote journal entries from the festival for *Salon*:

> Irresponsible: There's no other word for Limp Bizkit front man Fred Durst. He's goading the crowd, pumping them up, higher and higher. It's beyond working them into enjoying the show. He's encouraging the pit, working them into a frenzy. He wants people to "smash stuff." "C'mon y'all, c'mon y'all," he shouts. Below him, the pit is a war zone, a sweaty, dirty, roiling mass of vicious guys knocking the fuck out of one another. It's not a fun scene. It's nasty, and people are getting hurt—bad. Bodies on cardboard stretchers emerge from the audience a couple of times per song.[19]

Ann Powers reported that Mark Hoppus of Blink-182 invited women in the audience to service the band members, and she complained that both Kid Rock and Limp Bizkit "proclaimed they loved women even as they performed songs condemning them as whores."[20]

Many also believed that the behavior of these bands at Woodstock '99 emanated from outside of the festival's boundaries. Maria Raha wrote of the new male-oriented metal-rap bands of the late 1990s, "The only thing these new white acts seemed to demand was rampant, unchecked sexism, the right to freely appropriate black art forms, and the eternal sexual availability of women."[21] Writing in *Billboard*, Timothy White noted a basic shift in the music scene at the end of the 1990s:

> Recent articles have described the violence toward women at Woodstock '99 as sexism—i.e., attitudes and conditions promoting stereotyping and discrimination. This characterization is too tame. What's actually on the rise in popular music, as manifested at Woodstock, is . . . the hateful objectification of women as sexual toys and disposable human furniture. To rape and forcibly molest doesn't show a prejudiced sexual attitude; it shows psychopathic sexual contempt.[22]

If women within the music industry and society in general had made significant gains against the backlash during the 1990s, a new social movement seemed determined to level those gains and reenergize the backlash.

Afterglow

It has been easy to dismiss much of the women singer-songwriters in rock movement as nonsubstantial from multiple feminist and nonfeminist points of view. Third wave feminists who were grounded in politics were joined by riot grrrls in condemning popular women singer-songwriters as musically and lyrically watered down. Second wave feminists, for the most part, agreed. For alternative rockers, on the other hand, women singer-songwriters seldom warranted the same seriousness as grunge or rap. While there were exceptions like PJ Harvey, women singer-songwriters were either angry and shrill (Morissette) or New Age clichés (Jewel, McLachlan), hardly the stuff of which good rock and roll was made. To these critics, listening to Amos, Morissette, and McLachlan cover women's issues was like reading a feminist article in *Redbook*. Noting the acceptance of women singer-songwriters in the mainstream, Maria Raha wrote, "What the public so hungrily craved, apparently, was still only acceptable when packaged in typical forms of female expression (flowery, lovelorn lyrics) by commercially marketable (photogenic, heterosexual, and sexually available) women."[23]

To many who were critical of the movement, matters were made worse by the appearance and vast popularity of groups like the Spice Girls. As a phenomenon, the Spice Girls were viewed as the crass commercialization of women in rock, replacing an honest exploration of women's issues by riot grrrl bands with cliché slogans like girl power. "Never in pop history," wrote Karen Schoemer in *Newsweek*, "have female singers been quite so aggressively, shrewdly marketed on the basis of gender alone."[24] Mainstream women singer-songwriters, from Morissette to the Spice Girls, had simply borrowed heavily from the riot grrrls and adjusted the angry message for a broader audience, allowing them to rake in the money that rightfully belonged to the riot grrrls. Instead of focusing on stories about bulimia and anorexia, or stories about sexual and physical abuse, mainstream women singer-songwriters worried about self-esteem; instead of critiquing working class issues or analyzing life from an African American woman's point of view, their lyrics addressed the narrow concerns of a white, middle class audience; and instead of expressing concern for sexual diversity, they focused on traditional heterosexual relationships and traditional gender roles.

Because of these perceived shortcomings, critics could argue that this female rebellion in rock, like male rebellions in rock that dated back to the 1950s, was not revolutionary. In *The Sex Revolts*, Simon Reynolds and Joy Press noted the distinction between the rebel and revolutionary (a framework that they borrowed from Jean-Paul Sartre and adapted to rock). The male rebel was basically out for a good time and rebelled against anyone who tried to stop him from expressing his virility. The basic system, however (the patriarchy, capitalism, etc.), remained untouched. In fact, most male rebels, in time, take their place in the system: "We take it . . . that rock is not a revolutionary art, that its insubordination and ego tantrums are complicit with or bound within the terms of capitalism and patriarchy."[25]

It is easy to argue that for the most part, the female-led rebellion by women singer-songwriters also accepted much of the same system. This frequently included the acceptance of white, middle class status, and the economic system that supported that status. While they may have wished to expand traditional masculine/feminine boundaries, they never seemed interested in eliminating gender distinctions; and while they may have wished for more equality within male/female relationships, they seldom explored the possibility of nonheterosexual relationships. Maria Raha noted of mainstream women singer-songwriters, "They were polite and affable, they were always slender (almost frighteningly so), and for all their whispered 'fuck you's, they teetered on a feminist tightrope, revealing both their strongest and most stereotypical sides when it came to love and rejection."[26] Women in rock during the 1990s, then, wished for no major social changes, only an expansion of personal privileges within the existing system.

These criticisms, however, were too limiting. By Reynolds and Press' definition, any rock that challenges the system or part of the system—patriarchy and/or capitalism—is potentially revolutionary. And while the female-led rebellion of the 1990s often seemed complicit with capitalism, the movement's very existence was an assault on patriarchy. By suggesting that men and women might conduct themselves differently in relationships, that traditional gender roles might be expanded, and that female sexuality was as natural a phenomenon as male sexuality, the music and lyrics were potentially revolutionary. By challenging these basic issues, this female-led rebellion one-upped the male tradition within the rock paradigm itself: while the rock impulse had always been seen as generally liberal, it supported gender divisions within mainstream society along with the suppression of women as romantic objects and sexual conquests. By critiquing, deconstructing, and offering new examples of male/female relationships, by exploring women's sexuality, and by suggesting an expansion of gender roles, women singer-songwriters rebelled against both the larger social structure *and* rock music tradition itself. Reynolds and Press wrote,

> The women-in-rock question provided a sorely needed injection of animation and animosity at just the point at which rock culture seemed to be flagging. It's also partly a reaction against the masculinism of grunge. And finally, it's a grass-roots gust of impatience with the perennial marginalization of women, as if to say, "sure, things are improving—but not fast enough."[27]

An example of this radicalism might be understood by taking a closer look at the way women singer-songwriters focused on heterosexuality and heterosexual relationships. On the surface, it would be easy to mistake PJ Harvey's early work as conservative. On *Dry* and *Rid of Me*, she frequently focused on heterosexual relationships and the way in which gender is defined. Even while her depictions of heterosexual relationships are frequently violent in her early work, she never seems to be suggesting that women should abandon relationships with men, or that women should abandon all forms of culturally based femininity. Because Harvey does not push beyond heterosexuality, and because she does not push gender beyond some traditional form of a masculine/feminine split, she seems to stop short of suggesting anything that might be considered radical feminism. And in the wake of queer studies and ideas about gender as performance, a listener might even define Harvey's vision as reactionary. Despite the violence of masculinity and the masculinity's threat, women remain attracted to and involved with men.

But Harvey's exploration was more complex than these criticisms suggest. During the 1980s, a number of second wave feminists had defined heterosexual relationships and heterosexual sex as inherently violent. The debate would develop around figures like Andrea Dworkin and Catherine MacKinnon, and around issues like pornography and penetrative sex. Pornography was the visual equivalent of rape, and penetrative sex with men was sleeping with the enemy. Dworkin wrote in *Intercourse*: "Whatever intercourse is, it is not freedom; and if it cannot exist without objectification, it never will be. Instead occupied women will be collaborators, more base in their collaboration than other collaborators have ever been: experiencing pleasure in their own inferiority; calling intercourse freedom."[28] This new orthodoxy also seemed to shut down the sexual freedom that women were invited to explore during the 1970s, while suggesting that women only had one option if they wished to participate in nondominant relationships and equality sex: to become lesbians.

Many third wave feminists—both politically and culturally grounded—found these ideas limiting and oppressive. They were also, as psychologist Lynne Segal has noted, simplistic: "In fact, heterosexual institutions and relations, from marriage and coupledom to adolescent romance, have always been more contradictory than our dominant conception of them in terms of men's power and women's subordination would suggest."[29] As third wave women declared the right to embrace feminine roles when and if they wished, many also declared the right to have relationships with men and women or both, and to be as sexual or nonsexual as they wished. This rebellion against Dworkin and MacKinnon's views of heterosexuality, however, was about more than returning to tradition. Just because women chose heterosexual relationships, there was no reason to also accept traditional ideas of power inequality between men and women within those relationships. Through music, women singer-songwriters like Harvey would challenge the traditional meanings of heterosexual relationships and sexuality, and expand the concepts of masculinity and femininity. As Segal has noted, "All feminists could, and strategically should, participate in attempting to subvert the meanings of 'heterosexuality,' rather than simply trying to abolish or silence its practice."[30]

The mistake, Segal believed, was not in recognizing that heterosexual relationships had often been repressive to women (they often had), but in failing to recognize that "there are different heterosexual experiences and different heterosexualities."[31] Women singer-songwriters like Harvey, Love, Amos, and Phair would explore both the limitations of traditional heterosexual relationships and gender identity along with the potential for new "heterosexualities."

Populist Feminism

Many of the criticisms of the women singer-songwriters' movement—that it was too white, middle class, and heterosexual; that it failed to directly address political issues as had riot grrrl; and that the movement was too mainstream and watered down—failed to understand the aims of the individual artists and the nature of the singer-songwriter genre itself. The singer-songwriter wrote out of her own experience, not that of the broader body politic; and even when her lyric touched on political issues, the confessional style of the singer-songwriter tied her politics to her personal life and experience. The riot grrrls, for instance, may have offered a more forceful political message, but they offered it within the tradition of punk, not the singer-songwriter genre. To criticize a woman singer-songwriter for failing to broaden her social or political net, then, is to misunderstand her focus as a singer-songwriter and the tradition in which she worked.

These critics also failed to understand the relationship between the singer-songwriter and her audience. The power of this personal message and the import of its political content was centered on the bond the music formed between the performers and the listeners. In Ann M. Savage's study of women's response to feminist rock music during the 1990s, she noted the importance of this connection for women listeners: "Women clearly have a strong connection to female artists' music. All of the women [in the study] described moments of engagement with the text that in turn had implications in their lives."[32] The music and lyrics of these singer-songwriters, then, helped develop a dialog focused on women's issues that resonated with the everyday experiences of women's lives during the 1990s. Savage noted of the women in her study, "The women indicated that female artists were able to articulate emotions or feelings in a way they were unable to. In some instances, women actually used female artists to communicate with others and to express their thoughts and feelings to others."[33] The power of the music and the results of this connection and communication extended to all areas of women's lives. "In sum," wrote Savage, "the role of music by women in women's lives is one of political, social and cultural significance."[34]

Women singer-songwriters in rock during the 1990s, then, created what we might think of as populist feminism. As purveyors of populist feminism, women singer-songwriters opened up a social and psychological space within the popular culture landscape for girls and women. Sometimes these spaces were physical, as with Lilith Fair; other spaces were broadly social, as when recordings created connections between millions of women on common issues; and sometimes these spaces were psychological, generated by the fact that any woman could listen to and connect with recordings as they related to her own life and experience. Savage noted,

> Whether intentional or not, the artists, music and audience contribute to the development and perpetration of feminist-minded discourse. The mere existence and level of mainstream acceptance of this feminist and political discourse within a patriarchal industry alone exemplifies the political and cultural transformation that took place.[35]

This transformation of the popular culture landscape is perhaps most obvious with Lilith Fair. It has been argued that McLachlan proved music promoters wrong when she successfully staged Lilith Fair in 1997. From this point of view, the audience for women's music had always been there: all one needed to do was to create a festival like Lilith Fair and the audience would follow. It is easy to argue, however, that the reverse happened. No movement of women in rock before the 1990s had reached as many listeners, and never before had so many women become part of the mainstream rock scene. By building social, psychological, and physical spaces for women listeners during the early to mid-1990s, these women created a demand for a woman-centered festival in the mid- to late 1990s: Lilith Fair was a natural extension of the movement built by women singer-songwriters and their fans.

Women singer-songwriters in rock also built a movement in the 1990s by offering a populist aesthetic, one that pushed the boundaries of the singer-songwriter genre while never forgetting its audience. The movement borrowed the best from the past, mixing the poetic musings of songwriters from Joni Mitchell to Suzanne Vega with the anger of rockers from Chrissie Hynde of the Pretenders to Bikini Kill, and transformed it into a plethora of powerful soundscapes. It could be angry and visceral, or ethereal and quietly entrancing; it could be acoustic with folk sincerity, or electric with rock authenticity; and it could be all of these things at once within the constraints of a three-minute song. It was rock music as it might have developed ten or twenty years earlier, if women had followed or perhaps been allowed to follow in the footsteps of Patti Smith or Siouxsie Sioux. Consciously or not, these singer-songwriters generated a sound that was aimed at, and reached, a broad audience of young women born in the late 1960s and early to mid-1970s, women like themselves. In a sense, the movement created a vast communication network for a new generation of women.

It is ironic, in retrospect, that during the early 1990s—as many feminists, pseudo-feminists, and cultural observers were proclaiming that the feminist movement was dead and that young women were no longer willing to identify themselves as feminists—a broad cultural movement was loudly and publicly addressing women's issues for a new era. Between 1991 and 1998, the populist feminism of women singer-songwriters would permeate and infiltrate American culture, spreading ideas about heterosexual relationships, the limits of gender, and female sexuality to a new generation of women *and* men. By offering a broad populist vision within popular culture, the women singer-songwriters' movement also offered a vigorous counterattack against the ongoing backlash against women. Savage wrote, "The political and feminist nature of this music, the artists and fans challenge the status quo. The engagement of these performers, the music and the audience creates an ideological interdiscourse that works in opposition to, contests and contradicts the dominant ideology."[36] Mixing personal politics with rock guitars and delivering its often angry message from the public podium in the form of CDs, MTV videos, and radio hits, women singer-songwriters would prove that feminism, despite its much-rumored and publicized death in publications like *Newsweek*, remained more than a vital force: it had been absorbed into the mainstream.

In the 1990s, women singer-songwriters in rock created a broad populist rebellion by offering a loud, thoughtful, and socially poignant vision wrapped in a popular song. As women listened to *Jagged Little Pill*, *Fumbling towards Ecstasy*, and *Little Earthquakes* again and again, the music was woven into the very fabric of their lives; as they listened to "You Oughta Know," "Possession," and "Crucify" again and again, the experiences of other women were comingled with their own experiences. It was a rebellion that women could sing along to while riding in the car or jogging with a portable CD player, and it was a rebellion that women could sing along with while attending a festival with thousands of like-minded women. It was a rebellion that believed that music could be pleasurable *and* good for you at the same time; that art and politics were not the antithesis of one another, but could work in unison to create a more intoxicating musical cocktail. And finally, it was a rebellion that promised to persist—to continue offering psychological and social safe spaces—for as long as women and men listened and found meaning in the words that these women singer-songwriters had carved out of the emotional depths of their own lives.

Notes

1. Curtis White, *The Middle Mind: Why Americans Don't Think for Themselves* (New York: Harper San Francisco, 2003), 53.

2. Theodore Gracyk, *I Wanna Be Me: Rock Music and the Politics of Identity* (Philadelphia, PA: Temple University, 2001), 207.

3. Sarah Chauncey, "Alanis Morissette: Inside the Mind of a Supposed Former Infatuation Junkie," *Canadian Musician*, November/December 1998.

4. Alanis Morissette, "Reflections of a 'Supposed Former Infatuation Junkie': Alanis Morissette in Her Own Words," Mitch Schneider Organization PR. www.msopr.com/mso/morissette-words.html.

5. Chauncey, "Alanis Morissette."

6. Alanis Morissette, "Reflections of a 'Supposed Former Infatuation Junkie': Alanis Morissette in Her Own Words," Mitch Schneider Organization PR, www.msopr.com/mso/morissette-words.html.

7. Morissette, "Reflections of a "Supposed Former Infatuation Junkie."

8. Chauncey, "Alanis Morissette."

9. Chauncey, "Alanis Morissette."

10. Sylvie Simmons, "Tori Amos: *From the Choirgirl Hotel*," *Mojo*, May 1998.

11. Stephen Dalton, "The Dark Lady of Dorset: Polly Jean Harvey," *NME*, 1998.

12. Dalton, "The Dark Lady of Dorset."

13. Neva Chonin, "Backtalk with Liz Phair," *Option*, July/August, 1997, 146.

14. Maria Raha, *Cinderella's Big Score: Women of the Punk and Indie Underground* (Emeryville, CA: Seal Press, 2005), 223.

15. Ann Powers, "Critic's Notebook: A Surge of Sexism on the Rock Scene," *New York Times*, August 2, 1999, E1.

16. "In Woodstock's Wake, Hard Questions," *Billboard*, August 14, 1999, 1.

17. "In Woodstock's Wake," 1.

18. Jill T. Stempel, "Let Me Stand Next to Your Fire," *Rockrgrl*, September/October 2000, 24.

19. Jeff Stark, "What a Riot: Diary of a Woodstock '99 Survivor," *Salon*, July 27, 1999.

20. Powers, "Critic's Notebook," E1.

21. Raha, *Cinderella's Big Score*, 229.

22. Timothy White, "Sadly, the Times Are A-Changin'," *Billboard*, August 14, 1999, 5.

23. Raha, *Cinderella's Big Score*, 224.

24. Karen Schoemer, "The Selling of Girl Power," *Newsweek*, December 29, 1997, 90.

25. Simon Reynolds and Joy Press, *The Sex Revolts: Gender, Rebellion, and Rock 'n' Roll* (Cambridge, MA: Harvard University Press, 1995), 3.

26. Raha, *Cinderella's Big Score*, 224.

27. Reynolds and Press, *The Sex Revolts*, 385.

28. Andrea Dworkin, *Intercourse* (New York: Basic Books, 1987), 181.

29. Lynne Segal, *Straight Sex: Rethinking the Politics of Pleasure* (Los Angeles: University of California Press, 1994), xii.

30. Segal, *Straight Sex*, 259.

31. Segal, *Straight Sex*, 261.

32. Ann M. Savage, *They're Playing Our Songs: Women Talk about Feminist Rock Music* (Westport, CT: Praeger, 2003), 174.

33. Savage, *They're Playing Our Songs*, 175.

34. Savage, *They're Playing Our Songs*, 175.

35. Savage, *They're Playing Our Songs*, 177.

36. Savage, *They're Playing Our Songs*, 178.

Discography

Information for these charts has been compiled from *Billboard* and *All Music Guide*, and focuses on performers who were covered within this book. The performers are in alphabetical order, while the albums and singles are primarily in chronological order. Each entry provides two key pieces of information: (1) the top position for the single or album, and (2) the number of weeks the single or album remained on a specific chart.

The Billboard 200 is the primary album chart, though I have supplemented this chart with Heatseekers, which represents new artists, and Top Canadian Albums, which represents album sales in Canada. The Billboard Hot 100 is the primary singles chart; Hot Mainstream Rock Tracks follows the music played on mainstream rock radio; Hot Dance Club Play tracks music played in United States dance clubs, whereas Hot Dance Music/Maxi-Singles Sales represents the number of dance records sold; Hot Adult Top 40 Tracks records the number of plays a single receives on adult contemporary radio, while Hot Modern Rock Tracks mostly follows alternative rock radio; the Hot Adult Top 40 Recurrents represent singles that meet a number of Billboard recurrent requirements including the song's chart position and the time the song has remained on the Hot Adult Top 40 chart; Hot Adult Contemporary Tracks follows songs played on lighter pop radio stations; the Rhythmic Top 40 represents a mixture of dance, pop, hip-hop, and R&B singles played on mainstream radio stations.

Tori Amos

Albums

Album	Year	Chart	Peak Position	Weeks on Chart
Little Earthquakes (Atlantic, 1992)	1992	Heatseekers	31	3
	1992	Billboard 200	54	38
Under the Pink (Atlantic, 1994)	1994	Billboard 200	12	35
Boys for Pele (Atlantic, 1996)	1996	Billboard 200	2	29
Hey Jupiter (EP) (Atlantic, 1996)	1996	Billboard 200	94	3
From the Choirgirl Hotel (Atlantic, 1998)	1998	Billboard 200	5	20
	1998	Top Canadian Albums	10	1

Singles

Single	Year	Chart	Peak Position	Weeks on Chart
"Crucify" (Little Earthquakes)	1992	Hot Modern Rock Tracks	22	10
"Silent All These Years" (Little Earthquakes)	1992	Hot Modern Rock Tracks	27	4
"Cornflake Girl" (Under the Pink)	1994	Hot Modern Rock Tracks	12	12
"God" (Under the Pink)	1994	Hot Modern Rock Tracks	1	17
	1994	Billboard Hot 100	72	12
"Caught a Lite Sneeze" (Boys for Pele)	1996	Hot Dance Music/Maxi-Singles Sales	9	4
	1996	Hot Modern Rock Tracks	13	13
	1996	Billboard Hot 100	60	13

	Chart	Year	Peak Position	Weeks on Chart
"In the Springtime of His Voodoo" (*Boys for Pele*)	Hot Dance Club Play	1996	6	12
"Professional Widow" (*Boys for Pele*)	Hot Dance Club Play	1996	1	12
	Hot Dance Music/Maxi-Singles Sales	1996	14	35
"Talula" (*Boys for Pele*)	Hot Dance Music/Maxi-Singles Sales	1996	49	1
"Silent All These Years" (*Little Earthquakes*)	Hot Adult Top 40 Tracks	1997	26	18
	Billboard Hot 100	1997	65	20
"Jackie's Strength" (*From the Choirgirl Hotel*)	Billboard Hot 100	1998	54	10
"Spark" (*From the Choirgirl Hotel*)	Hot Adult Top 40 Tracks	1998	32	35
	Hot Modern Rock Tracks	1998	13	15
	Billboard Hot 100	1998	49	14

Fiona Apple

Albums

Album	Year	Chart	Peak Position	Weeks on Chart
Tidal (Clean Slate/Epic, 1996)	1996	Heatseekers	2	9
	1996	Billboard 200	15	91

Singles

Single	Year	Chart	Peak Position	Weeks on Chart
"Shadowboxer" (*Tidal*)	1996	Hot Modern Rock Tracks	34	6
	1996	Hot Adult Top 40 Tracks	32	15
"Criminal" (*Tidal*)	1997	Hot Adult Top 40 Tracks	17	26
	1997	Hot Modern Rock Tracks	4	26
	1997	Billboard Hot 100	21	20
	1997	Mainstream Top 40	18	17
"Sleep to Dream" (*Tidal*)	1997	Hot Modern Rock Tracks	28	13

Tracy Bonham

Albums

Album	Year	Chart	Peak Position	Weeks on Chart
The Burdens of Being Upright (Polygram, 1996)	1996	Heatseekers	9	4
	1996	Billboard 200	54	25

Singles

Single	Year	Chart	Peak Position	Weeks on Chart
"Mother Mother" (*The Burdens of Being Upright*)	1996	Hot Mainstream Rock Tracks	18	12
	1996	Hot Modern Rock Tracks	1	21

	Year	Chart	Peak Position	Weeks on Chart
"The One" (*The Burdens of Being Upright*)	1996	Hot Modern Rock Tracks	23	9

Meredith Brooks

Albums

Album	Year	Chart	Peak Position	Weeks on Chart
Blurring the Edges (Capitol, 1997)	1997	Billboard 200	22	47
	1997	Top Canadian Albums	11	10

Singles

Single	Year	Chart	Peak Position	Weeks on Chart
"Bitch" (*Blurring the Edges*)	1997	Hot Adult Top 40 Tracks	14	26
	1997	Hot Dance Club Play	34	5
	1997	Hot Modern Rock Tracks	4	21
	1997	Billboard Hot 100	2	30
	1997	Hot Adult Top 40 Recurrents	10	1
	1997	Mainstream Top 40	1	26
"What Would Happen" (*Blurring the Edges*)	1997	Hot Adult Top 40 Tracks	21	20
	1997	Mainstream Top 40	15	17
	1998	Billboard Hot 100	46	9
"Stop" (*Blurring the Edges*)	1998	Mainstream Top 40	40	1

Cardigans

Albums

Album	Year	Chart	Peak Position	Weeks on Chart
Emmerdale (Trampoline, 1994)				
Life (Minty Fresh, 1995)				
First Band on the Moon (Mercury, 1996)	1996	Heatseekers	3	14
	1997	Billboard 200	35	27
Gran Turismo (Mercury, 1998)	1998	Billboard 200	151	1

Singles

Single	Year	Chart	Peak Position	Weeks on Chart
"Lovefool" (*First Band on the Moon*)	1996	Hot Adult Top 40 Tracks	2	36
	1996	Hot Modern Rock Tracks	9	17
	1996	Mainstream Top 40	1	27
	1997	Hot Adult Contemporary Tracks	23	13
	1997	Hot Dance Club Play	5	13
	1997	Hot Dance Music/Maxi-Singles Sales	24	4
	1997	Rhythmic Top 40	18	16
	1997	Hot Adult Top 40 Recurrents	1	17
"My Favourite Game" (*Gran Turismo*)	1998	Hot Modern Rock Tracks	16	26

Sheryl Crow

Albums

Album	Year	Chart	Peak Position	Weeks on Chart
Tuesday Night Music Club (A&M, 1993)	1994	Heatseekers	2	9
Sheryl Crow (A&M, 1996)	1994	Billboard 200	3	100
	1996	Billboard 200	6	63
	1997	Top Canadian Albums	12	10
The Globe Sessions (A&M, 1998)	1998	Billboard 200	5	53
	1998	Top Canadian Albums	3	6

Singles

Single	Year	Chart	Peak Position	Weeks on Chart
"All I Wanna Do" (*Tuesday Night Music Club*)	1994	Hot Adult Contemporary Tracks	1	26
	1994	Hot Mainstream Rock Tracks	35	6
	1994	Hot Modern Rock Tracks	4	19
	1994	Rhythmic Top 40	31	7
	1994	Billboard Hot 100	2	33
	1994	Mainstream Top 40	1	26
	1995	Hot Adult Top 40 Tracks	32	26
	1995	Hot Adult Top 40 Recurrents	4	23

Single	Year	Chart	Peak Position	Weeks on Chart
"Leaving Las Vegas" (*Tuesday Night Music Club*)	1994	Hot Modern Rock Tracks	8	13
	1994	Billboard Hot 100	60	10
	1994	Mainstream Top 40	31	5
"Strong Enough" (*Tuesday Night Music Club*)	1994	Billboard Hot 100	5	26
	1995	Hot Adult Contemporary Tracks	11	26
	1995	Hot Adult Top 40 Tracks	34	26
	1995	Hot Modern Rock Tracks	10	14
	1995	Mainstream Top 40	3	24
"Can't Cry Anymore" (*Tuesday Night Music Club*)	1995	Hot Adult Contemporary Tracks	22	13
	1995	Hot Adult Top 40 Tracks	29	3
	1995	Hot Modern Rock Tracks	38	3
	1995	Billboard Hot 100	36	18
	1995	Mainstream Top 40	10	15
"D'Yer Mak'er" (*Encomium: A Tribute to Led Zeppelin*)	1995	Mainstream Top 40	35	4
"If It Makes You Happy" (*Sheryl Crow*)	1996	Hot Adult Top 40 Tracks	5	34
	1996	Hot Mainstream Rock Tracks	37	2
	1996	Hot Modern Rock Tracks	6	22
	1996	Billboard Hot 100	10	27
	1996	Mainstream Top 40	4	26
	1997	Hot Adult Top 40 Recurrents	2	19

Song	Year	Chart		
"Everyday Is a Winding Road" (Sheryl Crow)	1997	Hot Adult Top 40 Tracks	4	27
	1997	Hot Mainstream Rock Tracks	31	6
	1997	Hot Modern Rock Tracks	17	16
	1997	Billboard Hot 100	11	20
	1997	Hot Adult Top 40 Recurrents	2	23
	1997	Mainstream Top 40	5	24
"A Change Would Do You Good" (Sheryl Crow)	1997	Hot Adult Top 40 Tracks	5	26
	1997	Hot Modern Rock Tracks	25	9
	1997	Hot Adult Top 40 Recurrents	5	4
	1997	Mainstream Top 40	16	19
"My Favorite Mistake" (The Globe Sessions)	1998	Hot Adult Top 40 Tracks	2	35
	1998	Hot Modern Rock Tracks	26	11
	1998	Billboard Hot 100	20	10
	1998	Mainstream Top 40	5	25
	1998	Hot Adult Top 40 Tracks	2	35
	1998	Top 40 Tracks	7	24
	1999	Hot Adult Top 40 Recurrents	3	59

Garbage

Albums

Album	Year	Chart	Peak Position	Weeks on Chart
Garbage (Almo Sounds, 1995)	1995	Heatseekers	2	28
	1995	Billboard 200	20	81
Version 2.0 (Almo Sounds, 1998)	1998	Billboard 200	13	70
	1998	Top Canadian Albums	2	4

Singles

Single	Year	Chart	Peak Position	Weeks on Chart
"Queer" (*Garbage*)	1995	Hot Modern Rock Tracks	12	15
"Vow" (*Garbage*)	1995	Hot Modern Rock Tracks	26	9
	1995	Billboard Hot 100	97	2
"#1 Crush" (*Romeo + Juliet*)	1996	Hot Modern Rock Tracks	1	22
	1997	Mainstream Top 40	39	1
"Only Happy When It Rains" (*Garbage*)	1996	Hot Modern Rock Tracks	16	19
	1996	Billboard Hot 100	55	20
"Stupid Girl" (*Garbage*)	1996	Hot Adult Top 40 Tracks	36	4
	1996	Hot Dance Club Play	5	12
	1996	Hot Dance Music/Maxi-Singles Sales	30	4
	1996	Hot Mainstream Rock Tracks	39	2
	1996	Hot Modern Rock Tracks	2	25
	1996	Billboard Hot 100	24	20
	1996	Mainstream Top 40	25	12

Single	Year	Chart	Peak Position	Weeks on Chart
"I Think I'm Paranoid" (*Version 2.0*)	1998	Hot Modern Rock Tracks	6	52
"Push It" (*Version 2.0*)	1998	Hot Dance Club Play	5	13
	1998	Hot Modern Rock Tracks	5	21
	1998	Billboard Hot 100	52	18

PJ Harvey

Albums

Album	Year	Chart	Peak Position	Weeks on Chart
Dry (Too Pure/Indigo, 1992)				
Rid of Me (Island, 1993)	1993	Heatseekers	10	16
	1993	Billboard 200	158	1
4-Track Demos (Island, 1993)	1993	Heatseekers	10	5
To Bring You My Love (Island, 1995)	1995	Billboard 200	40	15
Is This Desire? (Island, 1998)	1998	Billboard 200	54	4

Singles

Single	Year	Chart	Peak Position	Weeks on Chart
"Sheela-Na-Gig" (*Dry*)	1992	Hot Modern Rock Tracks	9	10
"Down by the Water" (*To Bring You My Love*)	1995	Hot Modern Rock Tracks	2	14
"A Perfect Day Elise" (*Is This Desire?*)	1998	Hot Modern Rock Tracks	33	3

Hole

Albums

Album	Year	Chart	Peak Position	Weeks on Chart
Pretty on the Inside (Caroline, 1991)				
Live Through This (DGC, 1994)	1994	Billboard 200	52	68
Ask for It [EP] (Caroline, 1995)	1995	Billboard 200	172	2
Celebrity Skin (Geffen, 1998)	1998	Billboard 200	9	41
	1998	Top Canadian Albums	3	4

Singles

Single	Year	Chart	Peak Position	Weeks on Chart
"Doll Parts" (Live Through This)	1994	Hot Modern Rock Tracks	4	17
	1994	Billboard Hot 100	58	12
"Miss World" (Live Through This)	1994	Hot Modern Rock Tracks	13	10
"Asking for It" (Live Through This)	1995	Hot Modern Rock Tracks	36	4
"Softer, Softest" (Live Through This)	1995	Hot Modern Rock Tracks	32	5
"Violet" (Live Through This)	1995	Hot Modern Rock Tracks	29	10
"Gold Dust Woman" (The Crow: City of Angels)	1996	Hot Modern Rock Tracks	31	9
	1998	Hot Mainstream Rock Tracks	4	26
"Celebrity Skin" (Celebrity Skin)	1998	Hot Modern Rock Tracks	1	26
	1998	Billboard Hot 100	85	9
"Malibu" (Celebrity Skin)	1998	Hot Modern Rock Tracks	3	20

Jewel

Albums

Album	Year	Chart	Peak Position	Weeks on Chart
Pieces of You (East West, 1995)	1995	Heatseekers	4	26
	1996	Billboard 200	4	114
	1997	Top Canadian Albums	2	39
Spirit (Atlantic, 1998)	1998	Billboard 200	3	51
	1998	Top Canadian Albums	6	12

Singles

Single	Year	Chart	Peak Position	Weeks on Chart
"Foolish Games" (*Pieces of You*)	1996	Billboard Hot 100	2	65
	1997	Hot Adult Contemporary Tracks	4	26
	1997	Hot Adult Top 40 Tracks	1	28
	1997	Rhythmic Top 40	30	8
	1997	Mainstream Top 40	1	26
	1998	Hot Adult Top 40 Recurrents	2	14
"Who Will Save Your Soul" (*Pieces of You*)	1996	Hot Adult Contemporary Tracks	29	2
	1996	Hot Adult Top 40 Tracks	5	30
	1996	Hot Modern Rock Tracks	14	21
	1996	Billboard Hot 100	11	30
	1996	Hot Adult Top 40 Recurrents	3	21
	1996	Mainstream Top 40	3	26

Single	Year	Chart	Peak Position	Weeks on Chart
"You Were Meant for Me"	1996	Mainstream Top 40	1	35
(*Pieces of You*)	1996	Hot Adult Top 40 Tracks	1	46
	1997	Hot Adult Contemporary Tracks	1	42
	1997	Hot Modern Rock Tracks	26	10
	1997	Hot Adult Top 40 Recurrents	1	2
"Hands" (*Spirit*)	1998	Hot Adult Contemporary Tracks	7	26
	1998	Hot Adult Top 40 Tracks	2	26
	1998	Billboard Hot 100	6	16
	1998	Mainstream Top 40	4	24
	1998	Top 40 Tracks	3	19

Sarah McLachlan

Albums

Album	Year	Chart	Peak Position	Weeks on Chart
Fumbling Towards Ecstasy (Arista, 1993)	1994	Heatseekers	1	1
	1994	Billboard 200	50	100
The Freedom Sessions (Arista, 1995)	1995	Billboard 200	78	5
Surfacing (Arista, 1997)	1997	Billboard 200	2	108
	1997	Top Canadian Albums	1	51

Singles

Single	Year	Chart	Peak Position	Weeks on Chart
"Good Enough" (*Fumbling Towards Ecstasy*)	1994	Hot Modern Rock Tracks	16	14
	1994	Billboard Hot 100	77	10
"Possession" (*Fumbling Towards Ecstasy*)	1994	Hot Modern Rock Tracks	4	15
	1994	Billboard Hot 100	73	19
	1995	Hot Dance Club Play	30	8
	1997	Hot Adult Top 40 Tracks	19	26
	1997	Hot Adult Top 40 Recurrents	3	7
"Hold On" (*Fumbling Towards Ecstasy*)	1995	Hot Modern Rock Tracks	29	11
"I Will Remember You" (*The Brothers McMullen*)	1995	Hot Adult Contemporary Tracks	3	74
	1995	Hot Adult Top 40 Tracks	2	27
	1995	Hot Dance Music/Maxi-Singles Sales	24	2
	1995	Billboard Hot 100	14	20
"Building a Mystery" (*Surfacing*)	1997	Hot Adult Top 40 Tracks	4	28
	1997	Hot Modern Rock Tracks	3	26
	1997	Billboard Hot 100	13	22
	1997	Mainstream Top 40	15	20
	1997	Hot Adult Contemporary Tracks	28	5
	1998	Hot Adult Top 40 Recurrents	3	10

Single	Year	Chart	Peak Position	Weeks on Chart
"Sweet Surrender" (*Surfacing*)	1997	Hot Adult Top 40 Tracks	10	23
	1997	Hot Modern Rock Tracks	14	20
	1997	Mainstream Top 40	23	11
	1998	Billboard Hot 100	28	13
"Adia" (*Surfacing*)	1998	Hot Adult Contemporary Tracks	5	29
	1998	Hot Adult Top 40 Tracks	6	29
	1998	Billboard Hot 100	3	27
	1998	Hot Adult Top 40 Recurrents	2	6
	1998	Mainstream Top 40	20	20
"Angel" (*Surfacing*)	1998	Hot Adult Contemporary Tracks	1	82
	1998	Hot Adult Top 40 Tracks	1	36
	1998	Billboard Hot 100	4	28
	1998	Mainstream Top 40	4	26
	1998	Top 40 Tracks	1	26

Natalie Merchant

Albums

Album	Year	Chart	Peak Position	Weeks on Chart
Tigerlily (Elektra, 1995)	1995	Billboard 200	13	92
Ophelia (Elektra, 1998)	1998	Billboard 200	8	51

Singles

Single	Year	Chart	Peak Position	Weeks on Chart
"Carnival" (*Tigerlily*)	1995	Hot Adult Contemporary Tracks	8	26
	1995	Hot Adult Top 40 Tracks	8	23
	1995	Hot Modern Rock Tracks	12	23
	1995	Billboard Hot 100	10	31
	1995	Mainstream Top 40	6	26
	1996	Hot Adult Top 40 Recurrents	1	9
"Wonder" (*Tigerlily*)	1995	Hot Adult Contemporary Tracks	18	26
	1995	Hot Adult Top 40 Tracks	2	47
	1995	Hot Modern Rock Tracks	16	20
	1995	Billboard Hot 100	20	38
	1995	Mainstream Top 40	7	26
	1996	Hot Adult Top 40 Recurrents	1	35
"Jealousy" (*Tigerlily*)	1996	Hot Adult Contemporary Tracks	17	26
	1996	Hot Adult Top 40 Tracks	5	29
	1996	Billboard Hot 100	23	20
	1996	Mainstream Top 40	8	26
	1996	Hot Adult Top 40 Recurrents	1	11
"Break Your Heart" (*Ophelia*)	1998	Hot Adult Top 40 Tracks	24	16
"Kind and Generous" (*Ophelia*)	1998	Hot Adult Top 40 Tracks	3	26
	1998	Hot Adult Top 40 Recurrents	1	29

Alanis Morissette

Albums

Album	Year	Chart	Peak Position	Weeks on Chart
Jagged Little Pill (Maverick/Reprise, 1995)	1995	Heatseekers	2	1
	1995	Billboard 200	1	113
	1997	Top Canadian Albums	7	7
Supposed Former Infatuation Junkie (Maverick/Reprise, 1998)	1998	Billboard 200	1	28
	1998	Top Canadian Albums	2	15

Singles

Single	Year	Chart	Peak Position	Weeks on Chart
"All I Really Want" (*Jagged Little Pill*)	1995	Hot Modern Rock Tracks	14	16
"Hand in My Pocket" (*Jagged Little Pill*)	1995	Hot Adult Top 40 Tracks	25	27
	1995	Hot Mainstream Rock Tracks	8	16
	1995	Hot Modern Rock Tracks	1	23
	1995	Mainstream Top 40	4	26
	1996	Hot Adult Contemporary Tracks	30	14
"You Oughta Know" (*Jagged Little Pill*)	1995	Hot Mainstream Rock Tracks	3	19
	1995	Hot Modern Rock Tracks	1	19
	1995	Mainstream Top 40	7	26

Song (Album)	Year	Chart		
"Head over Feet" (*Jagged Little Pill*)	1996	Hot Adult Contemporary Tracks	27	8
	1996	Hot Adult Top 40 Tracks	1	35
	1996	Hot Modern Rock Tracks	25	11
	1996	Mainstream Top 40	1	26
	1997	Hot Adult Top 40 Recurrents	1	24
"Ironic" (*Jagged Little Pill*)	1996	Hot Adult Contemporary Tracks	28	4
	1996	Hot Adult Top 40 Tracks	5	30
	1996	Hot Mainstream Rock Tracks	18	12
	1996	Hot Modern Rock Tracks	1	21
	1996	Rhythmic Top 40	11	19
	1996	Billboard Hot 100	4	32
	1996	Hot Adult Top 40 Recurrents	1	12
	1996	Mainstream Top 40	1	27
"You Learn" (*Jagged Little Pill*)	1996	Hot Adult Contemporary Tracks	23	15
	1996	Hot Adult Top 40 Tracks	3	33
	1996	Hot Mainstream Rock Tracks	40	1
	1996	Hot Modern Rock Tracks	7	16
	1996	Rhythmic Top 40	32	14
	1996	Billboard Hot 100	6	30
	1997	Hot Adult Top 40 Recurrents	1	34
"Joining You" (*Supposed Former Infatuation Junkie*)	1998	Hot Modern Rock Tracks	16	13

Single

Single	Year	Chart	Peak Position	Weeks on Chart
"Thank U" (*Supposed Former Infatuation Junkie*)	1998	Hot Modern Rock Tracks	12	9
	1998	Billboard Hot 100	17	11
	1998	Mainstream Top 40	2	18
	1998	Top 40 Tracks	2	11
"Uninvited" (*City of Angels*)	1998	Hot Adult Top 40 Tracks	3	27
	1998	Hot Modern Rock Tracks	26	16
	1998	Top 40 Adult Recurrents	2	5
	1998	Mainstream Top 40	1	26

No Doubt

Albums

Album	Year	Chart	Peak Position	Weeks on Chart
No Doubt (Interscope, 1992)				
The Beacon Street Collection (Beacon Street/Interscope, 1995)				
Tragic Kingdom (Trauma/Interscope, 1995)	1995	Heatseekers	1	7
	1996	Billboard 200	1	90
	1996	Top Canadian Albums	1	33

Singles

Single	Year	Chart	Peak Position	Weeks on Chart
"Just a Girl" (*Tragic Kingdom*)	1995	Hot Modern Rock Tracks	10	26
	1995	Billboard Hot 100	23	29
	1996	Mainstream Top 40	24	16
"Don't Speak" (*Tragic Kingdom*)	1996	Hot Modern Rock Tracks	2	15
	1996	Hot Adult Top 40 Tracks	1	42
	1996	Rhythmic Top 40	9	23
	1996	Mainstream Top 40	1	66
	1997	Hot Adult Contemporary Tracks	6	26
	1996	Hot Adult Top 40 Tracks	1	42
	1997	Hot Adult Top 40 Recurrents	1	51
"Spiderwebs" (*Tragic Kingdom*)	1996	Hot Adult Top 40 Tracks	29	10
	1996	Hot Modern Rock Tracks	5	26
	1996	Mainstream Top 40	11	26
"Excuse Me Mr." (*Tragic Kingdom*)	1997	Hot Modern Rock Tracks	17	10
"Sunday Morning" (*Tragic Kingdom*)	1997	Hot Modern Rock Tracks	35	4

Liz Phair

Albums

Album	Year	Chart	Peak Position	Weeks on Chart
The Girly Sound (Bootleg, 1991)				

Album	Year	Chart	Peak Position	Weeks on Chart
Exile in Guyville (Matador, 1993)	1993	Heatseekers	12	20
Whip-Smart (Matador, 1994)	1994	Billboard 200	196	1
Juvenilia [EP] (Matador, 1995)	1994	Billboard 200	27	17
Whitechocolatespaceegg (Matador/Capitol, 1998)	1998	Billboard 200	35	9

Singles

Single	Year	Chart	Peak Position	Weeks on Chart
"Supernova" (*Whip-Smart*)	1994	Hot Modern Rock Tracks	6	19
	1994	Billboard Hot 100	78	14
"Whip-Smart" (*Whip-Smart*)	1995	Hot Modern Rock Tracks	24	7

Poe

Albums

Album	Year	Chart	Peak Position	Weeks on Chart
Hello (Atlantic, 1995)	1996	Heatseekers	4	19
	1996	Billboard 200	71	30

Singles

Single	Year	Chart	Peak Position	Weeks on Chart
"Trigger Happy Jack" (Drive by a Go-Go) (*Hello*)	1995	Hot Modern Rock Tracks	27	9

"Angry Johnny" (Hello)	1996	Hot Modern Rock Tracks	7	17
"Hello" (Hello)	1996	Hot Modern Rock Tracks	13	14
	1997	Hot Dance Club Play	1	12

Patti Rothberg

Albums

Album	Year	Chart	Peak Position	Weeks on Chart
Between the 1 and the 9 (EMI, 1996)	1996	Heatseekers	35	14

Singles

Single	Year	Chart	Peak Position	Weeks on Chart
"Inside" (Between the 1 and the 9)	1996	Hot Modern Rock Tracks	25	16

Bibliography

Ali, Lorraine. "Backstage at Lilith." *Rolling Stone*, September 4, 1997, 28–30, 32.
———. "Liz Phair." In *The Rolling Stone Book of Women in Rock*, ed. Barbara O'Dair. New York: Random House, 1997.
All Music Guide. www.allmusic.com/
Aston, Martin. "Liz Phair." *Independent Catalog*, September 1993.
Bangs, Lester. *Psychotic Reactions and Carburetor Dung.* New York: Alfred A. Knopf, 1987.
Barrett, Terry. *Criticizing Photographs: An Introduction to Understanding Images.* 2nd ed. Mountain View, CA: Mayfield, 1996.
Baumgardner, Jennifer, and Amy Richards. *Manifesta: Young Women, Feminism, and the Future.* New York: Farrar, Straus and Giroux, 2000.
Bitch, Winter 1996–Summer 1999.
Blanford, James R. *PJ Harvey: Siren Rising.* New York: Omnibus, 2004.
Borzillo, Carrie. "Maverick Finds Smooth Going for Morissette's 'Pill.'" *Billboard*, July 15, 1995.
Brownmiller, Susan. *Femininity.* New York: Linden Press/Simon & Schuster, 1984.
Brumburg, Joan Jacob. *The Body Project: An Intimate History of American Girls.* New York: Random House, 1997.
Burns, Stanley B. *Sleeping Beauty: Memorial Photography in America.* Altadena, CA: Twelvetrees Press, 1990.
Buskin, Richard. *Sheryl Crow: No Foot to This Game.* New York: Billboard, 2002.
Bust, 1993–1998.
Cantin, Paul. *Alanis Morissette: You Oughta Know.* Toronto: Stoddart, 1997.
Cassady, Carolyn. *Off the Road: My Years with Cassady, Kerouac, and Ginsberg.* New York: William Morrow, 1990.

Chang, Yahlin. "Blurring the Edges." *Newsweek*, May 26, 1997.

Chapel, Steve, and Reebee Garfolo. *Rock 'n' Roll Is Here to Pay*. Chicago, IL: Nelson-Hall, 1977.

Chauncey, Sarah. "Alanis Morissette: Inside the Mind of a Supposed Former Infatuation Junkie." *Canadian Musician*, November/December 1998, 34–37.

Chevalier, Jean, and Alain Gheerbrant. *The Penguin Dictionary of Symbols*. New York: Penguin, 1996.

Chickfactor, Fall 1992–1999.

Chideya, Farai. With Melissa Rossi and Dogen Hannah. "Revolution, Girl Style." *Newsweek*, November 23, 1992.

Chonin, Neva. "Backtalk with Liz Phair." *Option*, July/August 1997.

Christgau, Robert. "James Taylor." *Newsday*, November 1972; reprinted at Robert Christgau's website, www.robertchristgau.com/xg/bk-aow/taylor.php.

Covach, John. *What's That Sound? An Introduction to Rock and Its History*. New York: W. W. Norton, 2006.

Cummings, Sue. "Liz Phair Explodes the Cannon." *L.A. Weekly*, July 16–22, 1993.

"Daily News." *Rolling Stone*, July 8, 1997, www.rollingstone.com/.

Dalton, Stephen. "The Dark Lady of Dorset: Polly Jean Harvey." *NME*, 1998.

DeMain, Bill. *In Their Own Words: Songwriters Talk about the Creative Process*. Westport, CT: Praeger, 2004.

DeRogatis, Jim. *Milk It: Collected Musings on the Alternative Music Explosion of the '90s*. Cambridge, MA: Da Capo, 2003.

———. "Rock-Solid Response to a Stones Classic." *Chicago Sun-Times*, October 20, 2002.

DeSantis, Carla A. "Tori Amos: The Crispy Cornflake Girl." *Rockrgrl*, November/December 1998.

Dicker, Rory. *A History of U.S. Feminisms*. Berkeley, CA: Seal Press, 2008.

Dieckmann, Katherine. "Courtney Love." In *The Rolling Stone Book of Women in Rock*, ed. Barbara O'Dair. New York: Random House, 1997.

Dworkin, Andrea. *Intercourse*. New York: Basic Books, 1987.

Egger, Robin. "Sarah McLachlan: Her Own Woman." *Sunday Times*, January 11, 2004.

Evans, Liz. *Women, Sex and Rock 'n' Roll*. San Francisco, CA: Pandora, 1994.

Faludi, Susan. *Backlash: The Undeclared War against American Women*. New York: Crown, 1991.

Findlen, Barbara, ed. *Listen Up: Voices from the Next Feminist Generation*. Seattle, WA: Seal, 1995.

Fitzgerald, Judith. *Building a Mystery: The Story of Sarah McLachlan & Lilith Fair*. Kingston, Canada: Quarry Press, 1997.

Flanagan, Bill. *Written in My Soul: Rock's Great Songwriters Talk about Creating Their Music*. Chicago, IL: Contemporary Books, 1986,

French, Marilyn. *The War against Women*. New York: Summit Books, 1992.

Freydkin, Donna. "Fierce Feminists L7 Rant on with Live Album." *CNN*, December 11, 1998, www.cnn.com/SHOWBIZ/Music/9812/11/l7/.

Frost, Deborah. "PJ Harvey: Primed and Ticking." *Rolling Stone*, August 19, 1993.

George-Warren, Holly, ed. *The Rolling Stone Book of the Beats: The Beat Generation and American Culture*. New York: Rolling Stone, 1999.

Grace, Nancy M., and Ronna C. Johnson. *Breaking the Rule of Cool: Interviewing and Reading Women Beat Writers*. Jackson: University Press of Mississippi, 2004.

Gracyk, Theodore. *I Wanna Be Me: Rock Music and the Politics of Identity*. Philadelphia, PA: Temple University Press, 2001.

Grimm, Jacob, and Wilhelm Grimm. The Brothers. "Snow White." *Grimms' Tales for Young and Old*. Trans. Ralph Manheim. New York: Doubleday, 1977.

Herman, Tom. "It's a Fucking Debut Album." *Chicago's Subnation* 1, no. 6 (December 1993).

Heywood, Leslie, and Jennifer Drake. *Third Wave Agenda: Being Feminist, Doing Feminism*. Minneapolis: University of Minnesota Press, 1997.

"Hips. Lips. Tits. Power." *Q*, May 1994.

"In Woodstock's Wake, Hard Questions." *Billboard*, August 14, 1999.

Isenstein, Alyssa. "Liz Phair Interview." *Second Skin* 5 (circa 1993). Mesmerizing: Another Liz Phair Website, www.geocities.com/SunsetStrip/club/2471/00000049 .html.

Jackson, Joe. "Jagged Little Lady." *Irish Times*, April 12, 1996.

Jacobs, Jay S. *Pretty Good Years: A Biography of Tori Amos*. Milwaukee, WI: Hal Leonard, 2006.

Jervis, Lisa, and Andi Zeilser. *Bitchfest: Ten Years of Cultural Criticism from the Pages of* Bitch *Magazine*. New York: Farrar, Straus and Giroux, 2006.

Johnson, Joyce. "Beat Queens: Women in Flux." In *The Rolling Stone Book of the Beats: The Beat Generation and American Culture*, ed. Holly George-Warren. New York: Rolling Stone, 1999.

———. *Minor Characters*. Boston, MA: Houghton Mifflin, 1983.

"A Journey That Led to the Extremes of Human Kindness and Cruelty." *Muse*, Winter 1994.

Karp, Marcelle, and Debbie Stoller, eds. *The Bust Guide to the New Girl Order*. New York: Penguin, 1999.

Khoo, T. L. "Up Close with Alanis Morissette." *New Straits Times*, November 27, 1996.

Knight, Brenda. *Women of the Beat Generation: The Writers, Artists and Muses at the Heart of a Revolution*. Berkeley, CA: Conari, 1996.

Kot, Greg. "Gal in 'Guyville.'" *Chicago Tribune*, May 2, 1993.

Lamb, Sharon. *The Secret Lives of Girls: What Good Girls Really Do—Sex Play, Aggression, and Their Guilt*. New York: Free Press, 2001.

Lepage, Mark. "The Women Have It: No Bills on the Bill?" *Gazette*, August 16, 1997.

"Lilith Fair." *Entertainment Weekly*, May 9, 1997, (4).

Liss, Sarah. "The Gender Curse." *CBC News*, February 7, 2008, www.cbc.ca/arts/music/ womensongs.html.

Liu, Eric, ed. *Next: Young American Writers on the New Generation.* New York: W. W. Norton, 1994.

Love, Courtney. "Liner Notes." *My Body, The Hand Grenade.* City Slag, 1998.

Mackie, John. "McLachlan Gives Heart to Darkness." *Vancouver Sun,* October 28, 1993.

Marcus, Greil. "Days between Stations." *Interview,* April 1, 1996.

Maslin, Janet. "Singer-Songwriters." In *The Rolling Stone Illustrated History of Rock & Roll,* ed. Jim Miller. New York: Random House, 1976.

McDonnell, Evelyn, and Ann Powers, eds. *Rock She Wrote: Women Write about Rock, Pop, and Rap.* New York: Delta, 1995.

McLachlan, Sarah. *Fumbling towards Ecstasy: Live.* Vancouver, Canada: Nettwerk, 2005; originally *Sarah McLachlan—Fumbling towards Ecstasy Live.* New York: Arista, 1994.

———. *A Life in Music.* Toronto, Canada: Casablanca Media, 2005.

———. "Liner Notes." *The Freedom Sessions.* Arista, 1995.

Mifflin, Margot. "The Fallacy of Feminism in Rock." *Keyboard,* April 1990; reprinted in *Rock She Wrote: Women Write about Rock, Pop, and Rap,* ed. Evelyn McDonnell and Ann Powers. New York: Delta, 1995.

———. *VH1 Storytellers—Sarah McLachlan.* Chatsworth, CA: Image Entertainment, 2004.

Miller, Jim, ed. *The Rolling Stone Illustrated History of Rock & Roll.* New York: Random House, 1976.

Morissette, Alanis. "Reflections of a 'Supposed Former Infatuation Junkie': Alanis Morissette in Her Own Words." Mitch Schneider Organization PR, www.msopr.com/mso/morissette-words.html.

Morris, Chris. *Billboard,* April 12, 1997, (2).

Mundy, Chris. "Liz Phair: Last Train to Guyville." *Rolling Stone,* October 14, 1993.

Nehring, Neil. *Popular Music, Gender, and Postmodernism: Anger Is Energy.* Thousand Oaks, CA: Sage, 1997.

New York Times, 1991–1999.

O'Dair, Barbara, ed. *The Rolling Stone Book of Women in Rock.* New York: Random House, 1997.

O'Hara, Gail. "Girly Chat with Liz Phair." *Chickfactor* 3 (Spring 1993). Mesmerizing: Another Liz Phair Website, www.geocities.com/sunsetstrip/club/2471/00000300.html

Olden, Megan. "The Art of Contradiction." *Mondo,* Winter 1996/Spring 1997.

Oldenburg, Ann, and Karen Thomas. "Nose for Promotion Brings Skin Care to Lilith." *USA Today,* August 1, 1997.

Paglia, Camille. *Sex, Art, and American Culture.* New York: Vintage Books, 1992.

Pareles, Joe. "Cheers for Self-Determination (and Dumping Bad Partners) at All-Female Festival." *New York Times,* July 7, 1997.

Peabody, Richard. *A Different Beat: Writings by Women of the Beat Generation.* New York: High Risk, 1997.

Pendle, Karin. *Women in Music: A Research and Information Guide*. New York: Routledge, 2009.

Phillips, Lynn M. *Flirting with Danger: Young Women's Reflections on Sexuality and Domination*. New York: New York University Press, 2000.

Powers, Ann. "Critic's Notebook: A Surge of Sexism on the Rock Scene." *New York Times*, August 2, 1999.

———. "Houses of the Holy." *Village Voice*, June 1, 1993; reprinted in *Rock She Wrote: Women Write about Rock, Pop, and Rap*, ed. Evelyn McDonnell and Ann Powers. New York: Delta, 1995.

Raha, Maria. *Cinderella's Big Score: Women of the Punk and Indie Underground*. Emeryville, CA: Seal Press, 2005.

Raphael, Amy. *Grrrls: Viva Rock Divas*. New York: St. Martin's Griffin, 1995.

———. "Women: Look at Me I'm Famous." *Guardian*, October 10, 1995.

Reynolds, Simon. "PJ Harvey: What Makes Polly Scream?" *i-D*, October 1993.

Reynolds, Simon, and Joy Press. *The Sex Revolts: Gender, Rebellion, and Rock 'n' Roll*. Cambridge, MA: Harvard University Press, 1995.

Rockrgrl, January/February 1995–November/December 1999.

Roiphe, Katie. *The Morning After: Sex, Fear, and Feminism on Campus*. New York: Little, Brown, 1993.

Savage, Ann M. *They're Playing Our Songs: Women Talk about Feminist Rock Music*. Westport, CT: Praeger, 2003.

Schilt, Kristen. "'A Little too Ironic': The Appropriation and Packaging of the Riot Grrrl Politics by Mainstream Female Musicians." *Popular Music and Society* 26, no. 1 (February 2003): 5–16.

Schoemer, Karen. "Kitten, Bikini Kill and Boss Hog Maxwells." *New York Times*, February 6, 1992.

———. "Quiet Girls." *Newsweek*, June 30, 1997, (2).

———. "The Selling of Girl Power." *Newsweek*, December 29, 1997.

Segal, Lynne. *Straight Sex: Rethinking the Politics of Pleasure*. Los Angeles: University of California Press, 1994.

Shoales, Ian. "'You Oughta Know.'" *Milwaukee Journal Sentinel*, March 3, 1996.

Siegler, Dylan. "Lilith Fair: A New Women's Festival." *Ms.*, July/August 1997.

Simmons, Sylvie. "Tori Amos: *From the Choirgirl Hotel*." *Mojo*, May 1998.

Smith, Sidonie, and Julia Watson. *Women, Autobiography, Theory: A Reader*. Madison: University of Wisconsin Press, 1998.

Soccio, Lisa. "From Girl to Woman to Grrrl: (Sub) Cultural Intervention and Political Activism in the Time of Post-Feminism." *Invisible Culture: An Electronic Journal for Visual Studies*, Winter 1999, www.rochester.edu/in_visible_culture/issue2/soccio.htm.

Sommers, Christina Hoff. *Who Stole Feminism? How Woman Have Betrayed Women*. New York: Simon & Schuster, 1994.

Stark, Jeff. "What a Riot: Diary of a Woodstock '99 Survivor," *Salon*, July 27, 1999.

Stempel, Jill T. "Let Me Stand Next to Your Fire." *Rockrgrl*, September/October 2000.

Stevenson, Jane. "Beautiful Women, Beautiful Day: Lilith Fair Off to Noticeably Non-Rocky Start." *Toronto Sun*, July 7, 1997.

Sullivan, Jim. "Chapman, Hatfield Shine at Lilith Fair." *Boston Globe*, July 23, 1997.

Tanenbaum, Leora. *Slut! Growing Up Female with a Bad Reputation*. New York: Perennial, 2000.

Vaid, Urvashi. "Calling All Lesbians." *Advocate*, September 16, 1997.

Vowell, Sarah. "Throwing Ovaries: The Second-Grade Sensibility of the Pseudo-Feminist Lilith Fair." *Salon*, July 11, 1997, www.salon.com/july97/columnists/vowell970711.html.

"Vulnerable, Not Angry." *Winnipeg Free Press*, August 4, 1996.

Walker, Rebecca. *To Be Real*. 1995.

Warner, Marina. *From the Beast to the Blond: On Fairy Tales and Their Tellers*. New York: Farrar, Straus and Giroux, 1994.

Westmoreland, Kalene. "'Bitch' and Lilith Fair: Resisting Anger, Celebrating Contradictions.." *Popular Music and Society* 25, no. 1 (Spring/Summer 2001): 205–20.

White, Curtis. *The Middle Mind: Why Americans Don't Think for Themselves*. New York: Harper San Francisco, 2003.

White, Timothy. "Liz's 'Guyville': All Is Phair in Love." *Billboard*, May 8, 1993; reprinted in *Music to My Ears: The Billboard Essays*. New York: Henry Holt, 1996.

———. *Music to My Ears: The Billboard Essays*. New York: Henry Holt, 1996.

———. "PJ Harvey: A Lover's Musical Musing." *Billboard*, August 15, 1992.

———. "Sadly, the Times Are A-Changin'." *Billboard*, August 14, 1999.

William, Chris. "Meredith, She Rolls Along." *Entertainment Weekly*, June 13, 1997.

Wise, Nick. *Courtney Love*. New York: Omnibus Press, 1995.

Wolf, Naomi. *The Beauty Myth: How Images of Beauty Are Used Against Women*. New York: William Morrow, 1991.

———. *Promiscuities: The Secret Struggle for Womanhood*. New York: Fawcett Columbine, 1997.

Woodard, Joe. "Mellow-Sounding Demon: Feminist Neo-Paganism Goes Mainstream at Lilith." *Alberta Report*, September 8, 1997.

Woodworth, Marc. *Solo Women Singer-Songwriters: In Their Own Words*. New York: Delta, 1998.

Wurtzel, Elizabeth. *Bitch: In Praise of Difficult Women*. New York: Anchor Books, 1998.

Wyman, Bill. "Liz Phair's Suburban Blues." *Option*, September/October 1993.

Young, Charles M. "Alanis Morissette Is a Big Deal." *Playboy*, May 1, 1996.

Zak, Albin J., III. *The Poetics of Rock: Cutting Tracks, Making Records*. Berkeley: University of California Press, 2001.

Index